HITLER'S ENFORCERS

LEADERS OF THE GERMAN WAR MACHINE
1939–1945

JAMES LUCAS

CASSELL&CO

Cassell Military Paperbacks

Cassell & Co
Wellington House, 125 Strand
London WC2R 0BB

First published by Arms and Armour 1996
This Cassell Military Paperbacks edition 2000

British Library Cataloguing-in-Publication Data
A catalogue record for this book is available from the
British Library

ISBN 0-304-35450-3

Edited and designed by DAG Publications Ltd
Designed by David Gibbons; edited by Philip Jarrett

Printed and bound in Great Britain by
Cox & Wyman, Reading, Berks

Contents

Introduction, 8

Faithful Sepp, 13

Oberstgruppenfuehrer Josef Dietrich, Panzer General der Waffen SS

The Rosary Paratrooper, 26

Oberst Friedrich August Freiherr von der Heydte

Smiling Albert, 40

Generalfeldmarschall Albert Kesselring

'Grossdeutschland's' Panzer Commander, 54

Generalmajor Willi Langkeit

Master of the Field, 71

Generalfeldmarschall Erich von Manstein

The Fuehrer's Fireman, 86

Generalfeldmarschall Walther Model

Panzer Theoretician and Practitioner, 104

General der Panzertruppe Walther K. Nehring

Marine Soldier to Paratroop General, 119

General Hermann Ramcke

Hitler's Austrian Fireman, 129

Generaloberst Dr Lothar Rendulic

The Desert Fox, 146

Generalfeldmarschall Erwin Rommel

The Panzer Count, 163

Generalmajor Hyazinth von Strachwitz

The Airborne Innovator, 175

Generaloberst Kurt Student

The Finest Battlegroup Commander, 186

Otto Weidinger, Sturmbannfuehrer der Waffen SS

The Tiger Panzer Ace, 200

Michael Wittmann, Hauptsturmfuehrer der Waffen SS

Commander of the Eben Emael Attack, 215

Major Rudolf Witzig

Bibliography, 229

Index, 231

This book is dedicated
with every expression of deep love to my wife,
Edeltraude, as an expression of thanks for her
encouragement and support throughout
my writing career.

The writing of this volume and its preparation for publication have been made possible through the aid of a great number of friends and colleagues. So many were involved in the writing and the production that it is impossible to list them all. Through them I was supplied with original documents, and on my behalf they carried out document and photographic research in European and American archives. I acknowledge with sincere thanks my debt to them all for help so unselfishly given.

The names of just a few of them and of the institutions they used are given at the end of the book, and I ask the pardon of those who have had to be omitted. Shortage of space alone prevents their inclusion, but my gratitude includes them all.

James Lucas, London, 1996

Introduction

In every major army there are men who rise from lowly rank to the heights of military fame as a result of their own ability. These are the men of whom biographies are written, around whom legends are woven, to whom special names are given and who win respect not only from the soldiers of their own side but also from their opponents. When one considers the war in Africa it is Erwin Rommel – the Desert Fox – whose name is foremost in the minds and mouths of veterans.

The history of the German Army which fought the Second World War is filled with the names of soldiers like him, to whom nicknames or descriptions had been given. One of the most famous commanders was Model, celebrated as the 'Fuehrer's Fireman', who rose from the rank of Colonel to Field Marshal in a few short years. His fame rested not only on the fact that he was a successful and aggressive commander, but more upon his unsurpassed defensive skills, demonstrated during the middle and later years of the war. 'Smiling Albert' was the complimentary epithet given to Kesselring, an outstandingly successful commander both in the Luftwaffe and the Army who became Supreme Commander of the whole southern combat zone during the last weeks of the war.

Inevitably, some officers received nicknames which were not complimentary. August von der Heydte, who led the last major German paratroop drop in December 1944, during the Battle of the Bulge, was given the mocking title the 'Rosary Para' by Reichsmarschall Goering because he was a devout Catholic.

There are soldiers in these pages whose innovations influenced the way in which war was fought, in addition to those who gained military victories at the highest strategic level. Among the innovators is Student, whose Flieger Korps captured Crete, and Witzig, who, with a small number of men, seized the Belgian fortress of Eben Emael. Among the strategists is von Manstein, arguably the best of that *genre* of the Second World War. Others are included because their heroic acts demand acknowledgement, like panzer commander Wittmann, who almost singlehandedly halted the attack by an entire British armoured brigade by destroying more than twenty armoured fighting vehicles in a matter of minutes. Another is Hyazinth von Strachwitz, whose raids deep into enemy territory were legendary.

If, as I have written, the German Army had in its ranks a great many officers of outstanding ability, what was the rationale behind my selection of the fifteen men whose deeds are recorded in this book? Why, for example, was tank commander Wittmann selected and Barkmann, another successful panzer man, omitted? Why include Rommel and omit Guderian? Why choose Weidinger, who led a battlegroup on the Eastern Front, and exclude Scherer, who, isolated and surrounded, held the land bridge and village of Cholm for three months? Firstly, in a book of this length only a limited number of officers can be included. In my opinion, those selected had an extra dimension which, in military affairs, separates warriors of brilliance from those who are only first class. Although my choice is subjective, I believe it covers the widest possible spectrum of battle experience.

It will be appreciated that the accounts of many of the victories won by the men featured in this book will read as if they were citations for awards and medals. It has to be admitted that some of the accounts are based on citations. Others are post-battle reports written by the officers who were there, which I have expanded. The reports are factual, sober documents not given to exaggeration or hyperbole. Indeed, the report of one panzer commander who claimed an unusually high number of victories was not believed, and to establish its truth a commission of officers was sent out. It found out that he had, in fact, 'killed' more enemy machines than he had claimed. Because the wording of the post-battle reports and of the recommendations for decorations was restrained, I have endeavoured to give colour to those neutrally-shaded official records.

A text length of 80,000 words does not permit a detailed description of the actions of Hitler's men and, therefore, the reader must use his imagination to add the missing colours. Reading between the lines, he must visualise the dramas that can only be outlined in my words and see, in his mind's eye, the nature of the furious battles described. It will, perhaps, be of help if the reader is made aware that certain features are common to the lives of many of the officers whose careers are recounted in the following pages. To understand the reason for those common features, it is necessary for certain politico-military aspects of German history to be outlined.

Before the Great War of 1914-1918, Germany was an Empire whose eastern provinces included certain areas of what had once been Poland. In the 18th and early 19th centuries the territory of the former Poland was divided between the empires of Austria-Hungary, Germany and Russia. Those empires had common frontiers, and for the defence of their territories each held substantial military forces close to the national border. But, in addition to that defensive posture, all three countries prepared plans of military aggression against the neighbour State.

The creation of a German Empire in 1871 united the former kingdoms, principalities and dukedoms of Germany into a loose federal convention. That act of unification was viewed with alarm by nations bordering Germany, who saw it as a drift towards militarism. Those nations then expanded their armies to meet the threat which they thought Germany presented, and their expansions led in turn to Germany enlarging her own armed forces to meet what she saw as foreign challenges.

From the early 19th century conscription had supplied the rank and file for the human mass which formed the German Army. As explained above, late in the 19th century the Army's expansion had been so rapid that there was a shortage of commissioned ranks. To overcome that deficiency it was necessary to relax the rigid standards by which an officer's commission had formerly been gained. From the earliest days of a formally established standing army, the route to a commission had been for an 'Aspirant', as he was called, to enter a cadet school and to go from there into a military academy. Having passed out from that institution he took up service in a regiment. Such a route was the one preferred by the military authorities because the 'Aspirant' was already disciplined by having undergone basic military training. One element of that training was the skill of man management; the most necessary requirement of an officer.

Faced with a shortage of officers, the Army of the late 19th century had to open a second path to allow non-aristocrats to obtain a commission. That path was through higher education; the gaining of a matriculation certificate and/or an academic degree. As a generalisation it would be true to say that as late as the final decades of the 19th century the cadet school route was still the avenue used by the aristocracy and the traditional military families, while the education route was the path chosen by the bourgeoisie.

Until that new route was set up, an officer's commission had been viewed as the prerogative of the aristocrats. As a result of class distinctions and the fact that the Army was usually the instrument used by the State to put down rebellion and revolution, there had usually been friction between it and the common people. This was particularly the case after the year of Revolution – 1848. After that year the role of the military was more and more challenged by reactionary forces, and that hostility endured until well into the second half of the 19th century. Then hostility began to ebb and finally vanished. This came about chiefly because of a sense of national pride, of improved social conditions and because of the Army's new liberal views towards the bourgeoisie. In time the armed forces came to be seen as a national force, uniting all the people, and less and less as the instrument of royal oppression. Parents considering their sons' career prospects saw that an officer's commission offered a regular, pensionable post. More than that, it also had the advantages that promotion in the military field could bring about an improvement in one's social position. All of those things could be gained through application, diligence and hard work.

Once he was commissioned, the new officer had to be approved by the subalterns of his future regiment. It was for them to decide whether the new man would fit in and become a good regimental comrade. Service life in peacetime was a continual round of deadly routine and boring duties. Promotion was slow, but upon attaining the rank of captain an officer could elect either to remain with the regiment and await slow advancement to the next promotional step, or join the General Staff with its faster prospects of advancement but with the continual threat of his being returned to unit if he failed the many and difficult examinations.

After the First World War most of the senior officers featured in this volume elected for the General Staff route and rose, during the Second World War, to posts of high authority. Many had served during the First World War on the Southern, Eastern or Western Front, and in several instances some had fought on two, or all three. In addition to those, there are several men named in this text who had not served in the Great War. Two of them, Weidinger and Wittmann, were SS officers who gained their commissions by rising through the ranks. This had always been possible, and in time of war bravery in the field could result in the granting of a commission, although this was rare. In the years of the Third Reich, bravery and/or service led to many soldiers or NCOs being posted to an SS military academy where they were taught the duties of a junior officer. Thus a commission which, in the earliest years of German military history, had been almost exclusively a matter of birth, became available in the late 19th century to those with appropriate education. Then, after 1933, it could be gained by brave, skilled soldiers who had been imbued with the political, revolutionary spirit of National Socialism.

At the end of the First World War many men who were to rise to the highest ranks were still subalterns, and it seemed to them that their career prospects had suddenly ended. The Regular Army, as such, had almost ceased to exist. They faced the reality that whole regions of their country had been annexed under the conditions of the Treaty of Versailles and handed over to the Poles or to the French. In the eastern provinces there were also incursions and raids by Polish regular and irregular forces who claimed that territory which Germany had not had to surrender under the treaty was historically Polish. Under Versailles the German Army was a rump, and was not only forbidden to act against the Polish incursions, but was also forbidden to build either tanks or heavy artillery. Because the use of German Regular troops to counter the Polish incursions was forbidden by the Allies, the units which went out to defend the German East had to be volunteer contingents. A great many former ex-servicemen of the Great War served in one of the military volunteer bodies known, generally, as the Freikorps. The soldiers in those Freikorps contingents fought until the situation in the east returned to normal and the Poles had withdrawn from German territory. Many then volunteered for and were accepted into the ranks of the Regular Army.

The Versailles prohibitions on the construction of tanks or artillery were rigidly enforced by Allied inspections, and the German Army was also forbidden to have either a General Staff or troop training facilities. It is hardly surprising that, in the 1920s, the republican government of Weimar concluded a secret and illegal pact with Soviet Russia. Under the terms of the Rapallo Treaty, the tanks forbidden to be built in Germany were constructed in Russian factories, and were used in mock battles by German military units secretly undergoing training in restricted areas of the Soviet Union. That pact between the Weimar and the Soviet governments provided the opportunity for the future leaders of the panzer forces and of the Luftwaffe to practise battle tactics in remote areas of Russia. The German General Staff, which was forbidden by Versailles, was seen to be abolished, but the Allies did not realise that it had been promptly re-formed under an innocuous name and its leaders given experience, in the Soviet Union, of handling large forces of men.

It was obvious that Germany, restricted by the bounds of Versailles, would look for ways of circumventing the limitations, and the many attempts at seeking to salvage and regain national pride and honour are not to be wondered at. Adolf Hitler ended the period of Germany's subservience to the Treaty of Versailles and initiated a programme of rearmament which within years restored Germany to the status of a major European power. The Second Great War, which opened in 1939 and became a world-wide conflict, saw Germany and her allies, nations with finite resources in raw materials and manpower, facing a combination of countries whose resources, if not infinite, were considerably greater. Hitler gambled on winning all of his campaigns in swift and decisive blitzkrieg-type operations. He gambled and lost, for, in addition to the raw materials and manpower which the Allies possessed, they also had time on their side. Germany did not, and when the blitzkrieg tactics no longer brought results was certain to be defeated.

It is not to be wondered at that the military forces of Hitler's Third Reich triumphed in the campaigns which they initiated in the first years of the Second World War, for the aggressor always enjoys an initial advantage. But the soldiers and commanders of the Reich's armed forces gained victory after victory and continued to do so (admittedly in defensive warfare and only at a tactical level) up to the closing stages of that conflict, testifying to the outstanding military qualities and the battlefield skills of the commanders whose lives are recorded here, and who are representative of all of Hitler's men.

Faithful Sepp

Oberstgruppenfuehrer Josef Dietrich,
Panzer General der Waffen SS

Josef 'Sepp' Dietrich did not have a good press in the world except in those countries which, during the Second World War, were dominated or influenced by the Third Reich. In Germany's media, as well as in that of the countries allied to her, he was a military legend. Such is the power of negative propaganda, however, that while Red Army generals with working-class backgrounds were lauded by the Western media for their military ability, Dietrich, who had the same background, was looked upon as a bar-room brawler without any sort of military strategic skill.

He was born on 28 May 1892 in the village of Hawangen near Memmingen in Swabia, from where the family moved in 1900 to Kempten in the Allgau. His first employment was as a cart driver, but that position was uncongenial and soon, like many other German young men of the period, he became a Wandervogel, tramping the highways of his own country and subsequently those of Austria and Italy. In 1911 Dietrich returned to Germany to begin his compulsory military service, and much is unclear concerning this part of his early life. Although he claimed to have served as a regular soldier in a Lancer (Ulanen) regiment, documents indicate that he was an artilleryman who was invalided out of the Army after falling from a horse.

On 6 August 1914, two days after Britain declared war on Germany, Dietrich enlisted in the 7th Field Artillery regiment of the Bavarian army. For reasons which only he could know he was later to claim that he had joined the 1st Ulanen (Lancer) regiment and that he had transferred from the cavalry to the infantry and specifically into the 4th Infantry Regiment. What can be proved from the records is that, in October 1914, Dietrich was in action in Flanders with the 6th Bavarian Reserve Artillery Regiment. It is likely that in the last week of October he first fought against the British Army when the Division with which he was serving formed part of a major military grouping which had been ordered to capture Ypres. That town was the key to Flanders, and the British Expeditionary Force (BEF) fought as hard to hold it as the German Army struggled to capture it. The resistance put up by the British and French armies thwarted every German attack, and by the middle of November the mobile warfare which had characterised the first months had halted as both sides dug trench lines whose position was to remain almost unchanged for the four years of the Great War. During those years Dietrich was wounded several times; the first was a shrapnel wound in the lower part of his right leg and the second a lance thrust over the left eye. He was later to suffer other wounds, the most serious being that to the side of his head, inflicted during the fighting on the Somme.

Dietrich claimed to have served on the Italian Front and to have received an award for bravery from the Austrians. During 1916 the German High Command, seeking to break the trench-line stalemate on the Western Front, formed infantry and artillery Storm Troop battlegroups. The initial successes of these small assault detachments led to their being expanded to include machine-gun sections, light mortar teams, bombing squads and flamethrower groups. Such units were known as Sturmabteilungen (Storm battalions). Dietrich became a member of No. 2 battalion serving with German 3rd Army. Although the strategic intention had been to create a force of Sturmabteilungen strong enough to achieve a breakthrough on the Western Front, this did not happen. There were too few battalions, although at tactical level they proved invaluable in local operations.

At this point it is necessary to touch upon the character of the storm troops, for this has a bearing on the SS organisation which Dietrich later commanded. The storm troops were first-class fighting men, and both the officers and other ranks considered themselves an élite; the pick of the nation's warriors. Relations between the ranks were less formal than in conventional units and the officers and men often messed together. The storm troop units had to be rested more frequently than the standard formations, for the demands made upon them in battle were greater and more intense. Dietrich absorbed the characteristics of the storm units and in later years, when he commanded the Leibstandarte SS 'Adolf Hitler', applied similar principles to that SS formation, particularly in the concept of discipline based upon respect for the person and not upon the rank he carried.

During the Second World War SS officers and men were to fight with the fervour of the old storm troops, becoming with experience almost invincible in attack and rock solid in defence. But the implementation of Dietrich's concepts within the SS establishment were still many years away. Immediately ahead lay the great offensives of 1917 and 1918, during which new tactics of infiltration were evaluated, tested and applied, often with great effect. In November 1917 Dietrich won the Second Class Iron Cross, and three months later he was posted to the Bavarian Storm Tank detachment. The German Army's High Command acknowledged the value of an armoured fighting vehicle with cross-country capabilities and ordered male-type machines armed with an artillery piece and machine-guns. The tank arm was organised by battalions, each comprising five officers and 108 other ranks equipped with five armoured fighting vehicles.

British male-type tanks which had been captured were taken on charge and in time there were three battalions equipped with native vehicles and six others with captured machines. Dietrich served with a Bavarian battalion as a gunner in a captured tank.

His first 'mount' went into action on 1 June 1918, in the Chemin des Dames sector. Mechanical failure reduced the number of machines which took part in that operation, but Moritz, Dietrich's vehicle, performed well and gave excellent support to the advancing infantry until it 'bellied' in a large shell hole. The driver's efforts to bring the machine back on to firm ground caused the engine to overheat and a French counterattack which had driven back the German infantry threatened to capture the tank. Lieutenant Fuchsbauer, the vehicle's commander, decided that Moritz would have to be blown up to deny its use to the Allies. Dietrich was one of the three-man demolition team selected for the task, and in later years boasted of winning the respect of his comrades for salvaging a bottle of Schnapps under heavy fire. The demolition crew were awarded medals, and Dietrich received the Bavarian Military Service Cross, Third Class.

His next action occurred to the south-east of Soissons on 15 July, and during this operation Dietrich's tank was knocked out, together with all the others in the battalion. It was not until 9 October that his battalion went into battle again, but the mechanical failure of Dietrich's machine kept him out of that action. The unit's final mission came on 1 November 1918, when four vehicles supported a counterattack in the Curgies area of Valenciennes. This operation regained some ground which had been taken in an Allied attack, but it was lost again on the following day. Dietrich returned to Germany, which had not only lost the war but was degenerating into revolution, and was demobilised in March 1919.

In those immediate post-war years Germany was in turmoil, and the republican government saw the military as the only organised body capable of restoring order both internally and externally. But Germany's standing Army was not allowed to undertake military operations, so recourse had to be made to public-spirited ex-soldiers who were recruited into what were known as Freikorps Rifle Groups and organised along Storm Detachment lines. Nothing is known of Dietrich's activities during that period of post-war political unrest, but by 1920 he had enlisted into the Bavarian State Police, a paramilitary force in which his military training and former rank of sergeant brought him the command of men and a detachment of vehicles in the reconnaissance platoon.

The victorious Allies intended to detach from Germany, by *force majeure*, part of the province of Silesia, with its rich iron and coal resources, and to give it to the new Polish state. To legalise that proposed forced transfer of territory a plebiscite was held in March 1921. Although the Allies confidently predicted that the result would show that the electorate wished to stay part of Poland, it showed that a majority of the native population wished to remain German. The decision so inflamed the Poles that a group of their irregular and regular troops decided to seize the disputed territories, and crossed the frontier. The Allies would not allow German regular units to expel the invaders, and the local detachments formed to defend the area were not sufficiently strong. In desperation the German government turned for help to the Freikorps. Dietrich, who had been given leave of absence from the police force, served with 1st Battalion's No. 2 Company in the Oberland Frei Korps. The Oberlaenders' first objective was the Annaberg, whose convent was not only a place of pilgrimage but also an area of great emotional value to the German population. In a military sense its capture was important, for it commanded the ground on the right bank of the river Oder.

The attack to seize the Annaberg went in at 0230 on 21 May 1921, with two regiments 'up'; the Oberland on the left and another Freikorps formation on the right flank. The feature was quickly captured and held against furious counterattacks which persisted until the Poles pulled out of Silesia on 5 July. For his part in these military operations Dietrich received the coveted Order of the Silesian Eagle, 2nd and 1st Classes, and although the fighting had officially ended he remained in the disputed area long after the remainder of his unit. Eventually he returned home to resume his police career.

During this time he would have heard Hitler speak at open-air meetings. Although he sympathised with the Nazi Party's ideals to the extent of taking part in the abortive Munich putsch of November 1923, Dietrich did not join the party until several years later. It was, perhaps, because of his involvement in the November putsch that he either left or was retired from the police force in the following month with the rank of captain. He worked for several years in a succession of menial civilian jobs before joining the Nazi Party on 1 May 1928. Only days later he enlisted in the SS, the second of the Nazi party's paramilitary organisations and the one formed to protect its speakers at political rallies. The SS was, therefore, few in numbers compared with the SA (the Sturm Abteilung, or Storm Troops), the brown-shirted mass of Party soldiers which numbered over 72,000 as early as 1927.

Dietrich's rise in the SS was fast. Promotion to commissioned rank came in June 1928, command of the Munich Standarte (regiment) followed two months later, and by May of the following year he commanded the SS Brigade Bavaria. The Nazi Party did not pay its soldiers, and Dietrich worked in the Eber Publishing House. As a second duty he acted as a bodyguard to Adolf Hitler. In the 1930 elections Dietrich was elected to the Reichstag and was given command of the entire SS organisation in southern Germany. A permanent bodyguard detachment known as the SS Begleit Kommando 'Der Fuehrer' (SS Escort Group 'Der Fuehrer'), with a strength of twelve specially selected men, was formed in February 1931.

In 1933, with the Nazi Party now the official government of Germany, Hitler ordered that a new body be created to protect the Reichschancellery in

Berlin. Dietrich raised the 117-man-strong 'SS Headquarters Guard Dietrich'. That same year Hitler ordered military training to be given to the SS, and in particular to the élite SS Sonderkommandos Berlin, Juteborg and Zossen. These battalion-sized detachments were then amalgamated to form the Leibstandarte SS Adolf Hitler (the Adolf Hitler bodyguard regiment of the SS, or LSSAH). During the Roehm crisis of 1934 the Leibstandarte served under Hitler's direct orders to suppress Roehm's SA. The Fuehrer kept the Army out of this Party crisis, although military transport was used to carry the Leibstandarte to southern Germany. The SA leaders were arrested and shot, a task which Dietrich found distressing because so many of them had been his comrades in the Freikorps, but his unquestioning and unswerving loyalty to Hitler brought promotion to obergruppenfuehrer (lieutenant general).

The next step in the history of the SS and in Dietrich's advancement came when Himmler resolved to form the several types of SS unit into a 'Verfuegungs' Division (VT); armed units available for special duties. The Waffen or armed SS had come into being. When Dietrich learned that the Leibstandarte was to be amalgamated into the VT Division he realised that its independence was threatened and complained to Hitler, who ordered that it was to remain outside Himmler's control, which it did to the end of the war. Meanwhile there had been a series of political developments in Europe, in many of which Dietrich and his men took part. On 28 February 1935 Hitler ordered the Leibstandarte to move into the Saarland, where a plebiscite was to be held. The appearance of these tall, well-built and highly disciplined men illustrated the positive aspect of national socialism and must have influenced the Saarlander population to vote overwhelmingly to stay in the Reich.

Under Dietrich the LSSAH, an infantry formation, acquired a high reputation for turn-out and ceremonial drill, but he was dissatisfied with its infantry role and demanded to be issued with tanks. Although this first attempt at upgrading the LSSAH failed, the Standarte became better armed and was authorised to raise an armoured car platoon in July 1936. The Army's relations with the Nazi Party and the SS were not cordial, but it was soon noticeable that a distinct gulf yawned between the older SS commanders such as Dietrich, Steiner and Hausser, all of whom had been front-line soldiers in the First World War, and the younger officers, who were graduates from the SS Military Academies. The older men respected and trusted the Army, whereas the younger men were influenced against it by Himmler, a Party official determined to create an SS Empire.

In March 1938 the Standarte was on the establishment of Guderian's XVI Panzer Corps and Dietrich led the LSSAH, which was on Corps' establishment, into Austria. The Standarte returned to Berlin but was called out again, once more under Guderian, with whom Dietrich had a strong rapport, when the German Army entered the Sudetenland. Hitler's aggression finally resolved France and Great Britain to sign a pact with Poland, and the invasion of that republic on

1 September 1939 brought about a war in whose opening operations Dietrich and the LSSAH came under the command of XIII Corps as the only motorised formation in that corps.

The campaign in Poland was brief but bitter, and certainly not the easily-won 'lightning' war depicted by the Reich's war reporters. One interesting feature of that campaign came towards its end, when the Standarte was posted to Reinhardt's 4th Panzer Division to 'beef up' that formation's attack on Warsaw. What was not known either at Standarte or at divisional level was that two Polish armies which had fought well in western Poland were battling their way eastwards to strengthen the Warsaw garrison. Both were advancing on a line that would take them on a collision course with Reinhardt's 4th Panzer Division and the LSSAH. Unable to reinforce 4th Panzer, the German High Command (OKW) issued orders that not only was it to maintain pressure against the Polish capital, but it was also to block the advance of the two enemy armies. The attempts to carry out both tasks involved the 4th and the Leibstandarte in a two-front battle, during which many of their units stood back-to-back, some facing eastwards towards Warsaw and the others westwards towards the Bzura river. Urged on by Dietrich, the Standarte fought a superlative defensive battle and at Piastov forced the Poles back. The OKW then ordered an offensive to be undertaken in which the Standarte was to advance northwards along both banks of the Bzura river until the Vistula was reached. This successful operation trapped a major part of the Polish forces and the LSSAH played a leading role in the destructive fighting which reduced that pocket.

The participation of Dietrich's unit in the German-Polish war did not end there. He took it northwards to Modlin, where part of the Polish capital's permanent defence system was located. The Standarte had been given a defensive task, which was not one to the liking of Dietrich and his senior commanders, who all believed in aggressive action. The Leibstandarte fought an offensive battle with such determination that it quickly captured one of the principal forts. With Poland vanquished there was a brief period of rest and reorganisation before training began for the War in the West against France and Great Britain. The OKW battle plan also foresaw attacks upon Belgium and Holland, but the armed services of those nations presented little threat to the unfolding of the German plan. The French and British armies, being larger, were the main enemies and, if Germany was not to be involved in a re-run of the Great War, some new strategy would have to be devised to defeat them. This strategy is described in the chapter of this book devoted to Manstein, the officer who planned it.

For the campaign in the West the Leibstandarte served with 227th Division, and when operations began at dawn on 10 May 1940 it raced across the Dutch border, advanced 72km and succeeded in capturing, undamaged, a number of bridges across several rivers. Under the command of 9th Panzer Division, to which it had been transferred, the LSSAH was ordered to bring out the Fallschirmjaeger who had dropped near Rotterdam on the first day of the war, and when that task was completed it was to drive on to the Hague. During the advance to the seat of the Dutch government a potentially serious incident occurred. Dietrich's men in the southern part of Rotterdam opened fire on what they thought were armed Dutch soldiers. The enemy troops were, in fact, surrendering to General Student, Commanding the German airborne forces. In the fire fight which resulted from the confusion of mistaken identity Student was hit in the head, and evidence points to the shot having been fired by the Leibstandarte.

Dutch resistance was soon broken, and after a succession of temporary attachments to other units the Standarte rejoined Guderian's XIX Panzer Corps and took positions in the cordon of German units encircling Dunkirk, specifically along the line of the Aa canal to the west of St Omer. Hitler ordered the troops manning the Dunkirk perimeter to halt their advance, but Dietrich disobeyed the order and sent his 3rd battalion across the canal, where it captured a piece of high ground, the Wattenberg. He justified his disobedience with the explanation that the enemy defenders were 'looking down our throats'. Dietrich moved towards Wormhoudt when Hitler's restrictive order was lifted, and on 28 May, his birthday, he drove towards the combat zone to co-ordinate an attack upon the village. En route his car was shot up by British troops and he was forced to hide in a ditch.

The war in Flanders came to an end with the withdrawal of the BEF from Dunkirk, and Dietrich's Standarte was sent to fight in the second campaign, to destroy the French Army. Once again under the command of 9th Panzer Division, the Leibstandarte drove through central and southern France, arriving just south of Lyons on 24 June. The campaign in the west ended on 25 June, and many Germans were of the opinion that it was the end of the war. For his part in the successful battle for France, Dietrich was awarded the Knight's Cross to accompany the 1st and 2nd classes of the Iron Cross which he had won in Poland.

Then came news that the Standarte was to be expanded to Brigade size, and shortly thereafter Dietrich was advised that his formation was to take part in the Balkan campaign. It moved to south-western Bulgaria and came under the command of XL Corps (12th Army). The battle experience gained by Dietrich's formation during the fighting in the west had improved its fighting ability. In Poland the LSSAH had had élan, but lack of training had led to unnecessarily high losses. That deficiency in training was made good during the winter of 1939-40, and when the Leibstandarte took the field to fight in the west its battalions functioned well. In the Balkan campaign it evolved into a fine fighting instrument whose spirit and skill were praised by Army generals. Much of the credit for the unit's performance was due to the personal interest Dietrich took in his men's welfare. The basic tenet of every commander from the lowest to the highest is that the comfort and welfare of the men is the first consideration.

Dietrich had learned that basic commandment as an NCO, and he did not depart from it as a general.

Awareness that their commander was doing his best for them brought the response from the rank and file that they must do their best for him. This they did in Greece, capturing the vital Klidi pass in a three-day battle and then going on to seize the Klissura and Katarra passes. The capture of the Katarra pass hastened the end of Greek resistance. On 20 April Dietrich and General Tsolakoglou arranged the surrender between them, which included the Italian forces that had been fighting in the campaign. Mussolini was furious that the surrender had taken place without his being consulted, and insisted that the Greek general sign another surrender document. The Leibstandarte then raced down to Corinth, hoping to overtake and trap the retreating British Army, but much of the expeditionary force had already been taken off by the Royal Navy. Dietrich's style of leadership played a large part in the victory, and one of his officers wrote that if Dietrich had not been such an inspiration, the Greek campaign might have had a different outcome.

The war in Greece ended during April, and that against Russia opened towards the end of June. During that brief period of peace Hitler decided to raise the Leibstandarte to divisional status, and the war against the Soviet Union saw it serving with Army Group South and quickly acquiring a reputation for bravery and military skill which was acknowledged by General Kempf, commanding XLVIII Corps, in an order of the day issued at the conclusion of the bitter battle of Uman. It was during the fighting around Kerch, at the approaches to the Crimea, that Dietrich's Division first acted in the role of a fire brigade. During the night of 23/24 September the Red Army's attacks tore a gap in the front held by 3rd Romanian Army. The breach had to be closed quickly because there was a danger that German 11th Army would be cut off. Dietrich raced his formation to Gavrilovka, where its first assaults halted the Soviet forces flooding through the breach, then vigorous counterattack drove them back and sealed the line.

On 16 October 1941 the Division captured Taganrog, but then the weather broke. Heavy rain and more determined Russian resistance wore down the strength of the German attacking formations and so depleted the Leibstandarte companies that they were reduced to only a third of their strength. Indeed, a return dated 30 November showed that the Division had only 157 officers and 4,556 men, against a war establishment of 290 officers and 9,700 men. Shocked by the high losses suffered by all the military units, but particularly by the Division that carried his name, Hitler flew to Mariupol for a meeting with Dietrich. For his services in the campaign the Leibstandarte's commander was awarded the Oak Leaf to the Knight's Cross. He received this in Berlin, where his popularity among the Party's old guard was at it highest. He spent three nights in the Chancellery as Hitler's personal guest and at the celebration to mark Goering's birthday, was lauded as the pillar of the Eastern Front. Dietrich married on 19 January

1942, but before the end of the month had returned to his Division in Russia. Slowly more units were added to the Leibstandarte's Order of Battle, including a battalion each of panzers and SPs. Although these additions had been authorised during February, many did not come on charge until May.

Hitler's increasing concern about the situation in the west caused him to order the setting up of a special, fast, trans-European railway service. The concept was that, in the event of a crisis developing on either battlefront, he could transfer major units by the 'lightning express' network between the eastern and western theatres of operation. The first formation which Hitler sent westwards using the new 'lightning express' was Dietrich's Division, which arrived in the Paris area during the third week of July. Hitler decided that an SS Corps was to be formed, and ordered that the three motorised Divisions which were to form it, 'Leibstandarte', 'Das Reich' and 'Totenkopf', were to be upgraded to Panzer Grenadier status, but the serious military situation on the Eastern Front did not allow the three formations to be concentrated for many months.

During the autumn of 1942 the Leibstandarte's panzer battalion was enlarged to become a two-battalion regiment, but then, as if the problems concerning the expansion and reorganisation of the SS Panzer Corps were not a sufficient worry, Dietrich received a communication from Himmler condemning him for allowing 2,000 of his men to be infected with venereal disease during their service in Russia, and demanding an explanation. Dietrich checked the allegation and then replied to Himmler quoting the true facts; the actual number was 244. In that connection a surreal discussion was conducted at higher SS level about sexual intercourse between the racially pure Germans of the SS and racially inferior Russian women. Dietrich declared that the ruling which had been introduced by the SS authorities in Kiev did not apply to the Leibstandarte; it is likely that the Divisional commander, who had himself been a frontline warrior, subscribed to the old soldiers' claim that a rampant male member has no conscience.

The Leibstandarte returned from France to the Eastern Front and to Kharkov, a city under threat from the Soviet winter offensive, and which Hitler had ordered must be held to the last. Subsequent events connected with the fighting for Kharkov must have made Dietrich realise how vast a gulf yawned between the soldiers of the battlefront and the politicians in the Homeland. The Soviet offensive had breached the German line between the Leibstandarte and the Division on its right flank, the 320th. It was vital that the line be resealed, and Dietrich led a large battlegroup in bitter winter conditions to gain touch with the 320th and bring this about. The breach was sealed, but because the Soviets had all but surrounded Kharkov, Hausser, commander of 1st SS Panzer Corps, decided to evacuate the city despite Hitler's direct order. In later months, when Dietrich was asked what reserves he had had when the evacuation order was issued, he is said to have replied: 'Behind me was four hundred kilometres of empty space'. It was very plain that Fuehrer headquarters had no idea of the privations under which the troops on the ground were living, nor of the bitterness of the battles they were fighting. Manstein's strategy, which had brought about the deliberate evacuation of Kharkov, also brought about its recapture on 14 March, and Dietrich's panzers led the advance into the city, a success which brought to the LSSAH commander the Swords to the Knight's Cross. Only days later came the news that his second son had been born.

In April 1943 Hitler decided to raise a new 1st SS Panzer Corps and to renumber the existing 1st Corps, commanded by Hausser, the 2nd. The Fuehrer empowered Dietrich to raise the new 1st Corps, and his deep involvement in that task made it impossible for him to lead the Leibstandarte when it took part in the 1943 German summer offensive, Unternehmen Zitadelle (Operation Citadel). In fact the early summer of 1943 was the last personal and close contact that Dietrich had with his old Division. But there was consolation in his promotion to obergruppenfuehrer (general) of the SS.

At the end of October 1943, having paid a brief visit to the Eastern Front, Dietrich returned to France with the task of raising his SS Panzer Corps and training his men for the invasion they all knew was coming. The Allies landed on 6 June 1944, and Dietrich's Corps was moved to the beachhead area. Neither of its component Divisions, 1st SS nor 12th SS Panzer, was able to go into action immediately. Allied fighter-bomber attacks delayed the advance to the concentration areas, making German ground operations piecemeal and lacking in cohesion. Domination of the air was the key to the Allied victory, and any attempt by the Germans at mounting a ground offensive was hit by the 'Cab Rank' system of fighter-bomber attacks.

During the weeks of confusion which marked the course of the Normandy campaign on the German side, Dietrich spent most of his time visiting the frontline positions, encouraging and inspiring his soldiers. On 1 August he was promoted oberstgruppenfuehrer (colonel general), an appointment made retrospective to April 1942, and on 5 August he received the Diamonds to the Knight's Cross. Shortly before that award was made, orders came from Fuehrer headquarters that a new offensive was to retake Avranches, where the US forces had broken out of the restricting perimeter of the beachhead and into open country. Both 12th SS and 1st SS were to be committed, although the armoured strength of the Leibstandarte had sunk to just 60 machines. The operation, known as the Mortain offensive, was perhaps the first in military history in which air power alone halted and totally destroyed an armoured offensive. When that assault was smashed, Allied efforts were then directed at the capture of the city of Falaise, and these efforts were redoubled as it became clear that German 7th Army and Panzer Group West were being trapped in the Falaise pocket. Although a great many German soldiers were killed or captured in the Falaise encirclement, sufficient numbers escaped to hold the line north of the Seine river; but Normandy had been lost. On 11 September Dietrich reported to the Fuehrer head-quarters and was ordered to create an SS Army, initially titled 6th Panzer Army and then retitled the 6th SS Panzer Army during April 1945.

The headquarters of 6th Panzer Army were in Heilbronn in north-west Germany, and there, around an initial cadre of just ten officers, the constituent divisions and corps were formed. It was a difficult task, for there were two major problems; manpower shortages and fuel. The terrible casualties suffered during the five years of war had forced a reduction of the original high standards of the Leibstandarte, and for the first time some of the rank and file had had to be conscripted. The other major problem, the shortage of fuel, meant that panzer drivers received so few hours of instruction that they could neither handle their machines nor carry out tactical moves. To compound everything, there was a chronic shortage of battle tanks.

A plan which Hitler had in mind, and of which Dietrich was unaware until shortly before D-Day for the operation, foresaw 6th Panzer Army spearheading an armoured thrust to capture Antwerp, supported on either flank by 5th Panzer Army and 7th Army. This offensive was to become known as the Battle of the Bulge. During the briefing conference on 23 November, attended by most of the senior commanders, Dietrich advised Hitler that he doubted whether 6th Panzer Army would able to play its vital part in the offensive. Then, when he learned more about the operation, he was appalled. The roads allotted to his Army were narrow, unsurfaced and totally unsuitable for the passage of heavy armoured vehicles, and the operation was to be made in December, when there were few hours of daylight. The fuel arrangements were ridiculous. The 6th Panzer Army's stocks were sufficient for only 200km, and most of that stock was held in dumps located far behind the battle line. Fuel would have to be brought forward along roads which would be choked with the soft-skinned and armoured vehicles following the advance. If the 6th Panzer Army was involved in any sort of prolonged fighting, or had to carry out long diversions, the fuel tanks would run dry.

Among the units attached to 6th Panzer Army for the duration of the operation and added to bring the Army's advance forward were two specialist formations; Skorzeny's 150th Panzer Brigade and von der Heydte's 6th Fallschirmjaeger regiment. The arguments between the commander of 6th Panzer Army and von der Heydte came to a head when the paratroop officer asked for carrier pigeons to carry messages because the high hills in the drop zone made it impossible to communicate using standard wireless sets. To that quite reasonable request, Dietrich, who had been drinking heavily, remarked that he was running a panzer Army, not a zoo.

During a final briefing held on 12 December Dietrich repeated to Hitler that 6th Panzer Army was not ready to undertake the offensive, and his stand was supported by the other senior commanders. But it was a Fuehrer Befehl – an order which had to be obeyed. Dietrich's battle plan was for his Army to strike in two waves, with 1st SS Panzer Corps in the van and 2nd SS Panzer Corps eche-loned behind it. The ground over which the assault was to roll was appalling, and one road became an impassable swamp within hours of the first panzers cross-ing it. Despite these difficulties the 6th pressed on with its spearhead formation, Battlegroup Peiper, seeking to find a way out of the valleys in which it was trapped. The surrounding high hills meant that there was little communication between Dietrich and his subordinate formations, and the greatest number of messages received reported units to be low on fuel. In an effort to keep the offensive moving, Dietrich reinforced the point of maximum effort with troops taken from other sectors, but it was a vain effort.

By 27 December he was convinced that the operation had failed. Attempts to swing the main effort behind Manteuffel's 5th Panzer Army, which had made better progress than the 6th, had little effect. Before the end of the year it was clear, even to Hitler, that the Bastogne operation could not be won, and although he attempted to renew offensive operations on the Strasbourg sector, these too, were unsuccessful. Recriminations and accusations of military incom-petence were levelled against Dietrich personally by the other senior comman-ders, although those officers must have known that an Army Commander was, militarily speaking, less important than his Chief of Staff, and Dietrich's Chief of Staff was a very experienced Army officer.

On 12 January 1945 a major Soviet winter offensive opened on the East-ern Front, and Dietrich was called to Berlin to discuss the grave situation with the Army Chief of Staff, Guderian. The plans which had been agreed by those senior officers to defend the Oder river line were rejected by Hitler, who ordered 6th Panzer Army to Hungary to raise the siege of the capital, Budapest. In addition to the cares of military command, Dietrich also had the burden of personal worry about his family, which was living close to the combat zone along the Oder. He resolved that problem by moving his dependants to a flat in south-west Ger-many, but the task of recapturing Budapest, which had fallen to the Russians on 12 February, was an impossible one. Nevertheless, in his usual optimistic fashion Dietrich expected that the operation would take about twelve days, and then the 6th would be sent to the Oder to counter the Russian drive towards Berlin. That was not Hitler's intention. Of greater importance to him was the need to protect Germany's last oil reserves, in Hungary.

For the Fuehrer's new offensive, 'Spring Awakening', Dietrich was ordered to place his Army between two lakes, Balaton and Velence. His attack would be supported by Balck's 6th Army. In the course of an interrogation during his time as a prisoner of war, Dietrich recalled that the lack of success of 6th SS Panzer Army was due to terrain conditions; the ground was a marsh and could not bear the weight of a Tiger tank. The state of the ground could have been learned from a thorough reconnaissance, but Hitler had forbidden this, to keep the operation secret. 'Spring Awakening' failed to gain its objectives, and the consequences of that failure finally convinced Dietrich that all the fighting and bloodshed for Hitler had been in vain.

Enraged at the failure of Dietrich's 6th SS Panzer Army to gain a victory in Hungary, the Fuehrer ordered that the SS Divisions taking part in the operation were to be disgraced. The cuff titles, the visible signs of their allegiance, were to be taken off. The execution of that order is the subject of many stories, most of them apocryphal, like that in which all the armbands and medals, together with the arm of a fallen soldier of the Leibstandarte, were said to have been returned to Hitler in a chamber pot. One more plausible account is that Hitler's humiliating order was not passed down from the senior officers to the rank and file. Called to Vienna to receive a personal reprimand from the Reichsfuehrer SS, Heinrich Himmler, Dietrich tore the Knight's Cross from his throat and flung it down in disgust.

The Red Army captured the oilfields of Hungary on 2 April and Dietrich was then ordered to hold Vienna, a task which he knew to be impossible. One of Dietrich's bitter comments at this time was that his Command was known as 6th Panzer Army because it had only six tanks on establishment. General Rendulic, who was now commanding Army Group South, had received orders from Fuehrer headquarters that the Russians had to be prevented from penetrating deep into central Austria. Rendulic was also aware of the true military situation, but passed the order on to Dietrich as he was duty bound to do. The Red Army fought its way into the Austrian capital and 6th SS Panzer Army was ordered the cross to the northern bank of the Danube on 13 April and take up a line west of Vienna.

Although Dietrich was able to establish some sort of defence in the Gloggnitz area, the rapid pace of events soon brought the military situation to a point where little co-ordination existed between the remnants of Army Group South and 6th SS Panzer Army. On his own initiative Dietrich ordered the 12th SS (Hitler Youth) and the 9th SS (Hohenstaufen) Panzer Divisions to surrender to the American forces. The Leibstandarte was directed to form the rearguard while the sister Divisions surrendered. The headquarters of 6th SS Panzer Army was moved to Zell am See in Austria, and one morning, while he was en route to Kufstein in Tyrol, Dietrich and his wife were captured by the 36th US Division. After undergoing a number of trials as a war criminal and serving more than ten years in prison, Dietrich returned home to Bavaria, where he died on 21 April 1966 of a massive heart attack.

The Rosary Paratrooper

Oberst Friedrich August Freiherr von der Heydte

F riedrich August Freiherr von der Heydte was born in Munich on 30 March 1907, the long-awaited son of a Bavarian noble family. Shortly before Friedrich August was born, his father had retired from the Bavarian Army so that he could devote his whole time to raising his son. As he came from a military background it was accepted that the young Heydte would follow a Service career, and his first step along that road was enrolment as a page at the Bavarian Court. The end of the First World War in 1918, and the declaration of a Socialist republic, prevented the young boy from taking up that post at Court.

The political, revolutionary events in immediate post-war Germany affected him little, although in 1919, at the age of 12, he was one of a group of young lads who pulled down the red flag from a communist-held building in Traunstein. In March 1925 Heydte matriculated, and on 1 April he entered the Army as a recruit in the 19th Infantry Regiment in Landshut. Life as an infantry soldier was not his choice, for he would have preferred to undertake service with the cavalry. An outbreak of measles in the autumn of 1925 was for him a piece of good fortune. A vacancy for a cadet officer in the 18th Cavalry Regiment became available through illness, and Friedrich August entered the barracks of that regiment in Stuttgart-Cannstatt. His time as a cadet officer was not easy, as his instructors were former NCOs who had served in the Great War and who treated their subordinates harshly and trained them hard. This was not an unnecessary dependence upon harshness for harshness' sake. The former front-line soldiers knew the value of the Army dogma that sweat on the parade ground saves blood on the battlefield, and this article of faith was applied by them to every military activity.

By a paradox unforeseen by the victorious allied powers, the limitations of the Treaty of Versailles on the numbers who would be permitted to serve in the German armed forces served only to improve the quality of officers and men. Because of the restrictions the German Army was able to hand-pick its officers from the great mass of volunteers who came forward. Because there was a need to train as many men as possible for command positions, a number of officers or officer cadets were released each year from the Services in order to enter university, where they could improve themselves intellectually. The Army's was a long-term view that one day, when the limiting restrictions of Versailles were lifted and the armed forces were increased in number, those military academics would re-enter the Services as senior officers.

As one of those released into University life, von der Heydte left the 18th Cavalry regiment during the autumn of 1926 and took up the study of law at Innsbruck University. In his free time he devoted himself to religious studies and joined a Catholic society, in which each of the members had to lecture on particular themes. The lectures were followed by vigorous discussions, and those debates sharpened Friedrich-August's already alert brain. The von der Heydte family had fallen on hard times, for its wealth had been invested in war bonds which had lost their value and, in addition, the Bavarian State was too poor to pay pensions to its former officers. Rather than be a burden to his parents, Friedrich August took up the post of private tutor. He had learned to be self-reliant and had also gained a name for piety which later caused him to be mocked by Hermann Goering as the 'Rosary Paratrooper'.

Using the money he had saved from his salary as a tutor, the young Heydte studied for a year in Berlin University, where he learned that the German Foreign Office granted bursaries for students who wished to study in the Austrian Consular Academy. Heydte applied for and was granted a bursary. In the autumn of 1927 he travelled to Vienna and entered the Consular Academy, an institution set up to train foreign students, particularly those from the Succession States of the former Austro-Hungarian Empire. Those countries, chiefly Czechoslovakia, Hungary and Yugoslavia, lacked senior civil servants with diplomatic experience, and the Consular Academy was intended to provide the candidates from those States with the necessary diplomatic training.

Heydte's time in the Consular Academy ended abruptly in 1934, when he and a friend beat up a Nazi student who had insulted the Catholic church. The victim informed the Gestapo, who came to arrest the delinquent pair. Heydte rejoined his cavalry regiment, where the Gestapo had, at that time, no power of arrest. Then came a change of regiment, to 15th Cavalry, which brought with it promotion to full lieutenant. Of greater importance to him was that peacetime Service life still allowed him enough free time to study law in the Hague. During the autumn of 1935 the cavalry squadron with which Heydte was serving was converted to the status of an anti-tank Company. To a passionate horseman this was so great a blow that it came as a relief when, during the winter of 1938-39, he was selected to attend a course for General Staff Officers.

On a personal level, it had been Heydte's intention to marry on 4 October 1938, but the political crisis of that time did not allow him to be absent from his unit and the wedding was postponed for a fortnight. Upon the outbreak of war in September 1939, Heydte was returned from the General Staff course to his unit, where he once again took up command of his anti-tank Company. In the early spring of 1940 he was transferred to become the first assistant to the 1a of 246th Division, and although the part he played in the campaign in the west during May-June 1940 was, by his own account, modest, it was sufficient for him to be awarded the Iron Cross First Class.

With the end of the French campaign came another transfer, this time to become supplies and reinforcements officer in a newly raised Division. This was a boring post which he endured rather than enjoyed, and he was rescued from it when his application to join the paratroop arm of Service was approved. On 1 August Heydte transferred from the Army to the Luftwaffe, joining the 3rd Fallschirmjaeger regiment which was then being created. In that regiment he took over No. 14 Company, the regiment's anti-tank unit, and in an effort to make himself known to every man of his Company he interviewed each of them individually. As a result of the interviews he learned that there were two soldiers on the Company Nominal Roll for whom pay, supplementary pay and rations were being drawn but who did not exist. He stopped that abuse and others which he found. At the successful completion of his jump training Heydte was given command of 1st Battalion of 3rd Regiment, which he led in the invasion of Crete and in fighting for the island. The ground strategy of the campaign was that large battlegroups in approximately regimental strength were to be landed on the north coast of the island. The 3rd regiment, forming part of Battlegroup Centre, was to land and take position between the Western and Eastern battlegroups.

At 0300 on Tuesday 20 May Heydte and his men emplaned. The Junkers Ju 52s took off at dawn, arriving in sight of Crete shortly before 0700. The drop zone for his battalion was around the road running southwards from Canea. The centre of the zone was the prison, located on the south side of a ridge near the village of Galatas, and the greater part of the drop zone was covered with vineyards which led to difficulties when the Jaeger landed. Firstly, they were accustomed to touching down on flat, clear areas, and the sloping and rocky surfaces encountered in Crete caused a great many broken bones. The second problem was that troops dispersed over a wide area come under fire as they try to group, and, thirdly, the coloured weapons containers became targets for the New Zealand defenders, who realised very quickly that the German paratroops were weaponless until they had retrieved and opened the containers and distributed the arms therein.

Heydte descended into a fig tree, cut himself free and once on the road walked until he could see other individual figures unpacking the weapons containers. On the edge of the drop zone he set up a temporary headquarters and collecting point. In a short time he had a small group which he led in an assault to seize the ridge and thereby gain the tactical advantage of holding the high ground looking toward Canea. The New Zealanders holding the village of Galatas and the prison area as a strongpoint offered strong resistance. The Fallschirmjaeger group lacked heavy machine-guns and mortars, and it was clear that any frontal attack launched upon those features would result in heavy losses. Heydte decided upon an indirect approach, and his first attack upon Galatas was made from the north-east. It had to be broken off when ammunition ran short.

Heydte's Fallschirmjaeger group then went over to the defensive for two days, during which time it was strengthened by other, smaller German groups who had marched to the sound of battle. Despite this reinforcement, Heydte's group was still not strong enough to attack and to capture the village. The arrival of Ringl's Gebirgsjaeger allowed the paratroops to move from the defensive to the offensive, and Galatas was taken. The fierceness the fighting can be gauged by the fact that the village was won and lost six times during those few days. The capture of Galatas made it possible for Canea to be attacked, and on 27 May Heydte's battalion formed the right flank unit of the assault, which went in and captured the Akrotiri heights to the east of Canea. It was no easy battle. There was no liaison between Heydte's Jaeger and the mountain artillery battery whose covering fire had been intended to lift the paratroops on to the objective. The attack opened the south-eastern road out of the city, but as the paratroops were laying out air-recognition signals for an air drop a number of British soft-skin vehicles packed with New Zealand soldiers raced towards them. Through a fault in the battle plan Heydte's TAC Headquarters Group was actually marching in front of the paratroop companies and not behind them. There was no infantry to back up Heydte and his group against the approaching British, but, undaunted, he and his handful of men opened fired with a pair of machine-guns to such good effect that their opponents soon surrendered.

The advance towards Canea continued, and Heydte decided not to attack the village of Akrotiros but to bypass it in order to strike into Canea from the south. Against diminishing opposition his battalion entered the town and reached the main square. There he set up his HQ and ordered the Reichs War Flag to be hoisted on a nearby minaret to show that the place was now in German hands. Reconnaissance patrols sent out to determine Allied strength in the town soon returned with two civilians; the mayor and an interpreter. The mayor wished to surrender the city, but it took von der Heydte some time to convince the civilian that he was indeed a German officer. He had lost his cap, and wore on his head a handkerchief knotted at each corner; the trouser legs of his jump suit had been hacked off at the knees and he was in shirtsleeves. Only his waist belt showed him to be of commissioned rank, and after brief negotiation he accepted the surrender of Canea over a glass of wine in a nearby taverna. Heydte's reward for his part in the campaign was the Knight's Cross of the Iron Cross, which he received in the Fuehrer's Wolfschanze headquarters. There then followed a brief return to ordinary military life with parades and training until the call came for his unit to be sent to Russia.

As early as September 1941, only months after the invasion of the Soviet Union, German Army losses had been so great that reinforcements had to be taken from wherever they could be found and rushed to crisis points on the eastern battlefront. Among those units sent to bolster the battle line was, firstly, the 2nd battalion of the Paratroop Assault Regiment and then Heydte's 1st battalion of 3rd Paratroop Regiment. En route to the combat zone outside Leningrad, Heydte took the opportunity to 'organise' a supply of Luftwaffe heavy-duty overcoats for his men. Winter was coming and it seemed to him that no provision had been made to outfit the front-line soldiers to meet the approaching bitter weather.

By the middle of October, German 1st Army advancing south of Leningrad had forced its way over the Neva river and had reached the strategic area of Tichvin. The Red Army responded with an immediate counteroffensive, striking from north to south to recapture the line of the Neva. To meet the Russian thrust, Army Group North launched German counterattacks spearheaded by the Paratroop Assault Regiment's 2nd battalion. These had to be broken off after heavy losses had all but destroyed that unit. Heydte's formation, 1st battalion of 3rd Regiment, was hastily moved forward to maintain the impetus of the German counterattack. After a brief reconnaissance he decided on a night attack, to open at 2200. To reach the start line for that attack he and his men had to undertake a 5km march. Absolute silence was ordered so that the enemy would receive no warning of the impending attack, and Heydte headed the column as it made its advance to contact. He was accompanied by the forward observation officer (FOO), a signaller and a couple of runners, and as the group made its way forward a barrage of shells crashed down around them. They dived for cover, and Heydte found to his horror that he had flung himself into a slit trench layered with Russian and German dead.

At 2200 Very lights climbed into the sky, signalling the opening of the battalion's attack, and Heydte's paratroops charged forward and were soon engaged in hand-to-hand fighting with their Red Army opponents. There then followed a close-combat battle which continued throughout the night until first light on the following morning. Although losses had been low in von der Heydte's battalion, the mental strain upon the Jaeger of hand-to-hand fighting had been enormous. The terror of a battle using entrenching tools, bayonets and paratroop knives had reduced morale very sharply. It was essential for the paratroop officers to overcome the inertia which had set in, and the fact that they succeeded so quickly was due in great part to the realistic training which Heydte had insisted upon. The Germans fighting on the Eastern Front soon realised that when the Russians lost territory they immediately counterattacked to recover it. Heydte's battalion cut the road to the south of the Neva, along which Soviet supplies and reinforcements were moved, and there was no doubt that a Russian counterattack would be made to recapture the lost ground. It came earlier than anticipated when, shortly before midnight, Russian infantry were detected moving forward towards the German positions. Other groups joined them until a whole mass of

Red Army soldiers lay silent, waiting for the order to charge. The night suddenly exploded with the blood-chilling, long-drawn-out baying cry of 'Hooraaaah'. The counterattack had begun.

Heydte fired two Very flares which illuminated the ground in front of his battalion's trenches. Exposed in the harsh white light could be seen a great mass of Soviet soldiers charging towards the road. Two tripod-mounted machine-guns which were being moved to a fresh firing position were ordered to remain where they were, and at Heydte's direction opened fire upon the Russian host, now barely 100m away. The greater number of that mass of Soviet infantrymen died in the fire of those machine-guns, and the survivors fled back across the Neva. Their retreat meant that one enemy bridgehead had been wiped out, and Heydte's battalion was marched north-eastwards to take out a second Russian perimeter which had been created. That bridgehead was too strong to be driven in and destroyed, but German attacks to contain it and to prevent it being enlarged led to more bitter close-combat fighting.

When that died away, a period of relative quiet set in along the battalion sector. One morning Heydte was struck by a shell splinter as he came out of his dugout. Carried into the Regimental Aid Post (RAP), he was being treated when the doctor attending him suddenly fell lifeless across his body. A dagger-shaped piece of shell casing had killed the medical officer as he worked. Shortly after this, Heydte's battalion left the line for rest and recuperation. During that time it was initially detached from its parent formation, 3rd Paratroop Regiment, and renamed Training Battalion No. 2 (Lehr Bataillon 2). Training Battalion No. 1 had been sent to Libya to fight under Rommel's command, and Lehr Bataillon 2 was not to stay long in Germany, for in July 1942 it, too, was sent to Libya, where it formed part of Ramcke's Battlegroup. Heydte's battalion took up position in what the Germans called the El Alamein line, which ran southwards into the desert from Sidi Abd el Rahman on the Mediterranean coast and into the Deir el Shein on the Ruweisat ridge. Heydte's battalion was inserted into the positions held by the Italian 'Bologna' Division.

The Axis armies were preparing for a September offensive designed to out-flank the British position at El Alamein by capturing the vital high ground at Alam Halfa, to the south of Alamein. The plan was that, while the mass of the Panzer-armee attacked in a wheeling south to north move, part of the Bologna Division, with Heydte's battalion under command, was to make a feint attack on the British positions on the high ground of the Deir el Shein. The operation, which has passed into military history as the battle of Alam Halfa, was a complete fail-ure. Not long afterwards Heydte fell sick with dysentery, but upon learning that Montgomery had opened an offensive at El Alamein he returned to his unit, though not completely cured. His battalion was holding positions in a wadi to the west of a camel track and had lost heavily in the fighting of the past days. The offensive at El Alamein which Montgomery had launched was decisive, and within months the Axis armies had been forced to retreat into Tunisia. Heydte was not destined to fight there. An even more severe attack of dysentery caused him to be flown back to Germany.

Once he had recovered physically, he was given the post of 1a in 2nd Paratroop Division, which, in 1943, was being raised in Brittany and trained as a counterattack force to meet the expected Allied invasion.

The time spent in Brittany by 2nd Paratroop Division was brief. The uncertain political situation which was developing in Italy began to deteriorate to a point where the OKW feared that the government of Benito Mussolini might well abandon the Axis camp and sue for a separate peace with the Western Allies. To counter a possible Italian breakaway the Germans produced Operation Alaric, which foresaw the need to disarm the Italian Army and for the whole country to be occupied by German formations. In anticipation of the need for Operation Alaric, most units all round the Mediterranean were put on standby, and 2nd Paratroop Division was one of these. Then came operational orders. Heydte was to take an advance party and fly to the aerodrome at Viterbo, where further instructions would await him. The lack of firm orders was due to a fluctuating political situation which did not allow hard and fast directives to be issued. Everything had to be done with 'fingerspitzengefuehl' with sensitivity and delicacy.

The orders which Heydte received upon landing at Viterbo were to hold open the Viterbo-Rome road and secure billets for the Main of the Fallschirmjaeger Division which was to follow within a matter of days. The Division was flown in and billeted in the accommodation found by Heydte, but there was no immediate call to action. Instead, the Jaeger had a chance to rest and recuperate in the warmth of the Italian summer, but this period of relaxation came to an end during the second week of September. Mussolini's fascist government had been overthrown and replaced by one which intended to sign an armistice to take Italy out of the war. She would thereby cease to be an Axis partner and become an enemy. Alaric was activated, and Heydte was ordered to take prisoner the senior officers of the nearby Italian Division which was guarding the coast against an anticipated Allied invasion. He carried out his mission, and in anticipation of future orders first expanded his battalion's perimeter and then led a fighting patrol of his Fallschirmjaeger towards the Italian capital. En route he accepted the surrender of the entire Sardinian Grenadier Division, and upon his arrival in Rome he set up his TAC HQ in the Colosseum.

With a firm base now set up, he issued demands for the surrender of the Italian General Staff and, as a further piece of bravado, for the surrender of the city of Rome. Using bluff, he soon convinced the authorities that his paratroops had the necessary power to enforce compliance with his demands, and the Italians surrendered. With things apparently under control, Heydte carried out an aerial reconnaissance of the island of Elba, which he expected would be the next objective, and was injured when the aeroplane in which he was flying crashed mysteriously and burst into flames on the ground. In hospital he received orders to raise a new 6th Paratroop Regiment to replace the one which had been almost totally destroyed in the fighting on the Eastern Front and had had to be broken up.

He took his new 6th Regiment into Normandy and trained it intensively in jump procedures and close-combat fighting. At this stage of the war, recruits to the paratroop regiments were given almost no jump training or jumps to qualify them for their wings. The emphasis was now upon producing high-calibre assault infantry soldiers, but Heydte always reckoned with the likelihood of new airborne operations. In Normandy, although his regiment had an independent role it came, for administrative purposes, directly under the command of LXXXIV Corps, which was holding the Cotentin Peninsula. The 6th Paratroop Regiment occupied an area of that peninsula to the north of Periers.

On 5 June a war game was arranged for the senior commanders of 7th Army, but Heydte decided to stay with his regiment. When reports came in of unusually heavy air activity over south-eastern England, he brought it to first-degree readiness. Within hours his 3rd battalion signalled that enemy paratroops were dropping to the north of Carentan, and that report was followed by others telling of airborne drops being made to the east of that city. Heydte concluded that the Allies intended to make their principal effort along the main highway from Cherbourg to Caen via Carentan.

While the battalions of his regiment were moving forward to engage the airborne enemy, Heydte carried out a personal reconnaissance to establish whether St Michel du Mont, the last village before the coast, was still in German hands or whether it had been taken by the Americans. It had not, and 1st battalion was ordered to hold it. Heydte placed the 2nd battalion on the right wing, with orders to advance up the main road towards Cherbourg. The 3rd battalion he held in reserve. American pressure forced the paratroops to withdraw, and eventually they abandoned Carentan itself, an evacuation which led to violent arguments between Heydte and the SS Division 'Goetz von Berlichingen'. That Division had intended to pass through the town en route to the invasion beaches, and considered Heydte's evacuation treason. The SS officers were prepared to court martial the paratroop colonel, but the arrival of the Corps commander, praising the Regiment's staunch defence of the town unaided and unsupported, stopped the SS action.

For six weeks the 6th Regiment held a defensive line below Carentan, although by the end of that time its front was manned by only two Jaeger battalions. The 1st battalion had been almost wiped out in the fighting for Carentan, and the other battalions had suffered such heavy losses that the strength of most of their Companies was down to 40 men; less than a third of establishment.

The sector which the shrunken regiment was holding ran from north of Periers on the south-eastern side to the Seves flats, parallel to the small Seves river. The American positions, on the north-western side of the river, were held by a newly arrived unit. That formation opened an attack during the night of 22 July and soon broke into the sector held by Heydte's 3rd battalion. His counterattack Company, the 16th, was alerted and went in against an enemy of unknown but almost certainly battalion strength. The Company, whose own strength was five officers and 27 men, was given the task of throwing the enemy back across the Seves river and restoring the old front line. The first part of that counterattack involved the Company in a 5km march to contact, and the paratroops were armed only with light, close-quarter weapons. They made their march under a savage artillery barrage towards the sector of the line through which the Americans had broken.

A thorough observation of the ground showed that the US forces had created a gap some 800m wide, both flanks of which were held by small Jaeger detachments. The commander of the counterattack Company took those troops under his command and planned for his attack to go in against the American right flank, close to the village of Seves.

The operation began at 1800, and after a couple of hours of bitter fighting, mostly man-to-man, the American unit, part of 90th Division, was forced back and had lost half of its effectives. The paratroop counterattack Company had suffered only lightly when fighting ended at last light. Uhlig, the counterattack Company commander, intended to resume his attack on the following day, and in his search for reinforcements came across an SS Panzer unit whose commander promised three of his vehicles. A group of paratroops from 3rd battalion provided a heavy-machine-gun group and were positioned in a hollow from where their fire would cut off any American attempt to reinforce their front-line troops, or cut off any retreat if these pulled back under German fire.

The attack opened at 0730 on the 23rd, but soon halted when the SS panzer crews refused to advance unless the Jaeger scouted ahead of their vehicles. They claimed that the close-set bocage terrain favoured the defence, and that US bazooka teams posed too strong a threat. A light German bombardment at 0800 to 'lift' the paratroops into their attack brought in response a far heavier US box barrage which fell close behind the advancing paratroops, compelling their attack to be made at a faster than normal pace. Under Uhlig's attack the American infantry went immediately to ground, and because they offered little resistance the Jaeger advance raced on. Only one of the three SS panzers was able to give the promised support, but its presence forced the enemy troops to surrender. They were forced to do so because they could not withdraw; fire from the two heavy machine-guns stopped their retreat.

By 1100 the battle was over. The old front-line positions had been recaptured and a defensive front set up. This was the last successful attacking action by a unit of German 7th Army, and it was a short-lived victory. Heydte's 6th Regiment was cut off by other US advances, and although a single airdrop of ammunition kept the Companies fighting, it was clear that they could not hold their present positions for long. The 6th was then ordered to move to St Lô to stem an attempted US breakout, but American pressure was now so overwhelming that the remnant of the 6th was involved in three encirclements. Three times they managed to escape, although each time with heavy loss, until Heydte was left with only 40 unwounded men under command. The last encirclement was that at Falaise, from which he and his men broke out and reached Paris.

The survivors of the 6th were posted back to Germany, where they were to be rested, reinforced and retrained. They had little time to rest; the military situation in Belgium was critical. Every available man was rushed to hold the line, and the 6th, made up of tired veterans and untrained recruits, was put back into a sector near the Albert canal. During September 1944 it fought in the Arnhem area, and then in other parts of the Low Countries until October. On the 23rd of that month Heydte received two telegrams. One pleased him; the other did not. The first advised him that he had been awarded the Oak Leaf to the Iron Cross. The second posted him away from his regiment to the Fallschirm Armee Waffen Schule (the paratroop Army Weapons school), where he was to train new officers.

His disappointment in having to give up a combat command for a non-combatant one did not last long, for on 8 December General Student told him: 'The Fuehrer has issued orders for a new and major offensive. One element of this will be a para drop, and you will raise a battlegroup for that operation and will lead it.' To build the battlegroup, every paratroop regiment was ordered to furnish 100 fully qualified paratroop soldiers. Heydte was allowed to choose the NCOs and officers as well as the members of his planning staff, but he had the gravest misgivings that a unit so hastily assembled would possess the inner strength found in units welded together in battle. Without that strength produced by shared and common experience, he would be forced to depend upon the 'paratroop spirit' drilled into every Jaeger, and he was to find, during the mission in the Ardennes, that that spirit – the 'Springer Geist' – was present and filled each man with determination and the will to succeed.

Within 48 hours Heydte had under his command four Jaeger Companies, a 'heavy' weapons Company armed with twelve heavy machine-guns and four mortars, and a Signals and a Pioneer platoon. The battlegroup's units were brought to Aalten only to find that neither equipment nor parachutes had been delivered. From Aalten the group then marched to Sennelager, near Paderborn, but on reaching the aerodrome at 0300 in the morning they learned that neither the officer commanding the aerodrome nor the Luftwaffe senior officers in Mün-ster knew anything about them. This proved to be only the first of a series of dif-ficulties and accidents that dogged the last paratroop drop of the German forces in the Second World War. The missing equipment arrived on 12 December, as did Major Erdmann, the officer commanding the Ju 52 squadron which would fly the group to its drop zone. Erdmann's unit had a very small nucleus of skilled aircrew, the remainder of his men being little more than recruits with no training in formation flying or night flying. Nor had they ever carried out the dangerously intricate operation of dropping paratroops on to an objective. That was the second factor which threw doubt upon a successful outcome of the operation.

At a briefing at Luftwaffe HQ (West), Heydte and Erdmann were given only an outline of the forthcoming offensive. They learned that Model's Army Group was to advance out of the Eifel and head for Antwerp. The tactical questions raised by Erdmann were not gone into. To resolve these, he was told, he would have to liaise with the commander of the Fighter Force (West). Heydte and Erdmann then reported to the Army Group Commander, Model, during the night of 14 December, and were given further details of the operation. Heydte's battlegroup had the task of opening and keeping open a corridor through which 6th Panzer Army, the spearhead formation, would pass to gain the final objective, Antwerp. The commander of 6th Panzer Army, Sepp Dietrich, did not give precise battle orders when he and Heydte met during the morning of 14 December. His directive was a repetition of Model's briefing: 'Your battlegroup will hold the northwest crossing of the Schnee Eifel heights at the road junction of Malmedy-Vervier, 15km north of Malmedy, and keep those crossing points open for 6th Panzer Army's advance'. The drop was to go in on D-Day just before the German artillery barrage opened at first light.

Heydte and his staff worked hard to produce a battle plan. The mission would not be an easy one. The untrained paratroops, brought to their drop zones by untrained pilots, would jump by night over a heavily wooded and swampy area. The drop zone lay some 75km behind the American front line, and there was absolutely no information on the location, disposition or strength of the opposing American forces. Heydte requested that reconnaissance aircraft overfly the American area to establish the details essential to the success of the drop, but his request was brusquely rejected on the grounds of security. He then asked to be supplied with any aerial photographs of the drop zone, and when these could not (or perhaps would not) be produced, he pointed out that the high hills of the Eifel area would interfere with, and might even prevent, communication between units. To overcome that problem he asked for carrier pigeons which could be used by FOOs to direct fire on to enemy batteries, only to be told by Dietrich: 'I do not run a zoo'.

The next discussion was with General Pelz, with whom the problems of flying in the transport aircraft and the paratroop drop had to be hammered out. It was finally arranged that, because of the lack of training, the Ju 52s would take off from the Paderborn aerodrome and fly along a corridor of searchlights towards the target area. Upon approaching the objective, the machines would be regrouped so as to fly along another avenue of lights to the drop zone. Fifteen minutes before the drop time, a Junkers Ju 88 master bomber would release signal bombs so that they formed an area approximately 1 to 2km in extent which would be the drop zone for the whole battlegroup. In addition to having a master bomber illuminate the target, other aircraft would drop short-lived 'christmas tree' markers before and after the drop. These would illuminate the target area and allow the Jaeger who had landed to locate each other and regroup. At the same time as the operation began, the Luftwaffe High Command planned for two 'Chinese' attacks to go in. Bombers would illuminate two other areas, to the north and west of the real target area, and drop paratroop dolls. The Luftwaffe High Command reasoned that, faced with the threat of three paratroop landings, the US 18th (Airborne) Corps would be forced to waste time establishing which drop was the real one, and more time in taking action to contain it. That delay, it was hoped, would aid the battlegroup's operations.

Erdmann and Heydte returned to their headquarters, each exhausted, annoyed and deeply concerned about the outcome of the forthcoming mission. Awaiting their arrival was the executive order for the mission, which set the time and date as 0300 on 16 December. The schedule also laid down that at last light on the 15th an Army transport column would take the battlegroup to take-off airfields at Paderborn and Lippspringe. The early part of the 15th was spent issuing orders, checking and drawing weapons and preparing for the operation. The arrival of the transport column at 1700 eased the tension until it was learned that the fuel tanks of the lorries were empty and that there was no more fuel available. It took until 2200 for petrol to be located and for the soft-skin machines to be tanked up. Even then there was not sufficient for the whole battlegroup to be taken by lorry to the airfields. Heydte estimated that only a third, some 400 men, would be able to fly the mission. His estimate was rejected by High Command, who thereupon cancelled the operation.

Then, at noon on 16 December, a telephone call informed Heydte that, on the direction of the Chief of Staff of 6th Panzer Army, the operation orders had been changed. Hitler's offensive had not made the expected gains, and it was anticipated that the Americans would bring down troops from the Aachen area to strike into the right flank of the SS Panzer Army. The aborted paratroop drop was reactivated, and was to be made during the night of 16/17 December. The task was no longer to hold open the routes for the advancing troops of 6th Panzer Army. Now it was the mission of Heydte's battlegroup to block those routes and halt, or at least reduce, the flow of American troops and supplies.

For this new mission the full-strength unit was brought by lorries to the airfields. Shortly before midnight, after singing the paratroop anthem, the Jaeger emplaned and the transports took off, with Heydte flying in the lead machine. The group then encountered the final setback. There had been a miscalculation in flying time; the force of the headwinds blowing across the Schnee Eifel had not been taken into account by the inexperienced pilots. They had worked on a strict time factor to determine when to drop their 'sticks' of men, and were miles short of the Drop Zone when the signal came 'prepare to jump'. Heydte, pressing his broken arm in a sling, flung himself through the exit door of the machine. He had an unfamiliar triangular canopy of Russian design, and landed heavily. The drop had not been carried out in the forecast wind force of 4 to 6m per second, but had been made in a gale force wind of 12 to 15m per second, accompanied by snow showers. Finding himself alone, Heydte made his way to the road junction nominated as the first rallying point. As he moved towards the crossroads he was joined by other soldiers of his group. He was not to know that US anti-aircraft fire had dispersed the in-flying armada, and that the paratroops had been so widely spread across the countryside that some of them actually landed in Bonn.

By first light, 125 men had reported in, less than a tenth of the number dropped, but among them was the SS FOO, his signaller and his runner. All three had jumped for the first time, without any training in how to land. So far as arms and ammunition were concerned, the men of the battlegroup had only the weapons and ammunition with which they had jumped, and only six of the arms containers were found, and then only after a long search. Among the equipment in the containers was a small wireless set, a mortar and several rounds of ammunition.

As daylight grew the battlegroup melted into the dense forests and took up all-round defensive positions. Heydte's first priorities were to establish communication with 6th Panzer Army and to locate the position of the US forces. The wireless set was so badly damaged that it could send no signals reporting the battlegroup's positions nor pass on details of US infantry and artillery positions. It was particularly frustrating that messages captured from US despatch riders could not be sent to Army for evaluation. In a desperate effort to establish some sort of communication Heydte sent out runners, but not one made it across the 50km gap from the drop zone to the German front.

On the third day of the operation Heydte's group met up with another 150 men of the battlegroup. Shortly after that the first American prisoners of war were taken; a dozen or so men of a rear-echelon unit. After dark those men, together with several injured paratroopers, were sent off towards the US lines. Another group of American soldiers was captured on the fourth day, and were released that night. The first seriously wounded paratrooper had to be left behind with another group of prisoners. He could not be carried as he had been shot in the stomach. By this time Heydte's men were at the end of their tether. They had long since consumed the hard rations they carried, and ammunition was running short. The group could hear no sounds of battle, except at Elsenborn, towards which American vehicles rolled by day and night.

On the fourth day Heydte decided to break out eastwards in the hope of making contact with the main German force, and on the morning of the fifth day, having crossed a freezing stream with water running breast-high, the group clashed with US units supported by armour. Heydte's men pulled back into the forest, where, on 21 December, he decided to break his group into three-man detachments. He himself was among one of the last groups to leave the area, and his small party reached Monschau, where they found shelter in various civilian houses.

Heydte was quartered with a teacher, and on the morning of 24 December he sent the teacher's son to the nearest US military post with his offer of surrender. He expected that the Americans would summarily execute him. For him the war was over, but he then faced proceedings in respect of unfounded accusations that he was a war criminal. Not until the autumn of 1947 was he released, and he returned home to take up first a university post, and then a career in politics until his retirement. Heydte, who had been promoted to a General of paratroops in the Bundeswehr, died in 1994.

Smiling Albert

Generalfeldmarschall Albert Kesselring

In his book *Soldat bis zum letzten Tag*, Albert Kesselring describes how, as early as the 12th century, his forefathers had defended the Christian, teutonic Western lands against invasions by the Slav and Magyar peoples. With such a warrior tradition as an inspiration, it is no surprise that Albert set his heart on becoming a soldier.

He was born on 13 November 1885 in Marksteft in Lower Franconia, into a family of teachers, councillors and academics. Some branches of the family were landowners or farmers, and it was on their modest estates that the young boy roamed free and learned country lore and how to be self reliant. He attended school in Bayreuth and, after matriculating in 1904, enlisted into the 2nd Bavarian Fussartillerie Regiment, at that time stationed in Metz. The Fussartillerie lacked the panache of the Horse or Field branches and dealt with the heavy guns of the siege artillery. As Kesselring was not the son of an officer, his path to a commission had to come through educational ability. Once accepted into the Army he carried out cadet training, studied at the War School and in 1907 was promoted from Ensign rank to that of Leutnant. From 1909 to 1910 he studied at the artillery academy, and in an attempt to improve his career possibilities he volunteered for service as an observer in the Imperial Balloon Arm.

At the outbreak of the First World War Kesselring first served with his regiment but was then posted to act as an aide de camp to a Bavarian artillery general. His future participation in the Great War was restricted to Staff appointments, including periods as a general staff officer with 1st (Bavarian) Landwehr Division on the Eastern Front and, later, on the staff of III Bavarian Corps. The return of the defeated German Army was marked with incidents, usually armed attacks by civilians or by soldiers of the communist military councils. Despite these provocations, Kesselring's unit returned to its depot in Nuremberg in good order. Then came the threat to Germany's eastern territories from Polish insurgent bands, and Kesselring, by this time holding the rank of captain, was active in raising volunteer units and putting down communist attempts at fomenting revolution. Towards the end of 1918 he applied to leave the Service but was asked to stay on and assist in the demobilisation of the Army. The office in which he worked was a hotbed of newly-appointed communist, civilian political appointees who, in 1919, had him summarily arrested and imprisoned. No charges could be brought against him, and Kesselring was released.

Despite these events, the young captain entered the Reichswehr, the Army of the Weimar Republic, and served as a battery commander for more than three years. By this time promoted to major, he was transferred to the covert War Ministry and served in the office of the Chief of the Army. During his years in the Reichswehr Ministerium he was involved with all of the Army's administrative functions; training, organisation and weapons. Of his work at this time it could be claimed that Major Kesselring was acting as Chief of Staff to the Chief of the General Staff, Hans von Seeckt, and together with another officer of the Army's Organisation Department he wrote a memorandum on the necessity for a General Staff. The report was well received and Kesselring was then transferred to other headquarters where he undertook a number of Staff appointments. In 1930 he returned to active service as a battalion commander with 4th Artillery Regiment in Dresden.

His career in the Army ended abruptly when, on 1 October 1933, he was posted sideways into the newly-created Luftwaffe and joined its headquarters staff. His sideways transfer was almost brutal in its execution. The Luftwaffe Chief of Personnel offered him a prominent position, which he declined. A little later the Army Chief of Staff asked whether the offer had been made and accepted. When Kesselring sought to explain why he had not accepted the post, the Army Chief of Staff interrupted him, saying: 'You are a soldier and you will do what you are told to do'.

In 1933 the Luftwaffe was still considered a defensive force, acting as a shield against foreign aggression, and it therefore lacked any aggressive aircraft or weapons. This is not to say that the Luftwaffe intended to remain defensive in outlook. Its leaders looked forward to the time when the Service expanded and constituted the third arm of the new German Wehrmacht. Under General Hermann Goering this came about soon after the Nazi accession to power. All air units which had been on the strength of the Army or Navy were absorbed into the Luftwaffe under his slogan: 'Everything that flies in the Third Reich belongs to me'.

Kesselring's task when the expansion of the air force began was to liaise with civilian and air force officials in acquiring the ground for the future barracks and airfields, and to oversee their growth and development. As a reward for his outstanding performance in planning and construction, he was promoted to the rank of Generalmajor on 1 March 1935.

Despite Kesselring's excellent work in creating the infrastructure of the new Luftwaffe, numbers of aircraft in the new Force had not kept pace and were decidedly modest. By the end of 1934 the Luftwaffe order of battle consisted of just five bomber squadrons, three fighter squadrons and three long-range and two short-range reconnaissance squadrons. The next step forward in Albert Kesselring's service life was his advancement to the post of Chief of the Luftwaffe General Staff. He was appointed to that position by Goering's direct order on 3 June 1938, following the death of the incumbent, General Wever. One of Kesselring's first acts on taking over the post was to propose that Germany send an air force contingent to test the Luftwaffe's machines and equipment under active service in the Spanish Civil War. In 1936 the German paratroop arm had been created, and Kesselring devoted much time and energy to forming the new élite force. During his period of service as Chief of Staff Kesselring had a number of disputes with the Secretary of State for Air, General Milch, and as a result asked either for a transfer to other duties of for permission to leave the Service. As a compromise, Goering posted him to Dresden as Chief of Staff to the General Commanding Luftflotte (Air Fleet) 3 and promoted him from lieutenant general to General of the Air Force.

The Czechoslovak crisis of autumn 1938 brought Luftflotte 3 to full war alert. The Czech State projected into Reichs territory, making Germany's principal cities in the east likely targets for aggressive Czech air action. To counter this possibility, Kesselring had airfields constructed close to the frontier, from where German fighters would be able to intercept raiding aircraft coming from either France or Czechoslovakia. Acting upon Hitler's instruction, Goering changed the operational orders under which the Air Fleet was to operate. Now it was to not to act defensively but aggressively, and Kesselring was to plan operations against targets inside Czech territory. An additional aggressive mission was planned. This was for an airborne attack to be carried out by the newly formed 7th Flieger Division. The Fallschirmjaeger were to land behind the Czech fortress area and attack the emplacements from the rear. In the event, the Munich conference and the political agreement signed there made the planned attacks unnecessary. Kesselring's next posting was to Berlin, where he took over Luftflotte 1 on 1 October 1938.

The acute political crisis in Europe could not be resolved politically, and throughout the summer of 1939 armed conflict became more likely. When war did come, Kesselring's Luftflotte 1 collaborated with the other two Services in the campaign against Poland. Although it was chiefly his Luftflotte which carried the burden of the air battle, in addition to his role as Commander in Chief of an Air Fleet he insisted on visiting aerodromes to welcome the machines and men returning from raids on enemy targets. For his work in the campaign Kesselring was awarded the Knight's Cross of the Iron Cross, and this was presented to him in the Reichs Chancellery.

The declaration of war by both Britain and France, following Germany's invasion of Poland, demonstrated that the conflict had ceased to be European and local, and was now world-wide. Luftflotte 1 now had to prepare itself against the possibility of Allied air raids upon the Reichs capital, and this involved

Kesselring in the task of reorganising the anti-aircraft defences within his Luft-flotte's area. Early in 1940 Kesselring, together with the senior officers of the Luftwaffe, was ordered to report to the Supreme Commander, Goering. The only item on the agenda of that conference dealt with an officer who had been carrying the projected plans for the war against the Western Powers when his aircraft crash-landed in Belgium. Goering was furious because the battle plans had been compromised through the negligence of one of his Luftwaffe officers. As a consequence of the affair the GOC of Luftflotte 2 was sacked and replaced by Kesselring. He was now responsible not only for conducting the air war against Britain, but also for drafting new plans for air operations which would be carried out by his Luftflotte during the War in the West. The OKW battle orders were that his force was to co-operate with Army Group B, the formation which was to make the major effort for the War in the West, codenamed Unternehmen Gelbe (Operation Yellow).

Kesselring's time between assuming the post of Chief of Air Fleet 2 and D-Day for the new war was fully taken up with conferences and inspections of the units of his new Command, as well as with training practices and full-scale rehearsals dealing with the movement of his units. On 10 May the six Fliegerko-rps making up Luftflotte 2 and Luftflotte 3 opened the War in the West and had soon scored successes. Those initial victories, the result of careful planning and scrupulous attention to detail, were to be overshadowed by a major tactical defeat. Goering, buoyed up by the Luftwaffe's victories, proposed to Hitler that the Army's advance be halted so that his air force could carry out the destruction of the Allied hosts trapped in the Dunkirk perimeter. The Army commanders spoke out energetically against Goering's plan, as did the Luftwaffe's senior officers. Kesselring, whose air fleet would have the task of flying the missions to destroy the Allied forces on the ground, told his superior in no uncertain terms that even were his Luftflotte to be reinforced it would still lack the strength to carry out the proposed task. Goering insisted that Kesselring's air fleet carry out the mission, and on 25 May the squadrons went in action. Despite the rain of bombs from the Luftwaffe there was no pause in the evacuation of the British and French soldiers, and Dynamo, the operation to bring out the British Expeditionary Force, was concluded on 4 June, by which time the Royal Navy had brought off more than 300,000 men.

Generalmajor von Richthofen, who led VIII Fliegerkorps in Luftflotte 2, spoke for his comrades when he wrote that, as a result of Hitler's intervention, victory had been cast away. Goering's boast had not been fulfilled, and Kessel-ring in his memoirs wrote that the task laid upon his Air Fleet would have been beyond the capabilities of even fresh formations. His own squadrons were exhausted after the strain of nearly a month on active service, during which time they had had to carry out missions against the Dunkirk air operation and collab-orate with the Army in its ground campaign on other sectors. The weakness of his Luftflotte, about which Kesselring complained, was ignored at OKW when the second phase of the War in the West was ordered. Without time to regroup his squadrons, he was ordered to support ground operations along the line of the rivers Somme and Seine. Despite the strain of operational planning, he met all the demands that Army Group B laid upon Air Fleet 2, and within weeks the French Army had been shattered. An armistice was signed on 22 June, and the War in the West ended. It was clear that the next operations to be undertaken would be those against Britain, and that they would be made in conjunction with a planned seaborne operation, Seeloewe, which was to be launched in the summer or early autumn of 1940.

As the first move of his Luftflotte's role in Seeloewe, Kesselring set up *Freya* masts (a type of radar) and a highly powered wireless intercept system in order to listen in on the radio messages passing between the RAF ground controllers and the pilots flying operational missions. Action then passed from intelligence gathering to launching the first bombing raids against ships, during which there were duels between German and British fighter aircraft. Reichsmarschall Goering visited the front-line squadrons of Kesselring's air fleet in July, and in a speech to its senior commanders told them that Hitler had given the order that the Luftwaffe was to smash the RAF so that a German military and naval force could follow up and occupy the United Kingdom. Kesselring and Sperrle, the commanders of Luftflotten 2 and 3, spoke out against the tactics which the Reichsmarschall intended to use to fight the campaign. Both were opposed to deploying their bomber squadrons until Fighter Command had been overwhelmed and the RAF's infrastructure, notably its airfields and radar installations, had been destroyed or at least severely damaged. Despite the powerful arguments advanced by Kesselring and Sperrle to show that their combined forces were too weak for the task, their objections were overruled by the Luftwaffe's Supreme Commander. Goering had estimated the strength of their two Luftflotten to be 4,500 machines, and was visibly shaken when his two Field Commanders told him that the true number of aircraft available for operations was only 700.

Shortly after the declarations of the two commanders, Hitler made an appeal to Britain to end the war. In the confident expectation that this would be agreed to by Churchill's government and that the war would then end, he announced a series of promotions. Kesselring advanced two ranks to become a generalfeldmarschall. However, Churchill rejected the German Fuehrer's offer of peace, and the war continued.

At the beginning of August 1940 Kesselring chaired a conference of his subordinate commanders, to discuss future operations against the United Kingdom. Hitler had now authorised attacks upon mainland Britain, hitherto forbidden, and the problem facing the officers of the Luftflotte was still that of overcoming the resistance of Fighter Command. Luftwaffe Supreme Command decided to field all three air fleets in the west. Accordingly, orders were issued for air fleets 2, 3 and 5 to be combined to carry out the attacks. It was planned that a four-day intensive struggle, commencing on 'Eagle Day', would wrest air supremacy from the British. That phase would be followed by a four-week period to consolidate upon any gains made. The seaborne invasion would then follow.

It is said that if it is possible for something to go wrong, then it will. Eagle Day, 12 August, proved the truth of that statement. The first mission flown was intended to take out Eastchurch Aerodrome, Kent. At the last minute orders came for the raid to be cancelled because of poor visibility. These were acted upon by the fighter squadrons but not by the bomber units, because they had already taken off. The fighters detailed to accompany the bombers did not fly, and the bombers flew their missions unescorted, losing eight machines. It was a bad start for the battle that was intended to precede the invasion, and the situation did not improve. On 20 August, with no victory in sight, Kesselring was ordered to concentrate the whole of his fighter strength in the Pas de Calais area. The RAF would be overwhelmed by the sheer numbers of German fighter aircraft who were to escort the bomber squadrons to their targets.

Despite the strength and number of the missions flown against Britain, these were launched to conceal the fact that a new war was being planned. In late 1940 the Third Reich began to run down the forces gathered for Seeloewe and to move many of these in secret to the new projected operational area; the Eastern Front. As early as the autumn of 1940 Hitler had decided to attack Russia, and plans for the new campaign were in active preparation. The Luftwaffe formations on the Channel coast continued to carry out raids and sweeps as if Seeloewe was still under active preparation, and Army and Kriegsmarine units, although scaled down in number, also carried out manoeuvres and assault-landing exercises, but these were all a mask to hide the eastwards move, and a costly mask, at that. Losses suffered in the fighting during the Battle of Britain, which reached a climactic phase between 8 August and 15 September, considerably reduced the strength of Luftflotte 2.

On the morning of 6 September Goering arrived at Kesselring's headquarters on the Channel coast to take over command of air operations against Britain. Kesselring wrote: 'It was a bitter period. The Luftwaffe strained every nerve to destroy the British armaments industry and mined the coastal waters to halt the flow of supplies. It was the dissipation of the Luftwaffe's strength against so many objectives that caused the whole offensive to fail.' A far greater, strategic error on the part of the Reichsmarschall was that he had not built long-range, four-engined bombers as Wever and Kesselring had proposed. The air force was equipped with short-range machines with limited bomb-carrying capacity. In the immediate pre-war years Goering had demanded vast numbers of aircraft and had obviously not seen the need for strategic bombers.

When Kesselring reported to Goering that RAF Fighter Command had still not been destroyed in air battle, the Supreme Commander decided to intensify the air raids against London. He anticipated, wrongly as it transpired, that the RAF would be forced to put up its fighter squadrons to defend the capital. While the fighter squadrons were busy defending London, as Goering thought they must, the Luftwaffe's other objectives would lie unprotected and could be destroyed. Therein, declared Goering, lay the key to success in the Battle of Britain. The climax came on 15 September, and resulted in a defeat for Goering's tactics. The Reichsmarschall returned to Germany, and in a speech to the Luftwaffe commanders made the accusation that the fighter arm had failed him. Although raids against British targets continued, it was clear to Kesselring and his subordinates that the air war in the west was being scaled down. They could not at first understand the reason for this, but in time learned of the War in the East which was being planned, and in which Luftflotte 2 was to play a prominent part. There its task would be to support Army Group Centre, one of the three major military groups which would fight the ground campaign.

When Kesselring went on Christmas leave he became aware of the differences between active service conditions and those in the homeland, and noted in particular the inefficiency of the German air defences. He demanded and gained an improvement in the civil defences of the Reich. At the beginning of 1941 he flew to Warsaw to discuss the forthcoming war, as well as to study the state of the Luftwaffe's ground organisation. During a second visit he was alarmed to find that the construction work he had ordered on his initial visit had not been completed; nor would it be before D-Day for the new campaign.

Inspection trips to units in the field showed that his Luftflotte was too weak in aircraft numbers, in his opinion, to play the role demanded of it in Operation Barbarossa, as the new campaign was codenamed. Aware that his Command would be in no position to support Army Group Centre adequately, he visited Goering in May to detail his Luftflotte's weaknesses. During that first discussion, as well as in subsequent ones, Kesselring was repeatedly rebuffed. He was told that he was not the only Luftflotte commander who demanded more aircraft, but he insisted on pressing the point that there was no purpose served in hiding the truth. At its present strength his air fleet was too weak to undertake the dual tasks of destroying the Soviet Air Force on the ground and supporting the operations of Field Marshal von Bock's Army Group. By 15 June 1941 the concentration of Kesselring's Luftflotte had been completed, and the remaining days before Barbarossa opened were filled with troop inspections and conferences.

One problem which arose at that time was that 'H' Hour for the Army Group's opening assault was set for 0330. For the Luftwaffe to fly the first missions, planned to destroy the Soviet Air Force on the ground, it was essential for its machines to operate in daylight, but dawn was not until 0430. The one-hour gap between the Army and Luftwaffe 'H' Hours would give the Russian squadrons warning of impending attacks. To cover that gap, Kesselring formed a special squadron whose crews were trained in night flying. They would bomb selected

Russian airfields at the same time as the ground forces opened their assaults. The operation, mounted by Kesselring's Luftflotte, was a total success, and no Russian fighter opposition was met for several days. During that lull enemy air bases and airfields up to 300km behind the Soviet lines were attacked and destroyed. Kesselring reported to Goering that no fewer than 2,500 enemy aircraft had been destroyed on the ground, a claim that the Supreme Commander did not believe, for he had been told that the whole Soviet Air Force numbered only 6,000 machines. A check showed that Kesselring's figure had been, if anything, too modest. But then came the order that his squadrons were to concentrate on supporting the ground forces and were no longer to destroy the enemy's fighter strength. The Russians, relieved of the burden of fighting an unequal war in the air, were free to attack German ground targets.

The great advances of summer and early autumn 1941 soon halted when rain produced clogging mud and then winter weather stopped all operations. In November 1941 Kesselring and the greater part of Luftflotte 2 were posted away from Russia to southern Europe. There he took up the post of Supreme Commander South, subordinate to both OKW and the Italian Commando Supremo. At a Fuehrer conference Hitler told Kesselring that one of his principal tasks was to defeat the Royal Navy so that Axis convoys could reach the forces fighting in Libya. Kesselring's proposal that Malta be attacked and captured was turned down because Germany lacked the forces to carry it out, and Hitler did not trust the Italians to undertake the task. The Fuehrer decided that he needed a first-class administrator and not a Field Commander. He had become increasingly aware of the Italian State's inefficient handling of its war effort, and realised that only someone of Kesselring's proven ability and persuasive powers could master the situation.

For the next few years it was to be the Generalfeldmarschall's task to stiffen Italy's resolve, to encourage the military build-up and to ensure that Mussolini's fascist state remained a loyal ally of the Third Reich. It was no easy task. The greater part of the Italian officer corps, and especially the senior commanders, were loyal to the king and not to the dictator, and most had fought against Germany in the First World War and were therefore pro-British.

In his directive to Kesselring to defeat the Royal Navy, Hitler had set out the correct priority. The losses of ships convoying men and materials to the African Theatre of Operations were alarmingly high, and few convoys reached Tripoli without some ships being sunk. Kesselring was well aware of the vital importance of the island of Malta to the British desert army, and his air fleet mounted attack after attack against convoys sailing towards the island, as well as against the island's harbour installations. The plan which Kesselring had earlier proposed to attack and seize Malta was revived and codenamed Unternehmen Herkules. It was to be an airborne assault, and the decision to mount the offensive was reached by Hitler and Mussolini at a conference on 29 April 1942. In the opinions of Kesselring and Rommel, the capture of Malta was the *sine qua non* before an advance by the Panzerarmee to the Suez canal could begin. Despite the confident prophecies of Rommel, Kesselring and Paratroop General Student, Hitler suddenly cancelled the operation.

Kesselring's area of command was vast, covering the area from south of the Alps to the Libyan desert and from Gibraltar to the eastern end of the Mediterranean. He needed all his skills as an administrator, his ability as a diplomat and his command of military matters to master the complex problems which beset him. One of the greatest difficulties he encountered was that the decisions he made as a result of local knowledge, personal experience or military logic were either rejected or amended by senior officers in Berlin. He was convinced that an Anglo-American invasion of French North Africa was imminent, but when he relayed his assessment of the situation Goering refused to accept his conclusions. Hitler, the Supreme Commander and the High Command all believed that any invasion would be made against southern France. When Kesselring then proposed that a German Division be stationed in Sicily as a preventive measure he was considered alarmist. Nevertheless he moved his own headquarters guard Company to the island and placed a battalion of paratroops on alert.

The need for the measures he had taken soon became apparent when the Allies invaded Algeria and Tunisia in November 1942. Hitler was determined to hold Africa. Its loss would be a serious blow to Italian as well as German morale. He telephoned Kesselring and asked what troops could be sent to hold Tunisia. The Generalfeldmarschall's reply was that his own headquarters detachment and the 5th Fallschirmjaeger regiment were immediately available. Hitler then ordered Kesselring to rush anything and everything available to French North Africa. With that small force he was expected to create a vast perimeter in Tunisia, into which the Axis desert armies could be withdrawn and which he was to hold until reinforcements arrived.

Although Kesselring had often flown to Libya, either to confer with Rommel and the Commando Supremo or to determine for himself the situation on the ground, for some unexplained reason Hitler expressly forbad him to fly to Tunisia. Despite that prohibition the Generalfeldmarschall knew that his most important task was to hold a line along the Algerian-Tunisian frontier. He emphasised the importance of holding that perimeter when General Nehring reported to him in Frascati on 13 November. During that conference Nehring was told that he had been appointed to command XC Corps, but Kesselring pointed out that the formation existed only in name. The Corps had neither troops nor a Staff structure, and it would have to work by rule of thumb for the foreseeable future. But the troop movements which the Generalfeldmarschall had ordered were taking effect, and soon a stream of military units which he had either diverted or deflected began to reach Tunisia. That stream of reinforcements made Nehring's seemingly impossible task more feasible.

But the establishment of a Tunisian perimeter was not the only problem besetting Kesselring. The greater one by far was that of Rommel, who, although subordinate to him, simply refused to listen to his superior or accept orders which were not to his liking. So far as Rommel was concerned, his first responsibility was to ensure than the German desert army remained an independent fighting force, under his command. Although past relations between the two men had been agreeable, it was clear to Kesselring that Rommel's attitude was likely to create difficulties and disharmony between the German and Italian senior commanders, and that this would affect future military operations. A third problem besetting the Generalfeldmarschall was that, in addition to pursuing the land war in a country he was not allowed to enter, he had also to oversee the air operations of his Luftflotte over that forbidden territory.

Working almost by instinct gained from his long professional training, he decided to counter Allied air operations by moving every available Luftwaffe formation into Sicily and Sardinia. Despite Hitler's order forbidding it, Kesselring flew to Tunis to be briefed by Nehring on the situation. The thin screen of German forces had been able to halt the first eastward advance of the Allied 'Blade Force', but whether that screen could hold the Anglo-American units at bay for long was doubtful. At that conference the Corps Commander drew his superior's attention to the continued lack of a Staff structure and the inadequate bayonet strength of his formation. He stressed the need for complete and well-armed formations if the Allies were to be held. Kesselring assured him that these would be received, then had to fly back to Rome to try and resolve the difficulties which had arisen between Rommel and his Italian superiors.

Kesselring spent Christmas and the New Year in the desert with Rommel's Panzerarmee, and as a result of the inspections he carried out he was able to report that the morale of the German troops was high and that they were prepared to carry on fighting. At a conference between the German and Italian High Commands in Libya, Rommel made it very plain he wished to withdraw with all possible speed from the Italian colonies and take his army into the Tunisian bridgehead. Kesselring and the Italians protested against this, but by the end of January 1943, in defiance of their protests, Panzerarmee Africa had crossed the frontier and was embattled in southern Tunisia. The end of the war in Africa was close at hand.

When that end came, in May 1943, Kesselring faced new problems. The Allies had gained strategic freedom of movement and could land at almost any point they chose in the Mediterranean. For his part, as defender of the southern shore, he could only assess where an invasion might come and make dispositions to meet it. It had been clear to him for some time that the most threatened area was Sicily, the stepping stone to the mainland of Italy. He reasoned that the island could best be defended by flinging back the invading Allied forces before they could set up strong beachheads. As part of his defensive plan he ordered

Luftflotte 2 to bomb the ports along the North African coast in which the invading armada was concentrating. His measures had little effect. The invasion of Sicily began on 10 July, and the Allies had soon set up perimeters on the island's eastern side which they held against the attacks of the Axis forces.

The Italian commander, Guzzoni, proposed to withdraw troops from the western half of the island to reinforce the eastern sector, but Kesselring advised against this. There then followed a farcical situation with the Italian General issuing one set of orders and von Senger, the German General commanding the ground troops, sending others. Kesselring flew to the island, not only to bring order out of the confusion, but also to check on the story that Italian formations were surrendering without firing a shot. He found the story to be true, and to cover the loss of the Italian formations he ordered the immediate transfer of German troops from the mainland to the island. The first reinforcements to come in were paratroop units, and these were followed by 29th Panzer Grenadier Division. Kesselring sought in vain to wrest the operational initiative from the Allies, but had to accept that the west side of the island, garrisoned mainly by Italian formations, would have to be evacuated. The main resistance would have to be put up against the British Eighth Army, which was fighting its way up the mountainous eastern side of Sicily. By now the situation was irretrievable, and, accepting that he had done his best, Kesselring ordered a slow-paced withdrawal to allow the bulk of the German forces on Sicily to reach the embarkation ports in the north. From these they could be shipped to the mainland to defend southern Italy against the Allies.

Soon the inevitable happened and Sicily was lost. Serious though that disaster was, one of greater significance had happened on the Italian mainland, where a palace revolution had overthrown Mussolini. The Generalfeldmarschall had a conference with Marshal Badoglio, who had been charged by King Victor Emmanuel to take over the Italian government. During that discussion Kesselring asked to be taken where Mussolini was being held, saying that the Duce was his immediate superior, to whom he was duty bound to report. His request went unanswered because Badoglio claimed he did not know where the dictator had been taken. Although King Victor Emmanuel and the senior military commanders assured Kesselring that Italy would continue the war as a ally of the Third Reich, he was not convinced that they were telling the truth. Hitler shared that opinion, and directed Kesselring to concentrate units in preparation for a counter-revolution which would overthrow the Badoglio government and restore Mussolini to power.

First, it was necessary to liberate the Duce. His place of captivity was quickly established. He was in a mountain-top hotel in the Gran Sasso range. An operation was mounted and carried out by a battlegroup made up of SS commandos and Fallschirmjaeger. Almost concurrent with that rescue mission, units of 2nd Fallschirmjaeger Division arrived to reinforce the German garrisons in central and southern Italy. Then a new complication arose. Kesselring learned that the Italian General Staff intended to withdraw its troops which were occupying southern France and use them to block the Alpine passes on the French-Italian border against a French invasion. Were this to happen, communications between the German armies in southern France and those in Italy would be lost.

During the time that each of the several crises was being dealt with, not only had Sicily been lost, but Italy left the Axis and allied herself with the Western Powers, and the Italian mainland was invaded by Montgomery's Eighth Army on the Adriatic side as well as by the Anglo-American Fifth Army on the Tyrhennian side. Despite these blows the Generalfeldmarschall did not lose his optimism, and according to many German commanders his determined and optimistic feelings inspired the whole of his Command area. The area which he commanded was abruptly reduced in extent when Rommel arrived to take over a newly created Army Group in northern Italy, thereby creating a situation in which there were two supreme commanders; a recipe for military disaster. The situation lasted only a short time, but it was an embarrassment to both men.

On 8 September an American air raid on Kesselring's headquarters killed nearly a hundred of his staff and destroyed the headquarters' communications network. The first news to be received after the signals network had been restored was that the Italians had signed an armistice and had ceased to be an partner in the Berlin-Rome Axis. To restore the situation at the highest level, Westphal, Kesselring's Chief of Staff, called the senior officers of Carbonari's Corps together and threatened a Stuka bombardment if resistance was offered to German moves to take over the country. This was a threat to which Kesselring gave only reluctant support. Despite the actions of Badoglio's government, he still had a great deal of understanding for the position in which Germany's former ally was placed.

The Allied landings already referred to meant that Kesselring's main task had ceased to be a diplomatic one and had become a military one. He determined to defend southern Italy and ordered 10th Army, facing Montgomery, to delay the British advance, while he himself concentrated on driving Mark Clark's Fifth Army into the sea. His countermeasures were made by a few understrength formations and, realising the weakness of the force under his command, he sent urgent requests to Hitler to release both 24th Panzer Division and the Leibstandarte SS, so that they could be brought without delay from the north of Italy down to the combat area. His requests were denied. Those units, whose intervention might well have been decisive in the beachhead battle at Salerno, stayed in the north. The chance was lost, and that missed opportunity was to be the pattern for the rest of the Italian campaign; a succession of possible victories brought to naught because Kesselring was denied the formations which might have been decisive in holding the Allies to the deep south of the Italian peninsula. He was able to counter the Anglo-Americans, whose offensives were not co-ordinated, by switching units from one side of Italy to the other to meet any new threat.

On 18 July 1944 Kesselring was ordered to report to Fuehrer headquarters, and on the following day was awarded the Diamonds to the Oak Leaf and Swords. Several months later he was involved in a car accident on the road between Forli and Bologna, and suffered such severe facial and head injuries that he was kept out of the conduct of operations for nearly three months.

At the beginning of February 1945, after a short period of convalescence, he returned to his headquarters and resumed the visits to front-line troops that he considered essential to maintain morale. He strengthened the defences of both 10th and 14th Armies, preparing both formations for the Allies' spring offensive, and was then ordered to report to Hitler on 9 March. In the course of their discussion the Fuehrer told Kesselring that he was to replace von Rundstedt as Supreme Commander West. Despite Kesselring's protestations that he was still not fully recovered from his accident, Hitler insisted that he take up the post. The Fuehrer went on to assure him that he would find the Western Theatre of Operations in very good condition, but the Generalfeldmarschall soon learned the real state of affairs in his new Command from his Staff officers. Still unwilling to disbelieve the Fuehrer, and convinced that Hitler was telling the truth, Kesselring met Model and began to criticise not only the commanders in the west but also the operations which Model's Army Group 'B' had recently carried out. Model flew into a rage and the two commanders had a violent argument.

The advances of the Allied armies in the west could not be halted, and in April Model's Army Group was surrounded and destroyed in the Ruhr. It was the beginning of the end, for soon the western Allied armies had divided the as yet unconquered territories of Germany into a northern sector commanded by Doenitz and a southern one under Kesselring. At the end of April news was received that Hitler was dead, and shortly afterwards came details of the surrender of all German troops in Italy.

Although the war had ended in that theatre, there were still German armies in the Balkans. They were trying to make their way home, but were under attack from the Yugoslav army of national liberation, which did not intend to honour the terms of the German surrender. In an endeavour to bring back those stranded forces, Kesselring, still believing that he had authority, asked, perhaps naively, to be given a Fieseler Storch aircraft. He planned to fly down into 2nd Panzer Army's area in Yugoslavia and bring order to the confusion of the evacuation. The US commander turned down that suggestion, and General Eisenhower also rejected another of Kesselring's proposals, that a communications network be set up to help bring home the surrendered German armies. The Anglo-American supreme commander had no interest in improving conditions for the defeated enemy.

By this time a prisoner of war himself, Kesselring was confined in the criminal wing of a VIP camp and held in solitary confinement for five months. In 1947 he was taken to Venice to stand trial for war crimes, and after a five-month hearing he was condemned to be shot by firing squad. The outcry evoked by that sentence caused it to be commuted to life imprisonment, but in 1952 Kesselring's heart condition worsened after a series of operations and he was released from prison. He died on 16 July 1960.

In view of the accusations made against him regarding his actions during the years he spent as Supreme Commander in Italy, it is necessary to examine those charges. He was accused of carrying out the reprisals ordered by Hitler for the bomb attack in the via Rasella in Rome, and of conducting operations against Italian partisan forces. In the matter of anti-partisan operations, these were carried out by the SS, who were outside his competence. The reprisals had been carried out without his order and therefore without his authority. He was, in effect, being tried for the crimes of others. What was not brought out during the trial was that he had used large numbers of German trucks to bring foodstuffs into the cities to feed the starving populace. Nor was it mentioned that he had prevented the conscription of Italian men to work in Germany. His role in saving the art treasures of southern Italy from destruction by US aerial bombardment went unconsidered, as did his naming of certain Italian cities as hospital towns to save them from possible destruction.

All of those humane acts were disregarded by the Western Allies in an attempt to placate the Italian communists and the Soviet Union by putting Kesselring on trial. It was his good fortune to have been taken captive by the Anglo-Americans. Many other German senior officers taken by or handed over to the countries of communist eastern Europe were shot or hanged for their alleged atrocities.

'Grossdeutschland's' Panzer Commander

Generalmajor Willi Langkeit

Willi Langkeit, the son of an East Prussian farmer, was born on 2 June 1907 in Schuchten bei Treuberg. He volunteered for, and was fortunate enough to be accepted into, the small post-war Army of republican Germany. He was fortunate because, with its reduced numbers, the Army could afford to pick from those who wished to serve in it, and only the best were accepted. Langkeit entered the Service at the age of 17 and, given his natural aptitude with mechanical things and his fascination for machinery, it was perhaps inevitable that the unit into which he enlisted was No. 1 Lorried Battalion, stationed in Koenigsberg, the capital of East Prussia.

His keenness, efficiency and leadership potential soon gained him not only admission into the ranks of the professional Army but also marked him out as a future officer. Training in the post-war German forces was designed to produce potential commanders who would lead the Service when, in the confident expectation of the High Command, it eventually expanded to its pre-war establishment. That expansion took place in the years following 1933 and Hitler's accession to power, and by 1938 Lieutenant Langkeit had risen from a platoon commander to become a Captain commanding No. 8 Company in 36th Panzer Regiment.

His baptism of fire came in the Polish campaign, and bravery in action earned him the award of the 2nd Class Iron Cross. During the War in the West, in the summer of 1940, he led his panzer Company with such élan that on 5 June he was given temporary command of 2nd battalion in the 36th Panzer regiment. That formation played a prominent role in the second part of the war in France, and particularly in the battle which broke through the Weygand Line. Langkeit's skill in leadership was recognised in the award of the 1st Class Iron Cross. But it was on the Eastern Front in the war against the Soviet Union that he made his reputation, and it was in that theatre that he spent the middle and final years of the Second World War.

The Reich opened its war against the Soviet Union in the final weeks of June 1941, and during the first months of the campaign advanced deep into Russian territory. Despite the gains it soon became clear to the commanders at intermediate level, as well as those beneath them, that the campaign on which they were embarked was fraught with terrifying dangers seemingly unrealised by the Supreme Command. The Soviet Union had not collapsed as Hitler had so confidently predicted it would. Instead, the Russian soldiers and civilians were fighting heroically to defend their Fatherland. Then, too, as the German advance continued eastward it became clear that the battlefront would widen, and would soon reach a point where there would not be enough soldiers to man a battle line. As it was, there was no continuous battle line in the Soviet Union as there had been in the other campaigns. The 2,000km length of battlefront in the east precluded such total cover, and that enormous length would increase as the Army moved deeper into Soviet territory. Inevitably, there would eventually be whole sectors on which there were would be few, if any, German troops. To cover that deficiency and to counter the overwhelming strength of the Soviet Army in men and equipment, the Reich needed to devise new tactics. Rommel had introduced so-called 'panzer raids' and had created all-arms battlegroups for his desert operations. It should be possible to apply the same tactics and pattern of organisation in the steppes of Russia.

They were tried by every Army Group on the Eastern Front, but proved most successful with Kleist's 1st Panzer Group in Army Group South. In the advance towards the Don in the late autumn of 1941 the two Corps of 1st Panzer Group, the III Panzer and XXIV, advanced into the eastern Ukraine. On 8 October the headquarters of III Corps issued orders for its formations to pursue the retreating enemy and plan the capture of Rostov. The 14th Panzer Division, in which Langkeit was serving, was to guard the northern flank of III Corps, and from 13 October the 14th Panzer was engaged in that uninteresting but essential role as Corps pushed eastwards and crossed the Mius river.

Although the 14th was deeply committed to battle throughout this period, some units had to be withdrawn to practise the tasks and rehearse the new tactics they would use in the forthcoming battle for Rostov. It would surely be a hard and bitter struggle, because the town was the centre of an industrial and engineering complex important to the Soviet arms industry. Corps' intention was to continue to drive eastwards and then, at a given point, thrust southwards towards the town and take it. Pouring rain caused the offensive to be postponed. Frost then hardened the ground, but the rain returned and caused the offensive to be postponed again. Finally, on 15 November, Panzer Group 1 issued orders for both of its Corps to begin the badly delayed operation. Corps directed that: 'At 0600 on 16 November [its units] were to advance in the centre of the 1st Panzer Army, were to attack the Russian front and to break through these before swinging southwards to take Rostov...'.

Final orders for the offensive were issued late at night on 15 November, and Langkeit, once again in temporary command of 2nd battalion of Panzer Regiment 36, briefed his subordinates on the battle plan. The divisional route would take it eastwards to Generalski Most and then the advance would run south of and parallel with the river Ludin. At Messvatay, Corps would swing in a right wheel. The 14th would take position on the left of the SS LSSAH Division and drive southwards to Bolshiye Ssala, the first objective of the Panzer Regiment and of the 103rd Lorried Infantry Regiment which would be accompanying it. Then orders came from Corps that, in imitation of the desert battlegroups serving with Rommel, the armoured fighting vehicles (AFVs) of 36th Regiment were to be grouped into an 'Armoured Battlegroup Langkeit' which would also contain infantry carried in armoured personnel carriers and soft-skin trucks. Langkeit would lead other, larger battlegroups in the later years of the Second World War, but this was his first independent command, and he led it so successfully that its action deserves to be described in detail.

On the morning of 16 November the going was easy. The ground had been frozen by temperatures which fell to 20° below zero, but the weather was dry, allowing the vehicles to move well across the hard surface. Within minutes the leading machines were under fire from Soviet infantry, firing from expertly sited and well camouflaged trenches. Although this opposition was only machine-gun fire, the panzermen knew it would not be long before anti-tank guns and field artillery would be opened up on them. The armoured vehicles of Langkeit's battlegroup took up attack formation and raced at full speed towards and then across the first line of Russian field defences.

A hail of shells from Soviet field artillery fell around them, and a single Russian pak (anti-tank gun) opened fire on Langkeit's machine at a range of some 20m. There was no time for the commander to issue fire orders to his unit, but the following panzer fired a high-explosive shell and this first shot took out the pak. The single shell fired by that gun had hit but not penetrated Langkeit's machine.

Directly ahead lay another trench complex. The wave of panzers rolled over this, too, forcing the defenders to abandon their positions. The fleeing Russians were shot down by the lorry-borne infantry. After another short drive under fierce fire a third trench system loomed, and behind it could be seen a fourth, from which Russian guns were firing. By this time the machines of Langkeit's battlegroup were dispersed across several trench systems, with fire coming at them from all directions, and although they had an abundance of targets they were too few in number to engage then all. It was a potentially disastrous situation. The panzers could not advance without the support of the infantry, and the infantry were so tied up in close-combat actions that they could not free themselves to support the armour.

Indeed, the Grenadiers, who were now involved in a desperate struggle, sent out frantic appeals for the panzers to come to their aid, and Langkeit did his best to respond to all of the dramatic calls. The AFVs of 'Battlegroup Langkeit', trying to perform a wide variety of tasks, did not at first realise that Russian AFVs had begun to reach the battlefield. Fortunately these first arrivals were not the formidable T 34s, but T 26s with lighter armour and a smaller main armament. The first shots they fired struck Langkeit's vehicle but failed to knock it out. His response was almost immediate, and the shots fired by his much more powerful main armament 'brewed up' the first enemy vehicle. The second, struck a glancing blow by a 7.5cm projectile, turned to escape and was struck in its flank. It, too, began to burn. The remainder of the Soviet vehicles turned away and retreated from the field, pursued by the battlegroup.

At last light the panzers reached and captured the day's objective, Bolshiye Ssala. They laagered for the night, but there could be no rest for Langkeit or his exhausted crews. Fuel tanks had to be filled, ammunition racks replenished with fresh rounds and repairs made to the panzers' fabric. Then there was the evening meal to prepare and eat. Finally, the crews would go to rest, but for the commander and his officers there was tomorrow's battle to be planned. The round of toil was never-ending, and the Soviets were determined that the Germans should have no rest. Throughout the night their guns smothered with shot and shell the area on which the battlegroup lay laagered. Although vehicles were hit and only superficially damaged, the crews found it safer to sleep inside their panzers than in the open.

At 'stand to' the tired panzermen saw lines of Soviet tanks, more than a hundred machines, coming out of the dawn half-light and advancing towards them. The Russian counteroffensive had begun. Over the Command net Langkeit gave orders that the enemy machines were to be allowed to approach to within 600m. It was a calculated risk, because the mass of enemy armour now included not only weak T 26s of the type which had been driven off on the previous day, but the better-armoured and heavier-gunned T 34s and the super-heavy KV machines. Langkeit was gambling that his group's better firepower and stricter fire control would prove superior to the Soviet mass.

The wall of Russian vehicles rolled forward as if to strike the thin line of German machines, but from his vehicle's turret Langkeit saw that, under the cover of that frontal attack, other groups of Soviet tanks were working round his right flank. He detached a group of Panzer IVs to meet the threat from that direction. The vedette moved into action, halted, opened fire, then moved on again towards the Soviet group, using fire and motion tactics to fight it down. Under the impact of German armour-piercing shells a number of the enemy's AFVs burst into flames, exploded, or were knocked out and left impotent. The surviving Russian machines suddenly swung in a wide half-circle, hoping to gain the cover of deep woods where they hoped to find protection from the panzers' destructive fire.

The Russian flank assault which the Panzer IVs had flung back had been made to test the reaction and determination of Langkeit's battlegroup. The Soviet tank men in those first squadrons had been sacrificed. Now aware of what he faced, the senior Soviet commander demanded and received reinforcement. Then, with his force strengthened, he launched his armour into two successive frontal attacks. Both were repulsed, and soon twenty tanks, the equivalent of a Red Army battalion, lay destroyed or burning. With his armour temporarily thwarted, the Soviet commander ordered infantry assault regiments to carry out the next phase of the attack. The Soviet infantry marched forward, accompanied by anti-tank guns towed by their struggling crews. Langkeit observed the approaching infantry masses with pity, but with no weakness of resolve. Very few would survive once his panzers opened up with cannon and machine-gun fire. At 400m he gave the order to fire, and a rain of high-explosive shells burst over and among the leading infantry files. Then the panzers' machine-guns opened up and the Russian soldiers died in a rain of bullets. The Soviet anti-tank gun crews fell before they could fire a shot. The infantry attack had as little success against Armoured Battlegroup Langkeit as had the tank assaults, and on that single day Langkeit's men destroyed seventeen tanks, 70 field guns and two anti-aircraft guns, and took numerous prisoners.

At O Group on the evening of the 18th orders were issued for the group to take a southerly thrust line to reach the outskirts of Nackitchevan and smash a way through the enemy defenders. The infantry would then take over and clear the town. The pace of Langkeit's armoured charge struck and rolled over the enemy's barricades, and by 1330 his battlegroup had reached Nackitchevan, the objective. His group raced forward and Langkeit then saw a mass of enemy machines breaking out of well-concealed hiding places and advancing towards him. The Soviets had lured him into a trap. In the concentrated fire of the Russian armour some of his group's machines were hit and knocked out, but his men rallied and in the ensuing short battle one Soviet tank after another was hit and set alight. By the time twelve of their vehicles had been destroyed the Russians had had enough, and pulled back into the protection of the town.

The battlegroup's exhausted panzer crews and infantrymen halted for the night and prepared to resume the attack in the early morning of the 20th. That assault began to roll at 0800, with Langkeit's command vehicle forming the spearhead of the panzer wedge. He crossed, unscathed, belts of mines laid by Soviet pioneers, but two vehicles of his group which had been following him ran on to mines and were crippled. Langkeit's panzer, by this time isolated and unsupported, came under the enemy's concentrated fire. His immunity could not last long, and the vehicle was struck and disabled. Luckily it did not catch fire, but most of his crew had been killed.

Langkeit leapt from the panzer's turret, landed on all fours and immediately became the target of enemy fire. The closest Russian position was a trench filled with Red Army infantry who were firing a machine-gun at him. The panzer officer drew his pistol, charged forward, killed the gun crew, drove off the remaining Soviet soldiers and then, with bullets humming and whistling all round him, found and climbed aboard one of the soft-skin Kubelwagen cars of his battle-group. Allowing himself no time for rest, he directed and inspired his unit's attack so that by midday the battlegroup had penetrated into the centre of the town. It was a cardinal rule that armour should not be used in street fighting, for in such conditions the defender enjoys every advantage. Consequently, the panzer advance was soon halted and the infantry battalion passed through, taking up the task of fighting from house to house to clear the area.

On the following day, 21 November, Langkeit's battlegroup, supported by the infantry of 108th Regiment and of 64th Motor Cycle Battalion, reopened the attack which would take out Rostov. The reinforced group seized a bridge over the Don before the Russians could destroy it, smashed through the enemy defences and carried its advance forward until panzers and infantry were at the southern end of an island in the river. Armoured Battlegroup Langkeit had reached Rostov, the final objective, and the commander was recommended for the award of the German Cross in Gold. According to the recommendation sub-mitted by Colonel Jesser, Langkeit's superior officer, the group had destroyed 321 tanks, 45 field guns, thirteen pak, nine anti-aircraft guns, nine mortars, one armoured train, one goods train, one aircraft, one ferry boat and one river tug, and had taken 1,500 prisoners. The colonel's recommendation was turned down at that time, and it was not until July 1942 that Langkeit received the decoration for which his name had been put forward. Five months later, on 9 December 1942, he was awarded the Knight's Cross of the Iron Cross.

Not long after the capture of Rostov the bitter winter weather called a halt to military operations, and during the period of reduced activity Langkeit's unit moved into defensive positions along the Mius river and held them against sus-tained and violent attack. In time, campaigning weather returned, and in early summer 1942 orders came for the German summer offensive, Unternehmen Blau, which would send Army Group South advancing towards the Volga and the city of Stalingrad, which stands on that river. The preliminary to Unternehmen Blau was an action to tidy up the front, and 14th Panzer Division with Langkeit, now promoted to the rank of major (the youngest in the Panzer Arm of Service), led the regiment towards Suchiy Torez. There he closed the ring of German steel around a pocket to the south of Kharkov by capturing Barak on the Donets and gaining touch with 6th Army.

Rain falling with monsoon ferocity prevented the next stage of the planned offensive opening on time, but on 10 June the operation began. On 14 June Burluk was captured against fanatical opposition and Langkeit, now officially in command of 36th Panzer Regiment's 1st battalion, took a leading part in the fighting of those early summer days by thrusting into the flank and rear of the Soviet armoured forces defending the area. In the middle weeks of June 14th Panzer Division was in action against Soviet tank regiments lined up along the Donets river.

Symptomatic of the overwhelming confidence that the German commanders had in the capabilities of their men was a mission which Corps ordered to be undertaken. The 14th Panzer, which was moving southwards from the Donets, was ordered to detach its motorcycle battalion and two panzers. The little group was expected to capture Novocherkasak, a large town standing on a steep hill. The attack opened but was called off after it had been stopped dead by Russian artillery fire. A fresh and more powerful assault was made later in the afternoon of 23 July, when Langkeit led his regiment's 2nd battalion in a thrust to take the town. It was defended by lines of trenches and belts of mines, and the battle to take it endured well into the night. Although the Soviet Army units fought hard to hold the place, under the pressure of Langkeit's panzers they were forced back. That pressure was maintained until the AFVs and the infantry battalion had reached the western edge of Novocherkasak, and was continued until contact was gained with another formation of 14th Division. Even when that unit came under Langkeit's command it still took another day for his group to clear the town and consolidate his hold on it. For his success in this action he was recommended for the Knight's Cross of the Iron Cross and, as stated above, received this on 9 December 1942. By the time the award was made he had taken over command of 14th Division's panzer regiment. This was an unusual promotion. An officer so young did not usually take command of an entire regiment.

The Corps, forming part of Army Group South, with 14th Panzer Division under command, advanced towards the Volga, but at Stalingrad Russian resistance halted the advance. The 14th played little part in the fierce fighting inside the town; it was an infantryman's war. Army Group, aware that some of its foreign formations had a doubtful fighting reputation, positioned the 14th Panzer Division in the rear of those units, or placed it on a sector that was particularly sensitive. Langkeit soon gained a high reputation for carrying out the relief and rescue of formations encircled and cut off from the main German body.

At the end of November 1942 he was promoted to the rank of lieutenant colonel for conspicuous bravery in the face of the enemy. One of the most severe tests of his leadership came on 29 December, when a major Soviet tank formation broke through the line held by 376th Division on the Dimietrvevka sector. Langkeit, whose regiment was the Corps' counterattack formation, brought his panzer battalions to immediate readiness and led them into battle. The Soviet enemy proved to be too strong, and other German units had to be alerted and rushed to Dimietrvevka. Those reinforcement units were placed under his command.

There then followed a series of duels between AFVs, unusual because it was not German armour policy for one tank to fight another. Panzers had strategic tasks to fulfil, and were not to engage in single combat with enemy machines. Such restriction on tactical duels was particularly necessary at this stage of the war because many panzers which had been destroyed in battle were no longer being replaced. On 29 December Langkeit's regiment, already reduced by constant battle to just 23 machines, lost nine more in tank/panzer duels. The losses were not in vain. The Soviets had been thrown back and the gap in the battle line restored. But the respite could only be brief. In and around the Stalingrad sector Stavka, the Soviet High Command, had massed a great number of Soviet armies. Stalin had given the order 'Not another step back'. Russian morale was strengthened by that uncompromising statement, and the Red Army fought bitterly to destroy the German and Axis armies now encircled and trapped on the Volga. Langkeit was in constant action, leading attacks, encouraging his men and showing neither fear nor despair, although it must have been clear to him that the battle for Stalingrad could have only one outcome; the destruction of 6th Army.

On 19 January 1943 he was wounded seriously enough to be flown out of the pocket for treatment in Germany. The 14th Panzer Division remained in the Stalingrad encirclement and was destroyed. In March 1943 a new 14th Panzer Division was raised in France, and was operational within six months. The new Division returned to the Eastern Front, and upon its arrival found itself embroiled in a crisis. A major enemy armoured force had broken through and was thrusting forward in a seemingly unstoppable advance. To confront that challenge, Langkeit was ordered to form a battlegroup and, in addition to his own 36th Panzer Regiment, the 1st battalion of 103rd Infantry Regiment, a battalion of artillery and a Company of Engineers was placed under his command. The battlegroup concentrated around Vladimirovka and drove towards Charanovka, where it clashed with the Soviet advance guard and shattered it.

Then came a wireless message that the main enemy body, made up of masses of tanks and infantry, was at Pavlovka. Langkeit ordered his battlegroup to advance towards the new objective, and as it shook out into attack formation it came under the concentrated fire of Russian anti-tank guns formed into a pakfront (a box formation of anti-tank guns). Langkeit ordered his vehicles to drive at a faster pace, and the charge rode over the guns and their crews. The fury of that first assault disconcerted the Soviet commander. He decided to order his tanks to pull back, but delayed too long in issuing the order. Standing in the turret of his panzer, Langkeit saw the signs of confusion on the part of the opposing commander and ordered his battlegroup into another charge against the hesitating enemy. Duels between advancing German and retreating Russian machines ensued, and soon twenty enemy tanks lay 'dead' on the battlefield. But the fighting was not yet at an end. Although they were under accurate and destructive fire, groups of Russian tanks rallied and sought to continue the struggle against the battlegroup. It was a vain hope. The power of the panzers and the fury of the panzergrenadiers, battling hand-to-hand against the Red Army infantry, brought the battle to an end. Langkeit's group had destroyed 33 tanks and had taken a great many prisoners.

The battle north of Krivoi Rog was still not ended, however, and only days later the battlegroup was ordered to carry out a pre-emptive strike across the

Igluz river and attack a position in Vodyana, where Red Army troops were concentrating ready to undertake a new offensive. The pre-emptive blow began early in the morning, and with Stuka support Langkeit's battlegroup smashed through Russian trench systems and a pakfront, clearing a way for a following wave of vehicles whose grenadiers seized the town. Langkeit's reward for that victory was the Oak Leaf to the Knight's Cross.

The battlegroup then struck northwards, and in bitter duels between tanks and panzers destroyed more than twenty enemy machines. Within a week the battlegroup, already low in vehicle numbers, had been reduced to just 36, but it fought on and smashed a further 21 Russian AFVs, as well as destroying a Red Army attack launched by two regiments of infantry. The bitter fighting had all but destroyed the 14th Panzer Division, and its vehicle strength had by this time been reduced to seven Panzer IVs, four SPs and four flamethrowing tanks. From that remnant, as well as the survivors of an infantry battalion and an artillery battalion, Langkeit created a new battlegroup, and led this back into action.

On 24 January 1944 it was given the task of throwing back 4th Guards Army, which was attacking the sector held by 389th Infantry Division. A threatened breakthrough by Russian infantry and armour came dangerously close to succeeding. The battlegroup captured the village of Rossochovatka and went on to seize the high ground to its north-west. This dominated the surrounding area, and the fire of the battlegroup's guns stopped the prospect of a Soviet breakthrough. But the Soviet Command did not intend to be beaten so easily, and in the heavy fighting which followed Rossochovatka was lost and then regained several days later by Langkeit's battlegroup. Russian pressure finally broke the front of German 8th Army, and through the gap poured a flood of Russian armour.

In March 1944 Langkeit left the 14th Panzer Division on a posting to the élite Panzergrenadier Division 'Grossdeutschland', where he took command of the division's panzer regiment. 'Grossdeutschland' was at that time in action in Romania, where it was serving as rear guard to the German forces as they retreated westwards. The intention of Supreme Stavka was to drive through the Sereth valley and seize the oil-rich area of Ploesti. Determined to gain a major victory in the forthcoming operation, Stavka grouped more than twenty infantry divisions and a great mass of tank formations. The Russian offensive opened on 26 April 1944 and the 'Grossdeutschland' Panzer Regiment was soon deeply committed. The battle endured for four days before the Soviets called off their attacks. The mass assaults had cost them more than 150 vehicles, and had so exhausted their tank regiments that they needed to be rested and regrouped.

This was denied them when, at dawn on the last day of April, the German counterattack was opened with Hasso von Manteuffel, the divisional commander, riding in the first wave of his division's armour. The Soviets began to give ground in the face of this determined assault and, although they sought to stand and fight, their attempts were flung aside by Langkeit and his panzers. The

Wehrmacht communiqué announced the destruction of 386 enemy tanks and 92 guns. For his decisive participation in the battle between the Pruth and Moldau rivers Langkeit was decorated with the Romanian Order of King Michael the Brave. The decisive action for which he received the decoration was the destruction of 56 enemy tanks by his regiment.

In the autumn battles in East Prussia, where 'Grossdeutschland' was next in action, Langkeit was wounded. During his convalescence he learned that he had been posted to the divisional replacement regiment. At that time, in the last months of 1944, it was clear that only very radical solutions could stave off the total collapse of the Eastern Front. Faced with the real probability of such a catastrophe, the Reich leadership sought solutions and came to the conclusion that a few large and flexible battlegroups with greater offensive/defensive potential than a large number of smaller battlegroups could master the crisis by acting as 'the Fuehrer's super fire brigades'. Small battlegroups, which in the past had been of an impermanent nature, had always lacked heavy weapons support, and had also experienced difficulties in the matter of supplies and replacements. In accordance with the High Command directive known as 'Gneisenau A', under which the formation of 'super fire brigades' had been ordered, the officers of 'Grossdeutschland' Corps met and decided that a strong all-arms battlegroup should be formed around that brigade. This unit was unusual at that stage of the war, since it was at almost full strength. There was also on the battlegroup establishment another major component that had its full complement of men and weapons; Alarm Group Schmelter.

The issuing and implementing of the codeword 'Gneisenau A' was intended to confront and to check the Red Army's advance to the Oder. Zhukov's 1st Byelorussian Front was driving south of Posen in a direct line towards Frankfurt, and it was the Russian commander's clear intention to thrust aside the flood of retreating and disorganised German formations and gain the line of the Oder before they did. The German defensive plan was designed to meet the Soviet hosts with large 'fire brigade' all-arms battlegroups. Upon receiving the alarm codeword, 'Alarm Gruppe Schmelter', 'Kampfgruppe Gersdorf', 'Kampfgruppe Langkeit' and the 'Alarm Brigade Grossdeutschland' were all amalgamated into a single major grouping and placed under Langkeit's command.

German Supreme Command, aware that its forces lacked sufficient men or weapons, hoped to redress the balance and counter the overwhelming Russian manpower/material superiority through the advantages their troops had of familiarity with the terrain and the morale factor that they would fight hard to defend their native soil. Basing its defence plans upon those factors, High Command placed their confidence in a system of field fortifications, the so-called 'Tirschtiegel' positions which had been constructed east of the Oder. That defensive line, it was believed, would seriously delay the Russian onslaught and allow the 'fire brigades' time to group, attack the Red Army and win defensive battles.

The Tirschtiegel defences were set among a chain of lakes, a natural water barrier which would compel the attackers to advance across areas of ground between the lakes known as land bridges, which could be held in strength by the defenders.

In the matter of the Tirschtiegel positions, the confidence of OKH in the strength of those defences was misplaced. There had been almost no work undertaken to construct strong field fortifications in the land bridges because responsibility for their construction had been delegated to Nazi Party political officers who had deserted their posts and fled as the Russians approached. Such defences as had been constructed were rudimentary; a few lines of trenches, dugouts and in some places parts of an anti-tank ditch, and all showed evidence of hasty and unplanned work. A second-line defence system was in a worse state than the first, and only the most basic work had been undertaken.

Military commanders withdrawing their formations into the Tirschtiegel positions faced two main problems. They not only had somehow to recruit sufficient labour to complete the defences, but they also had to find enough soldiers to defend those positions before the Soviet offensive struck them. The only units immediately available, and upon which they could call, were local militia and Volkssturm detachments. These were poorly armed men with little or no training who, when it came to a battle, would be no match for the veterans of Marshal Zhukov's Byelorussian Front. Reports of the weakness of the Tirschtiegel positions came into OKH and forced it to cast about to find sufficient units and weapons to man the line. In the frenzy of activity created by the announcement of 'Gneisenau', the High Command raised formations which had staff officers but no soldiers, or had troops who had no commanders. Out of the panic situation which existed in the middle weeks of January 1945, order was soon restored, and from that chaos some sort of defensive system was at last constructed.

When the several component units of Langkeit's Kampfgruppe had been amalgamated, its order of battle was Panzergrenadier Regiment Kluever, whose 1st battalion, commanded by Major Petereit, was made up of 'Alarmgruppe Schmelter' which had three grenadier companies and a machine-gun company; and Schoettler's 2nd battalion which not only had three grenadier companies and a machine-gun company but, in addition, a mortar company. The question of artillery support was initially in doubt. It had not been decided by OKH to which of the three Grossdeutschland formations the batteries of the Artillery Training and Replacement School were to be sent. Langkeit acted swiftly and incisively, and appropriated them for his battlegroup. To an initial strength of just two heavy field howitzers there was then added a battery of light field howitzers, a light flak battery with four 2cm guns, four twin 2cm guns and four 3.7cm motorised flak guns.

There was, to begin with, no armour on the battlegroup's establishment, and in the matter of procurement of AFVs for his unit Langkeit once again acted ruthlessly. He took machines from factories and also requisitioned vehicles from training depots. Those machines which came from the 'Grossdeutschland' depot did not have petrol engines but were fuelled by charcoal gas. Some of the panzers had no turrets and others had no guns. Hudel, the commander of the panzer detachment, was encouraged by Langkeit to obtain panzers by whatever means necessary. Soon he had appropriated or commandeered sufficient to create a headquarters squadron, a panzer Company and a reconnaissance platoon equipped with armoured cars. He also fielded four tank destruction Troops, two armed with multi-shot Panzerschreck rocket launchers and two with the single-shot Panzerfaust projectors. To Langkeit's establishment there was later added an anti-tank Company and a motorcycle Company.

Not the least of the problems facing the battlegroup commander was that many of his men were not from 'Grossdeutschland' units. One whole Company of the Panzergrenadier Regiment was made up of men who had been ordered off trains passing through Cottbus and taken on to the strength of the 'Grossdeutschland' units. It is a shocking commentary on the state of the German military body in the final months of the war that the principal Kampfgruppe of the 'Grossdeutschland Korps', one of the Army's most prestigious formations, was made up of infantrymen who had not trained together and whose armoured support lay in a miscellany of machines. 'Grossdeutschland' Corps and Langkeit's group were fortunate in having on their strength veteran instructors, officers and NCOs who quickly inculcated their men with the 'Grossdeutschland' spirit. So successful were those instructors that the corps history comments on the high morale of the men marching out to do unequal battle. Those men were determined to fight and to win against an enemy whom they knew to be superior in numbers and equipment.

During the night of 26/27 January, although it was in no way ready for action, being neither completely raised nor forming an homogeneous group, the battlegroup was ordered to reach Frankfurt, where fresh orders would be awaiting it. These new instructions were that Kampfgruppe Langkeit was to concentrate around Reppen and was then to strike north-eastwards into the flank of the Soviet forces thrusting towards Stettin and the Baltic. The High Command orders continued that, once that operation had been successfully concluded, the battlegroup was to fight its way forward and take up positions in the Zielenzig sector of the Tirschtiegel defences. The battlegroup was never able to carry out the last part of that order.

Battlegroup headquarters was set up in a farm near Neuendorf, and it was to there that the other formations were directed. All of them, but particularly the artillery battalion, had slow and difficult journeys along icy roads. Army intelligence sources could give Langkeit no details on the location of the enemy, and he was forced to rely upon information obtained from refugees in the so-called trek columns. These reported that the Red Army was advancing fast and driving isolated German groups before it. Reports also spoke of an SS unit being located somewhere near Sternberg, and the headquarters of Bittrich's SS Corps was also said to be somewhere in the area.

Langkeit pulled in the outpost detachments of 1st Battalion of the Panzergrenadier Regiment, which were holding a line outside Reppen, and sent 2nd Battalion marching along the road to Pinnow with orders to reach Sternberg and liberate the encircled force of Army and SS units. Since Langkeit's battlegroup lacked accurate information on enemy positions and strength, it is not to be wondered at that, on its approach march, 2nd Panzergrenadier Battalion was surprised and attacked by strong Russian forces. Overcoming the confusion of the initial shock of that encounter, the battalion fought back and restored the situation. In this brief battle it was supported by the well-controlled fire of two batteries of the artillery battalion; the 2nd Battery positioned to the north-west of Reppen and the 3rd Battery at Pinnow. Covered by that barrage, the Grenadier attack was successfully completed and the headquarters of the Panzergrenadier Regiment was set up.

At Pinnow Langkeit created two small motorised battlegroups and ordered them to advance upon Sternberg, leaving only one Company and battery of flak artillery to garrison the village. The motorised groups carried out their advance to contact and were heartened by the sounds of small-arms and artillery fire, believing these to be made by the SS in their break-out attempts. This was not the case, for towards midday Soviet tanks appeared from the north-east and began firing into Pinnow. Patrols then reported to Langkeit that on the northern flank Russian armour and infantry groups had actually bypassed Pinnow and were moving on Reppen. In fact the Red Army forces were outflanking the Kampfgruppe. Later during the day the motorised battlegroups group made contact with Volkssturm groups in the Sternberg area. In the evening they gained touch with SS headquarters, but the commander, Bittrich, could only report that his units were spread across the countryside to the east and that he was out of contact with them.

In the latter stages of the operation to break through to reach the SS an independent Company of tank-destroyer vehicles took an active part. Langkeit, always on the lookout for reinforcements, took that unit on to the strength of his battlegroup. Covered by a rearguard furnished by the Panzergrenadier Battalion, the remnant of the SS Corps, escorted by the tank-destroyer Company, pulled back westwards towards Frankfurt. Langkeit then ordered the Panzergrenadiers to pull back, but his plan for the rearguard to withdraw as far as Sternberg could not be carried out. The Red Army had long since bypassed Sternberg, and its units were closing in on Pinnow from two sides and racing to set up bridgeheads on the western bank of the Oder. It was clear that the Kampfgruppe was isolated in a salient and was in danger of being cut off. To concentrate his force, Langkeit ordered the 1st Battalion to move to Reppen, where it would link up with the 2nd Battalion, which had the support of an 88mm gun.

Red Army tanks then opened fire on Reppen and bombarded the roads leading toward Kunersdorf. The main road was blocked by refugees fleeing westwards and hoping to gain the safety of the Oder, and very soon the civilian vehicles had become mixed with those of Langkeit's groups. When the first shots fired by the giant Josef Stalin tanks set fire to refugee carts the flames lit up the road, and immediately some Russian vehicles opened fire on the battlegroup's vehicles. Other Red tank units drove towards the Oder, occupying the high ground to the north of the Kunersdorf road and dominating it. On the south side of that highway the Soviet commander committed his infantry force. The last detachments of 2nd Battalion of the Panzergrenadier Regiment, backed by the 88mm gun and some Volkssturm units, were still holding Reppen while the main of the battlegroup, now divided into two separate bodies, was making desperate efforts to break free of the refugees and reach the road between Kunersdorf and Neu Bischofsee. The press of civilian vehicles made this impossible.

To break free from the Russian forces now almost encircling his Kampf-gruppe, Langkeit first directed that the thrust line should be south-westerly, but realised there could be no question of an advance towards Sternberg. Accordingly, 1st Panzergrenadier Battalion, backed by 88mm guns and other artillery weapons, moved back towards Reppen to reinforce 2nd Battalion, which was holding it. The 1st Battalion had had a nightmare journey trying to move along the Reppen road, for this, too, was blocked by slow-moving columns of refugees who panicked whenever Soviet heavy tanks opened fire on them. To add to the fraught situation, Russian armoured columns cut the road at a point some distance behind the sector where Langkeit's panzergrenadiers were holding out. As a consequence the battlegroup which had been put into action to smash one encirclement was now itself surrounded and cut off in another encirclement. It was also dangerously split up. The 2nd Panzergrenadier Battalion was holding Reppen, the 1st Battalion was moving towards that place, and the heavy vehicles and panzers of the main body were at Neu Bischofsee, trying to fight free of the refugee columns in order to engage the enemy armour.

Langkeit formed his remaining panzers into two columns, intending to lead them in a charge which would break the Soviet ring. He launched the attack but it did not succeed. Indeed, it could not succeed because only a few panzers were able to deploy off the road and reach open country. The remainder, trapped among civilian carts, became the target of Soviet infantry and tank gunfire coming from both north and south of the road. The rain of missiles smashed down upon the press of carts and people. Then a few more panzers managed to force a way through the civilian mob, went into action and charged the enemy road blocks, but these desperate, weak attacks died in the concentrated fire of the Soviet tank guns.

Back in Reppen, the panzergrenadiers of 2nd Battalion, squatting in their slit trenches, patiently endured air assaults and heavy barrages from both mortars and tank guns. The houses in the town were soon in ruins. The Russian commander, perhaps believing that the German troops were now dead, wounded or demoralised, ordered his tanks and infantry to go in and mop up the survivors. That fatal order at last gave the men of the 2nd Battalion the chance to exact revenge for the punishment they had suffered. Ten machines out of a wave of T 34s were shot to pieces by the 88s, and a Red Army infantry battalion which came in against No. 6 Panzergrenadier Company was wiped out almost to a man. Nevertheless, it was clear that 2nd Battalion's ability to resist was nearly at an end, and Langkeit ordered it to destroy its vehicles and fight its way back to him. During the night of 31 January, covered by a short barrage, the heavy weapons were put out of action and the Grenadiers and artillerymen marched out of Reppen.

The battlegroup's situation had now become so desperate that Langkeit decided to make the main breakout attempt through the woods to the south of the road. He realised that once his Kampfgruppe had concentrated in the forest it would face a difficult and tiring march, but it was equally clear to him that the Russian infantry in the woods represented less of a problem than the tank units on the main road. It should be easier, he calculated, for the Kampfgruppe to fight its way through and out of the encirclement if the main thrust was made through the woods. The battlegroup's last surviving eight-wheeled armoured car went into the forest to reconnoitre a route. Although the first reports it sent back encouraged Langkeit to order the march to begin, by 1 February the panzergrenadier units filtering along forest rides and secondary roads were once again entangled in the civilian treks and under fire from Red Army units.

Langkeit's light flak detachments, heavy machine-guns and anti-tank guns poured fire along the edge of the trees. The intention was not only to beat back the Soviet units in the fringes of the woods, but also to cover the slow-paced withdrawal. Stuka aircraft of Colonel Rudel's tank-busting squadron were called in and flew missions to create a corridor of flame through which the Kampfgruppe could escape. The efforts of that crack Luftwaffe squadron achieved little, and Russian pressure grew.

Langkeit's report to his O Group during the late evening of 2 February was a bleak summary of events. The battlegroup was surrounded, its guns were down to two rounds each and the breakout through the woods had failed. He proposed, therefore, to shift the battlegroup's main effort from the woods south of the road on to the road itself. A swift, direct thrust with the support of the last panzers might succeed, but only if the disengagement from the Russian troops in the forest was covered by a strong rearguard. That rearguard dug in and the main body of the Kampfgruppe, spearheaded by a panzer detachment, opened its breakout attempt along the road at first light on 3 February. It failed to smash through.

Meanwhile, on the northern side of the road, the 1st Grenadier Battalion had charged with such fury that it destroyed the Russian forces opposing it, often crushing enemy opposition in hand-to-hand combat. The attention of the Soviet commanders was drawn away from the road on which the panzers were grouping, to the sector north of it where 1st Battalion was fighting and winning. The enemy's lack of attention to the main road offered a chance that the flexibly minded Langkeit was quick to exploit. The 'Hetzers' of the tank destroyer unit and the last vehicles of Hudel's panzer Company were ordered to undertake a second thrust along the road. This went in during the early afternoon and was successful. By 1400 the Soviet ring had been broken open, and through the gap the westwards withdrawal of Kampfgruppe Langkeit to Kunersdorf could begin. The column moved swiftly, but before it reached Kunersdorf another obstruction was met. A Soviet armoured group had cut the road. Langkeit's men, aware that this Soviet group was all that stood between them and freedom, struck with great élan and destroyed the enemy armour.

The breakthrough by the Kampfgruppe acted like a magnet, and soon a stream of vehicles, both civilian and military, was pouring through the gap and heading for nearby Frankfurt. The units of 2nd Panzergrenadier Battalion held open the shoulders of the breakout point, and a their efforts were covered by fire from artillery units set up in the streets of Damm. It was in that Frankfurt suburb that the battlegroup concentrated. Then Langkeit was ordered to send part of his group across the Oder, where they were to take up positions on the river's western bank. The remainder of his Kampfgruppe was to remain in Damm, where it would form part of the suburb's garrison. On 3 February, while his units and subunits were making their various moves, Langkeit received an order that his Kampfgruppe had been upgraded to the status of a Panzergrenadier Division and was to bear the name 'Kurmark'. He was named as commander of the new formation. Included in its establishment would be four Companies of Panzer V (Panthers) and an Assault Gun Company. Over the following days other units were posted to 'Kurmark' and taken on charge. These included a reconnaissance squadron, panzergrenadier Companies and tank destroyer units, as well as an artillery battalion. Langkeit's new Division was soon in action, fighting close to the area where the battlegroup had broken out only days earlier.

'Kurmark's' principal task was to hold the high ground east of the Oder and thereby deny to the enemy the advantage of observation over the whole Frankfurt sector. How well Langkeit succeeded in this task can be seen from the report written by his superior, General Busse, commanding 9th Army. He wrote: 'The fact that Soviet operations on this sector failed was due principally to Colonel Langkeit, who never spared himself and who carried along with him the miscellaneous collection of units which made up his Division. I have myself witnessed his exemplary courage...' The citation of which the above is an extract was Busse's recommendation that Colonel Langkeit be promoted to the rank of generalmajor. The promotion was approved.

Generalmajor Langkeit led his Division in the fighting on both the east and west banks of the Oder, and during the last days of April 1945 had bestowed upon him the Panzerkampfabzeichen in Gold, the highest decoration for a panzerman, in recognition of no fewer than 75 successful tank engagements. Shortly before the war's end his decimated Division was still fighting in the area of 12th Army, and on 7 May it surrendered and passed into captivity. Langkeit was a prisoner of war of the Americans for six years, and upon his release in 1951 he enlisted into the Frontier Defence Force. In that Service he formed and led the special boat patrols.

Always a modest soldier, Langkeit rejected any praise for his actions in the Second World War. He described the decorations he had received as trophies for the bravery and loyalty of the men whom he had been privileged to lead.

Master of the Field

Generalfeldmarschall Erich von Manstein

Erich von Manstein was born into the Lewinski family but was adopted at his baptism by the childless von Mansteins, who were close relatives on his mother's side. An Imperial decree authorised Erich to use his adopted parents' surname, and henceforth he was known in official documents as von Manstein formerly Lewinski. Both families were of the West Prussian military nobility, the Mansteins having provided army commanders from the earliest days of Prussia's military rise, from the 18th century right through to the collapse of the German Empire in 1918. Erich von Manstein carried on the family's military tradition, and has been recognised as the German Army's most able strategist in the Second World War. According to military historian Liddell Hart, Manstein had a greater understanding of mechanised weapons than any of the generals who did not belong to the Tank School itself.

Erich was born in Berlin on 24 November 1887, and as an Army child lived in those towns where his adoptive father was stationed. After education at the Lycée in Strasbourg, he entered the cadet Corps at Ploen. From there he graduated into the senior cadet academy in the Gross Lichterfelde barracks, Berlin, and also served a brief period as a page at the Imperial Court. In 1906, after matriculation, he entered the 3rd Foot Guard Regiment as an Ensign and was gazetted a year later. The first important step in his career was the period spent as Adjutant of that regiment's Fusilier battalion, a post he took up in 1911. He entered the War Academy in 1913, received promotion to full Lieutenant status, and upon the outbreak of hostilities in 1914 rejoined his regiment and was then posted to become adjutant of 2nd Guard Reserve Regiment.

Manstein took part in the first battles on the Western Front, but when the Russian 1st and 2nd Armies invaded Germany territory his regiment was sent post haste to the Eastern Front. There it took part in operations which destroyed the attacking Tsarist armies. In the course of one battle in Poland von Manstein took part in a charge to capture a Russian position and was wounded, being struck by two bullets. Following hospital treatment and a period of convalescence he was declared fit for a return to active service. He did not go back to regimental duties, but was posted first to the staff of the Army Group commander, von Gallwitz, and then to Staff positions in other Commands. Serving in so many different appointments gave him insight into and knowledge of the workings of the General Staff. In Serbia at end of 1915, while still serving with Army Group Gallwitz, he attained the rank of captain, and a year later he returned to the Western Front and to another Staff appointment with 12th Army. After this came a similar appointment with 11th Army and then, in 1916, with 1st Army on the Somme. Other posts followed, including one as Ia in 4th Cavalry Division in Courland and, subsequently, in 213th Infantry Sturm Division. The defeat of Germany and the abdication of the Kaiser in 1918 was a particularly bitter blow to Manstein, whose ancestors had fought for Prussia in the years when she had been only a Grand Duchy.

Although the royal house had gone, Germany remained, and in the defence of his country's eastern borders Manstein volunteered for the Frontier Defence Force and served as a Staff officer in Breslau until 1919. When the danger of Polish invasion receded, the Defence Force was disbanded, but within months Manstein was again active in a Staff capacity, working with General von Lossberg in planning the new, 100,000-man German Army. In the summer of 1920 he married Jutta, the daughter of the von Loesch military family. In accord with the Army's standard policy of alternating an officer's posts between Staff appointments and regimental service, Manstein was appointed Company commander in the 2nd Battalion of 5th Infantry Regiment in 1920, and two years later served on the staff of a Corps stationed in Stettin.

By the end of 1927, after a series of Staff and regimental posts, he had risen to the rank of major and to a post in the Truppenamt; the bland name which disguised the General Staff that Germany was forbidden to have. He served initially in the department dealing with military operations, and one of his first tasks was to plan the Army's mobilisation in the event of war. He went from that post to devising a war game for the Commander in Chief, and later visited the military forces of a number of European countries. Returned to regimental service and promoted to lieutenant colonel, he took over command of the Jaeger (Light or Rifles) Battalion of 4th Infantry Regiment in 1932.

While he was in that post there was a change of government and Hitler came to power, bringing with him a new oath form, using words which were a pledge of personal allegiance to him as Reichs Chancellor. In 1933 Manstein received promotion to colonel, and he was appointed to the post of Head of the Operations Department of the General Staff in 1935. One of his duties in that position was to consider proposals for new weapons and tactics, and one result of his application was his suggestion that self-propelled guns, later to become known as assault artillery, should be introduced into the armoury of the Service. It was an uphill struggle to introduce such weapons, for not only the conventional gunners but also the panzermen thought that the assault artillery would weaken their respective roles on a future battlefield. In the event, assault artillery proved to be a powerful weapon, giving close support to the infantry and dominating any enemy whose army lacked such vehicles.

With his promotion to generalmajor in October 1936, Manstein became deputy Chief of Staff to General Beck, and in 1938, in a return to regimental duties, he took over the post of General Officer Commanding 18th Infantry Division in Liegnitz. His spell of regimental duty was broken when, during the Munich crisis of 1938, he was appointed to the post of Chief of Staff to General von Leeb. Then, on 1 April 1939, came promotion to lieutenant general.

Shortly before the outbreak of the Second World War Manstein was appointed to the post of Chief of Staff to von Rundstedt's Army Group South, which had concentrated in Silesia and Slovakia in preparation for the war against Poland. Following the successful conclusion of that campaign he was ordered to report to OKH, where final planning for the operation against the western Allies was in progress. Manstein was surprised to learn that the Supreme Command had no grand strategic design for the prosecution of the war. For example, it had not been decided whether to seek a political settlement to end hostilities, or whether it was intended to conduct the war by military operations until the western Allies were forced to sue for peace.

Manstein was given the task of planning the deployment of the field armies as they advanced to battle, and while checking the ideas and plans which OKH had already accepted, he thought these to be flawed. In his opinion they were a revamped version of the Schlieffen plan used in the First World War, which had precipitated a head-on clash of the opposing armies. Schlieffen's plan was flawed because it had failed to gain victory in the Great War. In the plan produced by OKH during 1940, Army Group B, on the right wing, was to make the major thrust and would contain in its three armies the greatest number of panzer and motorised divisions. Rundstedt's Army Group A, with which Manstein was serving, had a subsidiary role in the campaign; that of protecting the left flank of Army Group B. Manstein disapproved of the OKH plan and advanced his own ideas of the way in which the initial operations for the campaign in the west should be conducted. He proposed a single, overwhelmingly powerful assault by Army Group 'A' which would strike out of the Ardennes into the weakly defended flank of the Allied armies and go on to aim for the lower reaches of the Somme.

Manstein's bold plan was rejected by OKH. Indeed, its senior commanders sought to have him transferred to a field command so that he could not interfere with the final stages of the planning. On 7 February 1940 Manstein was ordered to brief Hitler on the respective battle plans. As General Commanding XXXVIII Corps, he reported to Fuehrer Headquarters, and during that meeting he advanced his own ideas of how the campaign should open. Hitler was attracted by his original thinking, and ordered that OKH's battle plan be changed in favour of Manstein's. A combination of that plan and the tactical ability of the panzer force brought victory in the west within six weeks. During the opening phases of the new war, Manstein, who had been given his first operational command when he took over XXXVIII (Infantry) Corps, was promoted to full general rank on 1 June. It was his corps which broke the resistance of the French armies, whose defensive plan was predicated on holding the great rivers of France. The swift thrust by his corps brought the German army storming into southern France, and for his part in the campaign Manstein was awarded the Knight's Cross on 19 July.

Seven months later he took command of the newly-raised LVI Panzer Corps and led that formation into the war against Russia, in which it served as part of Hoepner's Panzer Group 4 in von Leeb's Army Group North. The swiftly conducted opening operations carried out by his Corps were a demonstration of blitzkrieg operations and, among other successes, he captured intact the bridges across the Duna river. The speed of his advance left the sister Corps, the XXXXI, so far behind that Manstein's formation had to be halted to allow the sister formation to catch up. That enforced delay denied Army Group North the victories which Manstein's swift advances would have gained. The battles of late summer saw his Corps winning victory after victory. Some were achieved as the result of aggressive offensive operations, while others were gained by skilled defensive actions against Red Army units which had broken through the German line.

In the early evening of 12 September 1941 Manstein received an order from OKH stating that, with immediate effect, he was to take over 11th Army in Army Group South. That Army was fighting in the Crimea, and was battling to capture the city of Sevastopol. Manstein was brought in to command 11th Army because Schobert, the former commander, had been killed when the aircraft in which he was flying landed in a Russian minefield.

The 11th Army was made up of Kuebler's II (Gebirgs) and von Salmuth's XXX (Infantry) Corps, as well as 3rd Romanian Army. They were pursuing the fleeing Red Army towards Melitopol, but Manstein had been given a dual task to fulfil. Employing two Corps of his Army he was to carry out a vigorous pursuit to Rostov. Then with Hansen's LIV Corps, newly added to his order of battle, he was to drive through the narrow, 8km wide Perekop Isthmus, one of only two land approaches into the Crimea. Having forced the narrows he was to advance southwards into the Crimean peninsula, then swing eastwards and threaten the Caucasus. Manstein realised that his forces were too weak to carry out both tasks simultaneously, and chose as his first priority that of attacking at Perekop. This would be followed by a motorised thrust of such speed and weight that the Sevastopol fortress system would be taken in a rush.

The opening move of Manstein's offensive was made by Hansen's LIV Corps on the morning of 24 September 1941. Even before the offensive opened it was evident that the battle would not be easy. Hansen's Corps was confronted by a 15km-deep system of strong fortifications held by strong formations of the Red Army. Using Manstein's battle plan, the Perekop positions were to be taken in a swift assault, and they were indeed forced within a single day. Immediately ahead of LVI Corps lay a new Russian system of defences at Ishun held by at least six Divisions, and those positions took a further four days to overcome. In vain Manstein struggled to achieve a total breakthrough, and brought forward formations to exploit the anticipated penetration. But there was no breakthrough. Instead, there was a strong Russian counteroffensive. Soviet forces had attacked in strength between the Sea of Azov and the Dnieper river. These fierce attacks tore open a gap in 11th Army's battle line, and the formations which Manstein had brought forward to exploit the breakthrough had to be force-marched back to their original positions. The gap which the Russian counteroffensive had created was closed when Panzer Group 1 struck into the northern flank of those Soviet units. To relieve Manstein's Army of that part of its burden, which entailed carrying out a pursuit to Rostov, OKH handed over that part of its task to von Kleist's 1st Panzer Group. The Romanian Corps took over the duty of coast defence and, freed of those responsibilities, Manstein could plan a strike to overcome the last set of Soviet defences. Once they had been gained, the advance into the Crimea could begin.

Plans and preparations were made and the offensive opened, but despite the best efforts of Manstein's soldiers it was soon clear that a breakthrough could not be easily achieved. In view of the casualties his units had suffered and the exhaustion of the troops, the commander brooded on whether or not he should break off the operation. He decided to allow it to continue, and on the 28th, only two days later, the hitherto staunch Soviet defence collapsed completely. By 16 November 1941 the whole of the Crimean peninsula, with the exception of the fortress of Sevastapol, had fallen into German hands.

The fortress was too strong. The skilful Russian commander not only prevented its fall but even launched counterattacks which halted the advance of Hansen's Corps. The formations opposing 11th Army were those under the command of Lieutenant General Cherevichenko, who demanded that his men resist to the death. How well his orders were followed can be seen from the fact that the defenders of Sevastapol held out for 250 days and nights. While Manstein was fighting on the south-western side of the Crimean peninsula to seize Sevastapol, on the eastern side Supreme Stavka had launched amphibious operations to land an invasion force and recapture the territory which had been lost. Stavka gave orders to 3rd Red Army to retake the Crimea, and during December 1941 the first seaborne landings came in. To meet the threat Manstein could send only a single infantry regiment, but it was one whose skill in attack was sufficient to drive the invaders back into the sea. By this time the German commander realised that his Army was too weak in assault artillery to attack Sevastapol. His reasons for breaking off the offensive were laid before Hitler, who accepted them. Operations against the fortress would be scaled down until the heaviest pieces of siege artillery had been brought into the Sevastapol area, when the offensive could then be resumed.

Manstein then swung the main effort of 11th Army away from Sevastopol to the eastern side of the peninsula. He had managed to convince the Fuehrer that there was little danger from the Russian defenders of the Sevastapol fortress; they were impotent, could not be reinforced and presented no threat. In addition, if the offensive was temporarily halted a number of German units could be taken from the line and employed to clean up the situation on other sectors of the peninsula and bolster the defences against attacks from the sea. Manstein's concern about fresh Soviet landings was soon justified. By the end of January 1944, as the result of a series of seaborne assaults, thirteen major formations of the Red Army and Red Navy had been landed and had taken up position on the Kerch peninsula. That collection of Soviet units remained on the defensive until 27 February, when they went over to the attack in an operation lasting until the second week of April, and which ended only with their total exhaustion.

Manstein, who had been fighting a brilliant defensive battle, now capitalised on the Russian weakness and mounted a counteroffensive. This brief series of well planned and skilfully co-ordinated attacks ran for ten days between 8 and 18 May, and when it ended the formations of 3rd Red Army had been driven from Kerch; 170,000 were taken prisoner. For that spectacular victory Manstein was promoted to the rank of colonel general. With his eastern flank secure he could now turn once again to the reduction of the Sevastapol fortress, and he regrouped 11th Army for the final operation. To achieve the success which had so far eluded him he relied upon the shock effect of siege artillery.

On the morning of 2 June 1942 those massive weapons of destruction opened fire upon the Russian garrison of 106,000 men who were manning the permanent concrete and steel defensive positions, as well as the external trench systems ringing the city. Aware that the fortress was tremendously strong and could withstand conventional assault, Manstein planned a five-day bombardment to be carried out by the largest guns in the German Army's arsenal. Following the barrage of destructive super-heavy artillery fire, he planned to commit his infantry to the final assault. He himself carried out a seaborne reconnaissance of the area in an Italian motor-torpedo boat. During that sortie the vessel was attacked by Russian fighter aircraft and began to burn fiercely. One of his aides de camp jumped overboard, swam to the shore, commandeered a Croatian motorboat and brought off the survivors.

The offensive opened on time, but the fighting endured for 27 days before Sevastopol surrendered. The reduction of the massive fortress was protracted because each individual emplacement had had to be stormed and taken. The savagery of the struggle in the subterranean tunnels eclipsed anything which Manstein's soldiers had so far experienced. In a great many cases the warriors of both sides had fought in the stench of decaying bodies as well as in smoke clouds so thick that they had to wear gasmasks in order to breathe. In vain the

Red Fleet tried to bring in reinforcements and ammunition. The end came for the Russian garrison in the final week of June. A few units were evacuated by sea, but those others who sat on the shore, waiting for ships to take them off, waited in vain. On 1 July 1942, with the fortress finally reduced, Manstein received a telegram from Fuehrer Headquarters, announcing his promotion to the rank of generalfeldmarschall. More pleasing to him was the announcement that a special arm shield was to be struck and issued to every man who fought in the campaign in the Crimean peninsula.

The brief period of rest which Manstein and his soldiers were now able to enjoy was spent by him and his family in the Carpathian mountains. Earlier in 1942 his son, Gero, had been killed, and in writing of him the Field Marshal was perhaps describing himself. 'It was his heritage to come from a long line of soldiers. By the fact that he was a good German soldier, he was also a gentleman and a Christian.' There is no doubt that the Field Marshal embodied all the characteristics of the Prussian nobility; a dedication to the Protestant work ethic, loyalty and a concept of honour common to many of the men who rose to high position in the Armed Forces of the Third Reich.

During the second week of July Manstein returned to the Crimea and found that 11th Army was under orders to move northwards, specifically to Army Group North's Leningrad sector. He knew that, once the move was under way, the Soviets would strike swiftly at the German forces holding the Crimea, now weakened by the loss of 11th Army. And so it happened. The Soviets struck at the 18th Army, which held the peninsula, and the force of their assault compelled Hitler to rescind 11th Army's movement order, although Manstein, together with his Command group and the artillery, had already moved northwards. Hitler, very nervous about the Crimea, then directed Manstein to return and carry out an offensive against the Soviet forces. In fierce fighting the Russian advance was brought to a halt, and by 2 October Manstein's mastery of the battlefield had restored the situation and defeated the enemy forces.

Meanwhile, in Stalingrad, the Soviet counteroffensive was launched on 19 November 1942 against Paulus's 6th Army. On the following day Manstein received the order from OKH to take up command of the newly created Army Group Don, which was to operate in the Stalingrad area and would be made up of the German 4th Panzer Army and German 6th Army, as well as 3rd Romanian Army. He left immediately to take up his new post. During the five-day journey to reach the fighting zone, the Field Marshal's train was halted at Smolensk so that von Kluge, the commander of Army Group Centre, could brief him on the situation he would be facing. The news was not good. The rapid advance made by Army Group South during the summer months of 1942 had been halted on the banks of the river Volga. The German formations had fought fiercely but unsuccessfully to capture the sprawling industrial installations which made up the city of Stalingrad.

Slowly but inexorably the balance of the battle swung against the German forces and their allies. The Russian counteroffensive had struck with great force, although less against the well equipped and experienced 6th Army than against the satellite armies. The latter could not offer the same resistance as the German formations, and soon the Soviet penetrations of the satellite battle lines had brought about a situation where the foreign troops were in headlong retreat. As a consequence 6th Army, as well as parts of Hoth's 4th Panzer Army, had been partly surrounded and cut off from the main body of Army Group South. There was not a firm or continuous front either to the north or to the south of Stalingrad. Instead, the battle line was perforated by wide gaps through which the Red Army was racing westwards. There were neither formations nor reserves from which Manstein could draw reinforcements to plug those gaps. On the Malmuck steppe, for example, the only link between the German forces in Stalingrad and those thrusting into the Caucasus had been a single motorised Division holding a front more than 100km long.

Manstein knew that it was not just the fate of Paulus's 6th Army which was at stake, but that of the whole German southern flank. He also knew that the present precarious situation on the southern flank had arisen because of Hitler's unsound strategy, based on the premise that Stavka was incapable of acting swiftly and decisively. Through that false assessment of the enemy's capabilities Hitler had, in effect, presented the Soviet High Command with the opportunity to destroy Army Group South. The Fuehrer, finally made aware of the magnitude of the disaster facing Army Group South, laid upon the Field Marshal the dreadful task of preventing the military debacle. Manstein knew that if 6th Army were to be defeated at Stalingrad, and if the onrushing Red armies reached as far as the mouth of the Don, Kleist's Army Group A, fighting in the Caucasus, would be cut off. It was crystal clear to him that there was a danger that the war against the Soviet Union could be quickly and decisively lost. The most obvious course of action, if that collapse was to be prevented, was to withdraw 6th Army from Stalingrad. Hitler refused to accept that solution, and neither Paulus nor Manstein was courageous enough to disobey the direct order of their Supreme Commander and order a retreat on their own initiative.

In a final endeavour to lay the unpalatable but inescapable facts before Hitler, Manstein wrote a memorandum on 28 November in which he stressed that Stalingrad could not be held; the Russians had a numerical superiority of seven to one. But, if an attempt was to be made to create a corridor through which 6th Army could be evacuated, then that operation must begin with minimum delay. Hitler, for his part, was determined to hold on to the Stalingrad area for prestige reasons, and would not sanction a withdrawal. He deluded himself with the thought that Stalingrad could form a forward base for a new and stronger attack towards Astrakhan. Manstein conceded that to pull back from the Volga would be a blow to German morale, but pointed out the suffering being endured by 6th Army, which was fighting a winter war on the open steppes.

The response to the memorandum was not long in coming. Hitler telephoned during the following night and categorically forbad any attempt to bring out 6th Army. It was to stay where it was, and was to defend what he called 'Fortress Stalingrad'. In an effort to bring some sense of reality into the telephone conversation, Manstein proposed that, in addition to Army Group Don, he should also take over command of Army Group A, to give the Southern Front a unified command structure. He went further, and asked that the Fuehrer give him freedom of action, so that he could operate without having to receive prior authority. That proposal, too, was rejected. The telephone conversation between Hitler and Manstein was long but reached no conclusion because they had differing ideas of the priorities of the moment. To Hitler the important consideration was for 6th Army to hold out on the Volga so that Army Group A could gain the oilfields of Baku. Manstein saw the saving of 6th Army as the greater military priority, for thereby a strong defensive line could be constructed west of Stalingrad. His concluding proposal was to repeat that, if he were given the two Army Group Commands and the freedom to use them as he saw fit, he would win a decisive victory in southern Russia and the Baku oil supplies would be in German hands. Hitler rejected that suggestion and confirmed his decision in a telegraph message, although he did authorise an attack by Hoth's 4th Panzer Army to strike into the flank of the enemy. That offensive made good progress in its opening days but was soon halted.

In vain Paulus asked Manstein for an order to break out to the south, but this the latter would not give, although he did assure Paulus that, if he were to start a withdrawal on his own initiative, he (Manstein) would strongly support him. It should be understood that if Manstein and Paulus had disobeyed Hitler's order and initiated a breakout attempt, they would, in effect, have been challenging a decision made by Hitler as the leader of the German nation.

On Christmas Eve 1942 the Soviets opened a major new offensive, flinging back Manstein's Army Group Don with such fury that the Army Group commander was forced to accept a new military priority. The imperative was no longer to rescue 6th Army; rather was it the need to create a firm front at Rostov which would protect the back of Kleist's Army Group A in the Caucasus. After hesitating overlong, Hitler finally allowed Manstein to withdraw his Army Group westwards. The movement began during the first week of January 1943, and the 200km retreat of Army Group Don, conducted in bitter winter weather, has been given by many military historians as a classic demonstration of Manstein's skill. In his usual modest way the Field Marshal praised the officers who had been chiefly instrumental in forming a defensive front and who had closed the gaps in the battle line. On 12 January Hauptmann Behr, the most senior of Paulus's aides des camp, flew in to report to the Army Group commander in sober and factual terms the suffering being endured by the German soldiers. At the end of his report he handed over a letter from Paulus demanding freedom of action. It must have been clear to Manstein that Paulus was seeking authority to surrender what was left of 6th Army to the Russians.

It was at this time that Hitler sought to explain the necessity for 6th Army to stay on the Volga. In the telephone conversation described above he had outlined to Manstein his strategic plan for the following year. The German Army would cross the Caucasus mountains and join forces with Rommel's desert Army. That combined force would then march into India and bring the war against Great Britain to a victorious conclusion. It was imperative that 6th Army, holding the line of the Volga, stood fast in order to form the advanced base for a two-pronged advance; one through Astrakhan and the other over the Caucasus. Manstein, Hitler hinted in the telephone conversation, might well be the commander selected to carry out that wide-ranging and decisive operation.

After Behr's visit, Manstein, feeling that Hitler must hear the first-hand report on conditions inside the city, arranged for Paulus' envoy to have an interview with the Fuehrer. Behr returned to Manstein and repeated Hitler's words on the conduct of the next year's operations. The Field Marshal, disgusted at such unrealistic, amateur strategy, showed Behr the true military situation. On the operations map he set the picture in which the dying 6th Army was isolated hundreds of kilometres behind the Russian front. Many of those who visited Manstein at this time questioned Hitler's strategy, hoping to enlist Manstein in a plot to remove the Supreme Commander and Fuehrer. Although Manstein might and did disagree with Hitler on strategic grounds, he had sworn an oath of allegiance and could not break his word.

The principal cause of disagreement between the Fuehrer and Manstein was the Red Army's continuing advance westwards. Hitler, who had no knowledge of strategy, thought in simple terms of doggedly holding on to ground. The Field Marshal saw in movement and manoeuvre the opportunities to win victories. He was quite prepared to yield ground to bring about the conditions required to achieve a tactical or strategical success. Hitler refused to lose territory, and since the two men saw the problem from differing standpoints there could be no common ground.

Hitler came to Manstein's headquarters in Saporozhne during February 1943 to discuss the Field Marshal's plan for a strategic manoeuvre. In this plan Army Groups A and Don (renamed Army Group South in February 1943) would withdraw behind the Don and the lower Dnieper. The Red armies rushing into that evacuated area would soon exhaust themselves, and when their advance faltered, as it surely would, the German forces would go over to a counteroffensive and trap and crush the Russian hosts. Hitler rejected the plan because it would lead to the loss of Kharkov. It was precisely that point, Manstein argued, which would lead to the plan's success. Kharkov was a magnet, compelling the

Supreme Stavka to make every effort to capture the city. Those efforts would overstretch the Soviet forces and they would be unable to withstand the German counter-stroke. Hitler gave his grudging consent to this war of movement and manoeuvre and, as Manstein had forecast, the regrouped German forces swept back, retook Kharkov and restored a firm front between the Sea of Azov and Byelgorod. More importantly, the military initiative had passed back once again to the German Army. The operations conducted between November 1942 and February 1943 demonstrated Manstein's superior military ability, and in recognition of those skills he was awarded the Oak Leaf to the Knight's Cross on 14 March 1943.

When Manstein finally brought the Russian winter offensive of 1942/43 to an end, a large blunt-headed salient was left projecting into the junction of the fronts of Army Groups Centre and South. The obvious military solution was for those Army Groups to attack the walls of the salient and pinch it out. If such an operation were mounted and speedily brought to a successful conclusion, certain benefits would have been achieved. Firstly, the Red Army would have been dealt a mortal blow. The Intelligence Branch of OKH; Foreign Armies (East), reported that nearly 40 per cent of the strength of the enemy forces was concentrated in the salient, and a German victory there would not only destroy a major part of the Soviet strength but would also put the strategic initiative on the Eastern Front back into German hands. A third advantage lay in the fact that eliminating the salient would shorten the battle line by 500km, allowing the units released by that shortening to be used as a reserve for operations on other sectors.

Manstein argued that the objective of destroying the Kursk salient could be achieved if the operation were mounted quickly, before the Soviets could create their usual deep systems of field fortifications and minefields. Hitler was not prepared to act that swiftly. He was determined to have everything in place before opening the offensive, and his prevarication lasted several months. During those lost months the Red Army built a complex of strong defensive positions extending almost the entire width of the salient. Every day of delay aided the Russians.

Hitler's battle plan for Unternehmen Zitadelle was simple. Model's Army, which was lining the northern wall of the salient, was to strike southwards and make contact with Manstein's Army Group, which would be attacking from the south. The two German forces would meet and, having encircled the Red forces in the salient, would go on to destroy them. At a briefing of senior commanders at the Wolfsschanze in Rastenburg, Hitler gave the final details of the major operation, which was to begin on 5 July.

When it opened, Manstein's Army Group fought hard but initially without success to achieve a breakthrough. The two Corps of 4th Panzer Army (Army Group South) had a difficult battle, but on 11th July III Panzer Corps achieved a penetration and it seemed that at last the Panzer Army would be able to drive swiftly to meet 9th Army (Army Group Centre). But that Army had its own difficulties to overcome. A Soviet counteroffensive had struck into its flank, and much of the strength of the southward attack had had to be withdrawn to resist the Russian assault coming in from the east. Thus the drive by 9th Army was seriously weakened. Because it was known that the bitter fighting had caused the Russians enormous casualties, it was the opinion of OKH the that Soviets had already committed their last reserves. It soon became clear that this was a false judgement. A Guards Tank Army was put in to support and strengthen the Russian units fighting against 4th Panzer Army. When it came, the clash produced the greatest engagement of armour in military history.

Although slow progress was made by Manstein's Panzer Army, the struggle caused the Fuehrer to reconsider 'Zitadelle'. He made a decision and unexpectedly called off the offensive, giving the invasion of Sicily by the western Allies as the principal reason. It was vital, in his opinion, for Germany to defend the southern flank in order to support Mussolini's tottering empire. In vain, Manstein argued that 'Zitadelle' must be allowed to continue; it was on the point of achieving a splendid victory. Hitler was adamant, and with that decision the military initiative on the Eastern Front passed into Russian hands and was never recovered.

As a result of the Kursk offensive the Soviets gained absolute confidence in their ability to conduct wide-ranging operations and, without pause, moved into a full-scale summer counteroffensive. When Hitler visited Manstein at Vinnitsa on 27 August 1943, the Field Marshal stressed that the Donets area could not be held with the present resources. The Fuehrer promised lavish reinforcements, but none arrived. Faced with a defensive task beyond the capabilities of the forces under his control, Manstein decided on 15 September to withdraw them behind the strong defensive water barrier of the Dnieper river. The operation was carried out under the Red Army's constant pressure, and was hindered by poor terrain conditions. It was a vast and complex task. Three whole armies holding a front of over 700km had to be funnelled through only five river crossings. Once on the west bank of the Dnieper they had to take up a front as wide as their former one. They were expected to do more. They were to hold the Dnieper line and repulse the Soviets, who were determined to cross the river and establish bridgehead positions on the far bank.

The German withdrawal was completed by the end of September, and was a master-stroke of military planning and organisation. Manstein had intended to hold the Soviets east of Kiev, but during October the enemy gained footholds on the west bank of that river and were threatening the city. The onset of winter slowed, but did not halt, the Red Army's westward drive, and the pressure it exerted brought the need for yet another withdrawal. On 4 January 1944 Manstein flew to the Fuehrer Headquarters to ask for authority to withdraw from the bend of the Dnieper. Backed by his closest associates, Hitler refused the

Field Marshal's request, and Manstein demanded a private interview. In a heated exchange of words Manstein vigorously put forward the proposal that Hitler appoint a Chief of Staff to advise the Fuehrer and to prepare operational plans that were realisable. The burden of carrying responsibility for all the battle fronts was, Manstein said, too much for one man; a Chief of Staff must be appointed. He then suggested that, for both the eastern and western theatres, a Supreme Commander be appointed who had full powers of authority. Hitler rejected both proposals and, thinking to conclude the argument, said that as his field marshals did not obey his orders, it was hardly likely that they would obey Manstein. The angry Manstein retorted that any orders he gave would be obeyed, even by other field marshals.

On 27 January 1944 there was another conference. A new Soviet major offensive had opened against Army Group South and was making considerable gains. During the Fuehrer's briefing to the generals Manstein interrupted the Supreme Commander with a sarcastic comment on the conduct of the war. The interjection was noted, but no action was taken against him at that time. Early in March the spearhead units of 1st Soviet Tank Army were approaching Chernowitz in Poland, and another tank army was about to cross the Dniester at Kemenez-Podolsk. Were those two tank armies to gain touch with each other, 1st Panzer Army would face encirclement. Hitler's response to the Russian advances was to propose setting up 'fortress cities' which would be defended to the last man and the last bullet. Manstein, after great argument, forced from Hitler the authority for the Panzer Army to pull back westwards out of the threatening encirclement, and then asked the Fuehrer to revoke the nonsensical 'fight to the last round' order.

On 19 March there was a third meeting, attended by all the field marshals and senior commanders. They were there to witness the handing over of declarations of personal loyalty to Hitler that each of them had signed. That meeting provoked an argument and resolved Hitler to rid himself of Manstein. On 25 March, at the Berghof in Bavaria, Hitler attempted to heap responsibility for the current military disasters on Manstein's shoulders. Manstein retorted in kind, and the men parted on bitter terms.

Manstein returned to his Command convinced that if he were given a free hand he could, by strategic manoeuvre, gain the Reich a breathing space for Hitler to exploit. He believed that the time could be used in the political arena to bring an end to the war on terms favourable to Germany. Manstein was recalled again to the Berghof on 30 March, where he had bestowed upon him the Swords to the Oak Leaf of the Knight's Cross, and was then told by Hitler that Army Group South was to have a new commander, Field Marshal Model, and that he was relieved of command. In an attempt to justify the dismissal, Hitler told the Field Marshal that the days of strategic manoeuvre were gone and had been succeeded by military situations in which defence to the last man was the requirement.

Previously, during the third week of February, the Field Marshal, feeling he had nothing to lose, ordered two of his Corps, the XXXXII and the XI, both positioned to the west of Cherkassy, to break out of the Russian encirclement in which they were trapped and fight their way through to the main body of Army Group. This operation was ordered in defiance of Hitler's direct order. Manstein had somehow gained the moral strength, and the determination he had hitherto lacked, to defy the Supreme Commander openly. The break-out of the units of both Corps was carried out during the night of 16/17 February. Hitler accepted the act of disobedience by issuing orders for the break-out to take place – after it had been completed.

Following his dismissal, Manstein returned home and almost immediately entered the eye clinic of the Breslau hospital. After an operation he went into convalescence near Dresden. As a consequence of his dismissal, and because of the operation on his eye, Manstein was no longer directly involved in military activities on any battlefront, but he did manage to be kept informed of developments, particularly those on the Eastern Front. Thus he was aware of the threat building up against Army Group Centre; a threat which became a reality when that Army Group was destroyed during the summer of 1944. The Field Marshal took no active part in the bomb plot which failed to kill Hitler on 20 July 1944, but he was certainly aware that the attempt would be made. In his post-war work *Verlorene Siege*, Manstein agreed the logical case for not participating in a coup against the Reichs government. Such an act, in wartime, would have led to an immediate collapse of the battlefronts and to chaos inside the Reich. In later years, during his trial on war crimes charges, Manstein justified his lack of action in the following words: 'No senior military commander can expect his soldiers to lay down their lives for victory and then precipitate defeat by his own actions'.

During the third week of January 1945 Manstein collected his family from their home in Liegnitz in the east of Germany and sought to drive through Breslau and bring them into the safety of the west. The small column of vehicles was halted at the exit of one village by two Nazi Party functionaries, who stated that the Gauleiter had forbidden any evacuation. Manstein's aide de camp threatened the two men that if they held up the column he would personally shoot them. The column passed, and in time the Manstein family was billeted in military accommodation in Celle in West Germany.

Before that move took place, Manstein went once again to see Hitler to discuss with him the future of Germany. Hitler refused to see him; nor did any of the Fuehrer's immediate circle come to meet the Field Marshal. As the war entered its final weeks, Manstein motored to north-west Germany to discuss with Field Marshal Busch, the commander of the Army Group there, the situation facing the German army in the west. Senior officials of the Reichs government, including Armaments Minister Albert Speer, visited Manstein, and then came the announcement of Hitler's death. That prompted the Field Marshal to write a letter which he had delivered to Field Marshal Montgomery.

The defeat of the Reich was followed by the arrest of those who had held high posts in its government and armed forces. Included in the latter group was von Manstein, who was first taken to an ordinary prison camp in Luneburg, and then transferred to Nuremberg, where he the war crimes trials were to take place. Thanks to Manstein's preparation, the collaboration of other senior commanders and the skill of the defence lawyer, the accusation that the General Staff was a criminal organisation was not proven.

In the autumn of 1946 Manstein was transferred to a special camp for general officers in the United Kingdom. He was returned to Germany in the summer of 1948 to stand trial with von Rundstedt, von Brauchitsch and Strauss, charged with being a war criminal. Of the four defendants only Manstein was tried. The others were released on medical grounds after one of them had died in a British hospital. It was widely accepted in the rest of the world that the trial, which opened during August 1949, was not a fair one, but had been initiated out of a spirit of revenge. Despite the eloquent pleas of Reginald Paget, Manstein's defence lawyer, that his client be acquitted, the sentence handed down was one of 18 years' imprisonment. Manstein was released from Werl prison after three years to undergo another eye operation. The state of his health did not allow him to be returned to prison, and he was moved, together with his family, to Bavaria, where he lived in Irschenhausen in the Isar valley until his death on 10 June 1973.

In 1956, nearly twenty years before he died, Manstein was called upon to advise the West German government on the setting up of a new Army. It was to join with the forces of Germany's wartime enemies in a projected military alliance against the powerful and threatening might of the Soviet Union. The cynicism of such a move could not have been lost upon the Field Marshal.

The Fuehrer's Fireman

Generalfeldmarschall Walther Model

Walter Model, full name Otto Moritz Walter Model, was born on 24 January 1891 in Genthin, in the Prussian province of Brandenburg. Although some ancestors had served as soldiers, the family was not a military one, being more connected with education and music, and particularly choral music. Shortly after Walter's birth the family moved up in the German social scale when his father became a civil servant and took his family to Haumburg an der Salle. The young Model did not have a robust constitution, and grew up a sickly lad who was excused physical exercise at school. Despite that handicap it might well have been the seduction of the uniform worn by the soldiers of the garrison town to Haumburg that led him to apply for a commission in the Army, specifically in the 62nd Regiment (6th Brandenburg). The fact that he had an uncle serving in the regiment was an important advantage, for in those days the subalterns of a military unit could blackball any candidate they considered unsuitable. Model was accepted and became an Ensign in No. 11 Company of the regiment's 3rd Battalion. For an unfit youth the training was so hard and strenuous that Walter seriously considered resigning his commission and taking up a career in medicine. The sarcastic comments of an NCO on the training staff about Cadet Model's poor physique and weakness served only to stiffen his resolve to succeed, and by a strict regime of self-discipline Walter brought himself to a peak of physical fitness that he was never to lose. The rigours he inflicted upon himself were later to be reflected in the strict manner in which he treated his subordinates. However, he would never expect any of his soldiers to do anything that he himself could not do, or would not be prepared to undertake.

In 1909 Model entered the War School in Neisse, and he was promoted to second lieutenant in September of that year, being gazetted to 52nd Infantry Regiment. His diligence and energy led to an appointment as adjutant of 1st battalion, and it was in that post that Model marched out to war with his regiment in the autumn of 1914. By the end of the year he was the regimental adjutant, but he did not allow that post to take him away from the front-line trenches, where he felt himself to be most at home. In May 1915 he was wounded for the first time, being hit by a bullet which passed through his shoulder and narrowly missed severing an artery in his neck. For his bravery in action he was awarded the Iron Cross First Class.

It was at this time that Oberleutnant Model attracted the attention of Prince Oskar of Prussia, who was serving on the staff of 5th Division. Impressed by Model's ability, the prince recommended that he be sent on a General Staff course. This began in April 1916, and Model passed with honours. His high marks led to him being appointed adjutant of 10th Infantry Brigade and then, in keeping with the army policy of rotating officers between staff posts and front-line duty, to the command of a Company of the 52nd and then one in the 8th Leibgrenadier Regiment. While in command of that unit he was wounded again; shot through the shin. Upon return from hospital he was appointed second-in-command of a battalion of the Leibgrenadier Regiment before taking up a Staff post in the Supreme Command which he held until March 1918.

Promoted to the rank of captain, he then took up a post as GSO II in the Guards Replacement Division, and from August with 36th Reserve Division. The outbreak of mutiny in the Imperial Navy and the defeats in the field forced Germany to sue for an armistice, and Model, thinking his military life at an end, once again considered a career in medicine. His regiment had recruited in West Prussia, and that province was threatened with attack by Polish military forces. The 17th Corps, which administered the province, ordered Model to stay on in the army, serving in one of the Grenzschutz units (local defence forces) then being created.

The Service authorities, taking a long-term view, were considering ways and means of preserving intact the framework of the Army. Under the terms of the Treaty of Versailles there was a limit to the number of men under arms. Moreover, the Army was denied heavy weapons and, most importantly, was forbidden to have a central General Staff system. It has been shown in earlier chapters how the military and political authorities sought to circumvent the restrictions of Versailles and retain the shape, if not the substance, of the Army, and it is not necessary to repeat here the methods used by the Reichs government. Suffice it to say that the directing genius of the Army of the Weimar Republic, General Hans von Seeckt, required keen and efficient officers who were apolitical. Model was just such a man, and he was posted to 7th Brigade's 14th Regiment, at that time garrisoning Westphalia. There followed for Model an alternating succession of troop and Staff posts. During one Staff appointment he had so bitter a confrontation with his superior that he asked to be returned to regimental duties and was given command of a machine-gun Company in one of the regiment's battalions.

During a political attempt to overthrow the central government, Model's battalion played its part in putting down the putsch. The civilian population, inflamed by left-wing agitators, turned on the troops, and Model had his first lesson in urban warfare, an experience which cost the regiment twelve men killed and 100 wounded. The military authorities, deciding that the soldiers should not be called upon to fire on their own countrymen, withdrew the regiment and it entered illegally (i.e. without permission) the zone of Germany occupied by British forces. The British promptly interned the regiment. Once released, Model was given other staff and regimental appointments, and as part of his military education he wrote a paper on the great Army reformer of Napoleonic days, Gneisenau. This was so well received that by 1928 he was lecturing to officers of the General Staff on military history and tactics. In that capacity Model, now a Major, thought through the attitudes of the Reichswehr, which were required by the restrictions of Versailles to be strictly defensive, towards the time when Germany would once again have heavy weapons and a General Staff. He was particularly interested in the concept of airborne forces, and in 1931 was sent on one of the illegal missions to Russia. He there put into practice the military theories which the German Army had developed since the end of the war, but which it was still forbidden to use.

Like his forefathers, Model was a Protestant, reared in the ethics of loyalty, hard work, thrift and charity. Pastor Niemoeller, a frequent visitor to Walter Model's home, interested him in the concept of aiding unemployed German youth, suggesting that these young men could be organised at a national level along paramilitary lines. This would ensure that their lives had direction and, more importantly, that they were properly fed. Model's proposals to the Army High Command foresaw, perhaps, the need to create paramilitary units to defend Germany's eastern borders in the event of a Polish invasion while within the German homeland such units could be used to quell any attempt at revolution. The enlisting of young Germans would provide a mass of disciplined, physically fit men, the raw material upon which the country could draw when the Army was expanded. It was argued that the young, non-uniformed army proposed by Model could be created without contravening the manpower restrictions imposed upon the Army by the Treaty of Versailles.

Model's proposals were approved, and to give him the authority he needed for this work of organisation he was promoted lieutenant colonel in 1932. Opposition was expected from the youth groups of the major political parties, particularly the communists and Nazis, who wished to retain a firm hold on their own young people. So far as the Nazis were concerned, Hitler was adamant; not one Party member would be allowed to serve in the youth army. When the Nazi Party came to power, the creation of the national Labour Corps (Reichsarbeitsdienst) and the reintroduction of military conscription eliminated the need for Model's Youth Training Programme (the Reichskuratorium). He returned to regimental service in 1933, taking command of 2nd Battalion of 2nd Infantry Regiment, and then, in 1934, with the rank of colonel, he took command of the whole regiment. On 15 October 1935 he was appointed to head Section 8 in the Army General Staff and promoted to major general.

In the post of Section Head he was responsible for studying and evaluating foreign arms and equipment, and went to Spain in 1937 to check on the weapons and tactics being used by both sides in the Civil War. He was sent on another secret mission in 1938, to spy out Czechoslovakia's defensive fortifications along the Sudeten border. In the matter of weapons, Germany had cast off the defensive role and could now think aggressively. Model proposed and designed a motorised replacement for the horse artillery; assault guns, or motorised gun carriages.

On 10 November 1938 he took up the post of Chief of Staff of IV Corps, and in March of the following year entered Prague, the capital of Czechoslovakia. The next promotion should have been to command a Division, but political events developed too quickly and war came on 1 September 1939 with the invasion of Poland. The arduous post of Corps' Chief of Staff gave Model scant opportunity to spend time with the fighting units during the brief German/Polish war, but his Staff work had not gone unnoticed and he was next posted to the Western Front. There he was employed as Chief of Staff of 16th Army, part of Army Group 'A', which was to carry the principal burden in the now imminent War in the West.

Model, promoted lieutenant general in April 1940, proposed a sort of commando operation. A group of Fieseler Storch aircraft were to carry an advance guard of assault troops, men of 34th Division who would land in the Luxembourg-French frontier area and capture tactically important areas in the path of 16th Army. The war in France and Flanders was brought to a successful conclusion, but on his way home for leave Model was injured in a car accident. Upon his return to active service he learned that he had been given his first independent major command; 3rd Panzer Division. To his dismay he found that this formation was a rump and not a full formation.

Adolf Hitler had decided at the end of the French campaign to double the number of panzer Divisions on establishment. He achieved this not by raising tank output to equip the increased number of Divisions, but by dividing each Division. Each separate half of the Division was then administered as if it were a full-strength, complete Division. The 3rd, already at only half of its former establishment, was further weakened by having to hand over its panzer regiment, reconnaissance battalion, artillery regiment and anti-tank units. All of these were sent to Tripolitania to 'flesh out' one of the formations which would form part of the German Afrika Korps.

Model's arm of Service had been the infantry, and he had a poor understanding of the workings of mechanical equipment. However he grasped the principles of armoured warfare as if by instinct, and was determined to make his Division élite. Slowly, its several component formations came on to strength, and once these were concentrated he undertook a series of inspections to make himself known to every man under his command. His units carried out exercises practising the type of warfare that they would be carrying out on the battlefield. Once they had proved their proficiency and were skilled in the disciplines of their role they were put through more advanced schemes to absorb the techniques of inter-arms co-operation. These were followed by battlegroup operations, and the whole formation was worked up to such a state of efficiency that it was selected to give a demonstration to the High Command with the theme, 'A panzer Division's advance across two defended water obstacles'.

Being now in every respect ready for war, the 3rd, forming part of XXIV (motorised) Corps, moved eastwards to take its place in the battle line that was being formed to undertake Operation Barbarossa, the invasion of the Soviet Union. Even during the move the Division could not relax, for Model used every opportunity to give the units tactical exercises. It was not only the fighting echelons who carried these out, but also the men of the train units, formations not normally called upon to do battle but whom Model insisted be trained in infantry tactics. That insistence was to be justified in the winter battles of 1941-42. It was not all hard slog, however, for Model was well aware of the need for relaxation and of the psychological impact of song to raise morale. Singing on the march was a routine of German military life, but Model arranged and often participated in choral competitions, using such occasions as a form of relaxation.

During the middle weeks of June 1941, 3rd Panzer concentrated in an area of dense woods to the west of the Bug river. Guderian's Panzer Group 2, on whose establishment was Schweppenburg's XXIV Panzer Corps, with 3rd Panzer under command, swept into action from an area 20km south of Brest-Litovsk. Model's Division was to capture intact the river bridge across the Bug at Kodern. In the late hours of the night before the battle opened, Model walked among the soldiers of his front-line units. He was confident that his formation would gain the day's objectives. The number of armoured fighting vehicles he controlled was impressive; the greatest number, 108, were the short-gunned Panzer III, and there were 50 of the Panzer II type and 32 Panzer IVs with the powerful long-barrelled main armament.

The opening attack was brilliantly successful, and the Kodern bridge was seized intact. The Division crossed the Bug to the south of Brest Litovsk, swept over the Beresina near Bobruisk and struck out for the Dnieper. Model was determined to follow the Corps commander's directive: 'Through and forward' – smash through the Russian defences of the Stalin line and drive forward into the open country to exploit the breakthrough. Model believed that only a sustained advance could bring victory. He shared the conviction of the senior panzer commanders that it was vital to keep the enemy on the run and disorganised, so that they could not set up firm lines of defence.

The early autumn of 1941 was the time of the great German encirclements of entire Russian armies. During the massive operation at Kiev, Model, whose Division was to the north of the city, created and sent into action a divisional battlegroup. That detachment was the advance guard of the northern pincer which was intended to gain touch with the leading elements of Army South, which formed the other pincer. To accomplish this link-up his battlegroup drove 200km in a seven-hour drive through the Red Army's rear areas. It was a perfect demonstration of Model's training methods and of his command of the battle-field. During the later stages of the encirclement battle Model was wounded while visiting front-line units in the woods around Kalista.

After a great deal of prevarication Hitler finally took the decision to advance upon Moscow, and Panzer Group 2's thrust line was changed from east-erly to northerly. The Group was to attack via Tula and close the ring around another group of Soviet armies to the west of the Soviet capital, but Panzer Group's resources were almost spent. Third Panzer Division, for example, had been reduced to a strength of just ten battle tanks, and the other Divisions in the Corps were in little better shape. Nevertheless, Panzer Group 2 took up its allot-ted sector of the line. Model's 3rd Division, still acting as Corps' spearhead, played a major role in the great encirclement between Orel-Briansk and then, dis-engaging from that operation, struck towards Tula. From there, Guderian's panzer Group was to open the advance to take out Moscow and thereby end the war in Russia.

Model was not to lead the 3rd in that battle, for on 26 October he was given command of XXXXI Panzer Corps, with the rank of panzer general, to which he had been promoted three weeks earlier. He took over his Corps at a time when the German Army's offensive was losing momentum. Although Operation Typhoon, the operation intended to seize Moscow, was still moving forward, the bitter weather had already caused terrible privation to the troops fighting on the Eastern Front, and conditions would worsen as the winter deepened. The feroc-ity with which the Red Army fought to hold Moscow was shown when the crack 36th (motorised) Division of Model's Corps was forced on to the defensive and had to battle hard to keep its bridgeheads on the Volga near Kalinin.

Model spent much of his time visiting his forward units and was well aware of the strain his soldiers were under, but even he was shocked when, during one visit, he found all the soldiers of one unit asleep. They were completely exhausted. His men were burnt out, and he demanded that they be taken from the line and rested. At his insistence a brief respite was given them, but in the middle weeks of November Army Group Centre decided to reopen its offensive against Moscow. For this new phase Panzer Group 3, to which Model's Corps had been posted, had the task of protecting the left flank of 4th Army. For that oper-ation Model's Corps, returned to offensive operations, captured the bridges of the Moscow reservoirs and continued to advance until it was only a short dis-tance from the capital itself.

The strain and wear of battle had so worn down the Corps' striking power that the tank regiments of its panzer Divisions were little more than weak battlegroups, but Model was determined to press on with his attack. Soon the leading elements of his Divisions stood only 20km from the Soviet capital. They were to approach no closer than that, for the Red Army's counteroffensive, which opened on 8 December, forced the German Army back. Because of Model's firm grip on his Corps it was able to conduct a fighting retreat, in contrast to other formations, which broke under pressure. For his part in stabilising the front, Model was named temporary commander of 9th Army, a formation which had shown signs of dissolution during the retreat and had ceased to be battleworthy. Model was just the man to provide the backbone it needed.

There can be no doubt that the longest and happiest period in Model's military career was as General Officer Commanding 9th Army, although it was marked with times of crisis and bitter arguments with Hitler. Model came to command of that Army in January 1942, when the Russian winter offensive had driven a blunt-headed wedge into the northern wing of 9th Army, between Systshevka in the south and Rzhev in the north. Two Red Army Fronts, Kalinin and West, then opened offensives which threatened the back of 9th Army and had the intended aim of attacking the deep flank of Army Group Centre. The gap which the Red Army had already torn in 9th Army's battle line was not only too great for that formation to close, but was likely to grow wider under the heavy and continued assaults of the Russian masses.

General Strauss, the former commander of 9th Army, was sent home on sick leave and replaced by Model on 18 January. The new commander was confronted with a stark choice; either pull 9th Army back to the so-called 'Koenigsberg' defensive line or counterattack the Red hosts. Model was well aware of the vital importance of holding Rzhev. Were he to pull back his battle line, the move would jeopardise the whole Army Group front. He decided to attack, and it was expected that the pincer movements he proposed would close the gap and cut off the Russian spearheads. Those Soviet units which had broken through would be isolated once the line had been firmly sealed, and could then be attacked and wiped out. Model opened offensive operations on 5 February, and had soon trapped a large number of Russian units within a giant pocket. After a brief but successful battle the line was closed with a loss to the Russians of 26,000 dead.

The triumph at Rzhev restored morale in the German army on the Eastern Front, marking a victory after the whole catalogue of defeats which had occurred during December-January. On 28 February Model was promoted to colonel general and awarded the Oak Leaf to the Knight's Cross. In the course of a briefing at Fuehrer Headquarters which followed the presentation of that award, Model proposed that a Panzer Corps be sent northwards to reinforce the Rzhev sector. Hitler rejected the proposal, stating that the Corps was needed in the south, near Gshatsk. A heated argument between the two men then developed which only ended when Model asked Hitler the direct question: 'My Fuehrer. Who commands the 9th Army – you or I?'. Hitler, who had always stood in awe of the fiery

Model, accepted the suggestion, but added that if things went wrong Model would pay for it with his head.

This was not the first time that Model had clashed with Hitler, and it would not be the last. Later in the war, following Operation Citadel, the summer offensive of 1943, Hitler remarked that the German soldiers of 1943 were not of the calibre of those of 1941, and wondered where that fighting spirit had gone. Incensed by Hitler's remarks, Model told him in impassioned words: 'The reason is because the men of 1941 are dead. Yes, my Fuehrer, dead. Their graves lie strewn across the whole of Russia. The men of 1943 are no less good soldiers, but they are fewer and their equipment is old.' On another occasion, when a Staff Officer tried to defend Hitler against Model's outbursts, the Field Marshal retorted: 'What are you talking about? You know nothing of the situation. The men in the front line fight against tanks, masses and masses of tanks. They are bombarded day and night and lie, often hungry and cold, in holes in the ground. You sleep each night in a warm, comfortable bed and are well fed. What do you know of the sacrifices of my soldiers? I forbid you to talk in such a fashion.'

Many of the stories about Model may well be apocryphal, but he stood in fear of no one in the defence of his men. He had a rough tongue, a fierce temper and a temperament which demanded the best from his Staff at all times. Small wonder, then, that officers on his staff had nervous breakdowns and that applications for transfers away from him were the norm.

As a result of the clash with Hitler on 28 February 1942, Model was allowed to direct 9th Army as he saw fit, and within a day the enemy forces near Byeloi were trapped and destroyed, as he had planned. Many Russian soldiers who had avoided capture by hiding in the deep woods joined partisan units operating in the rear of the German armies and soon became a problem. With his Army now holding a firm front, and with the encircled Russian forces defeated, Model turned to the hunting down and destruction of the guerrilla groups. He directed operations in person, flying over the combat zone in an unarmoured Fieseler Storch light aircraft. This proved hazardous for, during one operation to round up the guerrilla forces, his aircraft was fired at from the ground and he was struck by a bullet which passed through the length of his body from leg to shoulder. The pilot managed to land the damaged machine near the headquarters of 2nd Panzer Division, and Model was taken to a field hospital and given an immediate blood transfusion.

The Rzhev sector was highly sensitive throughout the spring of 1942 and remained so during Unternehmen Blau, the German summer offensive of that year. In outline this was a two-pronged operation, one pincer striking into the Caucasus and another driving for the Volga at Stalingrad. The vast forces needed to launch the operation could only be obtained by drawing troops from other sectors of the Eastern Front battle line, and Stavka, aware that the postings had weakened Model's force, opened fresh and massive assaults to take Rzhev. One of these, mounted by the Kalinin Front and employing more than 3,000 AFVs, was beaten back by 9th Army with great loss to the Russians. The next Soviet offensive followed almost immediately and struck at men and formations which had already been strained by weeks of battle. Model knew the importance of Rzhev to the summer offensive. Were the town to fall, Unternehmen Blau would collapse. Determined that it would not fall, he issued the uncompromising order: '... we shall not give way'. Then, leading from the front in his usual fashion, he restored the situation on one threatened sector after another.

Commanders who failed to gain the objectives he set them were sacked, and he even removed general officers when it became clear that they were not equal to their tasks. The strain under which he worked was enormous, but his tenet was that a leader had no right to think of himself. The welfare of his men was the greater consideration. On those occasions when no formally constituted units such as regiments or battalions were to hand to confront a battlefield crisis, Model created battlegroups, and by such means and through his own personal example restored the situation time and again.

When the third battle for Rzhev ended, the Soviets had lost 380,000 men killed in action, 2,943 tanks destroyed and 453 aircraft brought down. Stavka was not deterred by such casualties, and on 24 November the fourth battle opened. Two whole Red Army Fronts deploying nearly six armies and totalling 60 infantry divisions, 5 cavalry divisions and 35 tank brigades struck 9th Army. The Russians had soon almost surrounded Model's Army, and he found himself fighting not a one-front or even a two-front struggle, but one on three fronts. Against so great a force 9th Army's battle line eventually ruptured, and to the south-west of Byeloi the Russians swarmed through the gap they had created. Model immediately counterattacked with the only forces to hand; 1st SS Cavalry Division and 2nd Luftwaffe Field Division. The speed and determination of the counter-thrust quickly isolated elements from ten Russian infantry divisions and four of their cavalry divisions, but the ensuing battle to subdue that great mass of soldiers lasted until the second week of January 1943. Then, with the last of the Soviet units destroyed, the fighting died away.

With the Red Army on his sector no longer an aggressive force, Model returned to mounting local offensives and to undertaking operations against the partisan bands. Although the 9th had won a victory on its sector, the German operation to capture Stalingrad on the Volga had failed with the loss of Paulus's 6th Army. That disaster left a vast gap through which the Red Army drove forward, intent upon the destruction of the Army Group Centre. However morally defensible it had been to hold the Rhzev salient, militarily, by January 1943, it had become a wasteful exercise and Hitler finally agreed to a withdrawal. Model then constructed the new roads which he needed to move his military units and the thousands of tons of stores, food supplies and other materials that had to be brought out. The operation was to begin on 22 February 1943 and to be completed by 1 March. Such a massive movement could not, of course, be hidden from the Russians, who launched in quick succession six offensives to overwhelm 9th Army as it retreated. In those battles the Soviets lost 42,000 men without seriously affecting the pace of the German withdrawal. By contrast, 9th Army's move gained it an advantage. It had a shorter line to defend and a Reserve of eight Divisions with which to strengthen other sectors of its front. For his success in the evacuation Model was awarded the Swords to the Oak Leaf on 3 April 1943, and when Manstein was removed from his post as commander of Army Group South it was Model whom Hitler chose to be the temporary replacement.

Undaunted by the debacle at Stalingrad, late in April 1943 Hitler laid out the plan for Operation Citadel, the German summer offensive. The operation was designed to take out the Russian salient around Kursk which had been created in the last stages of the Soviet 1942/43 winter campaign. Camouflaged under the name 'White Group', 9th Army was to form the northern pincer arm of Hitler's new operation. Under Model's command were eight Infantry, six Panzer and one Panzer Grenadier Division, but these no longer had their former power. How much the German Army's strength had been diminished by the war in Russia is shown by the fact that 9th Army had only 227 Panzers immediately available. Another 95 vehicles, including 70 Tigers, had been promised for the end of April, and a force of Ferdinand Jagdpanzer were also expected to be delivered before Citadel opened. On 9th Army's left flank stood 2nd Army, a seriously weakened force with an establishment of only fifteen understrength Divisions. Opposite 9th Army, holding positions on the southern side of the Kursk salient and thus form-ing the second pincer for Operation Citadel, stood 4th Panzer Army. This was strong formation. Between 9th Army and 4th Panzer Army extended the vast bulge of the Kursk salient which was held by two Russian Fronts, both of which had improved their already strong defences with field fortifications, barbed wire and minefields. In reserve the Soviet Fronts had tank masses and infantry armies.

Model had the gravest doubts about the wisdom of undertaking the oper-ation. It was clear to him that when the offensive began and the German forces were deeply committed, the Russians would launch a massive counterattack against 2nd Army, on his left, with the twin aims of throwing the German offen-sive off balance and of capturing the Orel sector held by 2nd Army. Model fore-saw that when that great Soviet counterattack was launched he would be compelled to divert troops from 9th Army's attacking force to counter the Russ-ian thrust. The Soviet operation would be a diversion which would weaken and thus prejudice the successful outcome of the whole operation.

So great were Model's doubts of the ability of his Army to play a full part in the operation that he demanded two additional panzer and four additional infantry Divisions, as well as heavy artillery assault guns and extra Engineer for-mations. He intended to create a strong counterattack reserve in the Orel-Karachev area. At briefings, Model repeated his advice that Citadel should not take place at all. Rather than open offensive operations, he argued, the German forces should either stand on the defensive and defeat any Russian assaults or withdraw from the Orel bend and pull back as far as the Desna river. Hitler was not prepared to take the latter course, but he did postpone the launching of Citadel until July.

By June, the reinforcements and extra panzers promised to 9th Army had still not been received, and Model again proposed that the operation be cancelled. Hitler would hear no more. Citadel would take place. For the offensive Model placed XXXXVII Panzer Corps in the centre of his Army's battle line, with XXIII Panzer Corps on the left flank and XX Panzer Corps on the right. The XXth had the task of maintaining touch with 2nd Army in the Orel bend. Model's battle plan was for 9th Army to advance under a strong artillery barrage and only after aircraft had bombed the Russian forward positions. The operation began, but so strong were the enemy defences and so bitter was the opposition that XXXXVII Panzer Corps gained only 8km in the first day's fighting, while XXIII Corps was halted short of its given objective, the town of Malo-Archangelsk. Fuel shortages played a significant part in dramatically reducing the air support vital to Model's attacks. Denied that support, 9th Army's principal objectives, the areas of high ground at Ponyri and Oboyan, remained uncaptured.

On the second day of the battle the Red Army began its own counterattacks against 9th Army, using fresh troops. During his visit to XXXXVII Corps on the offensive's third day, Model learned that Citadel was paralysed. Drawing his own conclusions from the reports he had received, he tried to revitalise his army's offensive by regrouping and moving the point of its maximum effort to a 10km-wide stretch of front along the line Olkovatka-Ponyri. The regrouping had little effect, and the new attacks which his troops launched gained little ground. Model attributed the lack of success to insufficiently trained panzer crews, and decided that the armour should be deployed in small groups rather than mass formations. All such considerations were academic, however, for on 11 July 2nd Army came under attack and on the following day the main Soviet counteroffensive opened. Model's promised reinforcements did not arrive, but were diverted to 2nd Army.

A major Russian thrust broke through and threatened 9th Army's main supply depot at Orel. To prevent its loss Model was forced to deflect two of his panzer Divisions from the main attack towards Kursk and divert them northwards to 2nd Army. His superior, Kluge, then ordered that he take command of 2nd Army as well as 9th Army. On 13 July Hitler cancelled Citadel, but that did not end the battle, for on the 15th a new Russian assault opened and forced 9th Army on to the defensive. Accepting the situation for what it was, Model requested and received permission to withdraw his Army to previously prepared positions, and when the move was completed 9th Army had a shorter battle line and four Divisions to put into reserve.

Right: A studio photograph of Dietrich taken years before the outbreak of the Second World War. He is here seen wearing the black uniform of a Gruppen-fuehrer of the SS.

Right: A photograph of Dietrich taken in 1942, while he was serving on the Eastern Front.

Left: Dietrich is here seen shaking hands with Wilhem Mohnke, the officer accused of murdering British troops near Dunkirk in 1940. This photograph was taken on the occasion of the raising of the 12th SS Panzer Division 'Hitler Youth', in Belgium during the winter of 1943/44.

Left: August von der Heydte, here seen in the rank of Major commanding the Fallschirmjaeger Lehr battalion (the Paratroop Training battalion) in Doberitz.

Right: Von der Heydte here seen leading his battalion through Braunschweig, 27 July 1941.

Below: Von der Heydte, commanding 6th Fallschirmjaeger Regiment, (centre, wearing steel helmet) here seen with SS Brigadefuehrer Ostendorff, GOC, the SS Division, 'Goetz von Berlichingen'. Normandy, June 1944.

Left: A formal portrait of Albert Kesselring, taken in the first year of the war.

Right: Kesselring made a great number of visits to front-line units. This 1944 photograph shows him during one such visit to his soldiers in Italy.

Left: A snapshot photograph of Kesselring taken in Italy, during the late summer of 1944.

Right: Kesselring made frequent visits to Libya to confer with Rommel and with the Italian commanders. This snapshot picture was taken during t spring of 1942.

Left: Shortly after the capture of Tobruk, in the summer of 1942, Kesselring made another visit to the desert army. He is seen here shortly after touchdown in Libya.

Below: Colonel Willi Langkeit (second from the left) wearing the black panzer uniform, with Lieutenant General von Manteuffel (with his hands in his pockets), during the defensive fighting at Jassy Roumania, May/June 1944.

Right: Langkeit here seen wearing the Oak Leaf to the Knight's Cross.

Below: In the spring of 1943, Hitler visited von Manstein at Saporozhne on the Dnieper river.

Left: Field Marshal von Manstein often visited the front-line trenches. He is here seen in the forward zone in the Donets river region, May 1943.

Lower left: A snapshot of von Manstein taken in his work room in the Ukraine headquarters at Vinnitsa, July 1943.

Right: Captain Model as a company commander in the 8th Infantry Regiment. Goerlitz.

Left: Colonel General Walter Model, commander of 9th Army, here seen wearing the award of the Swords to the Oak Leaf of the Knight's Cross.

Above: A snapshot of Model during the period he spent as GOC of Army Group North. He is here seen in conversation with an unnamed divisional commander.

Below: Model often visited the combat area and is seen here with two Grenadiers. Eastern Front, winter 1943/44.

Right: A young subaltern officer explaining the tactical situation to Field Marshal Model, Western Front, 1944.

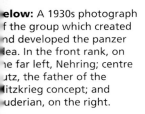

Below: A 1930s photograph of the group which created and developed the panzer idea. In the front rank, on the far left, Nehring; centre Lutz, the father of the Blitzkrieg concept; and Guderian, on the right.

Left: A snapshot of Nehring in North Africa, as commander of XC Corps, 1942.

Lower left: A formal portrait of Nehring after his appointment to command XC Corps in Tunisia, 1942.

Right: A snapshot of Nehring taken during the campaign in Poland, 1939.

Right: After Ramcke's battlegroup was abandoned in the desert during the battle of El Alamein, he led his men out to rejoin the main body of the German forces. This photograph is of Ramcke's battlegroup driving through the desert.

Left: General Hermann Bernhard Ramcke.

Right: A formal portrait of Ramcke, after the award of the Swords to the Oak Leaf of the Knight's Cross.

Below: When the German Army annexed Austria in 1938, Lothar Rendulic was recalled from retirement and given a new command. He is here seen in the uniform of a colonel in the Austrian Bundeswehr (but wearing the Reichs eagle on his right breast) at the ceremony which incorporated his Austrian Army unit into the forces of the Third Reich. (Photograph supplied by the Heeresgeschichtliches Museum in Vienna and reproduced by kind permission of the Rendulic family.)

Above: Another shot of the parade in Vienna when Colonel Rendulic's unit was absorbed into the German Army, 1938. (Photograph supplied by the Heeresgeschichtliches Museum and reproduced by kind permission of the Rendulic family.)

Below: In October 1942, General Rendulic, who was serving in Yugoslavia, celebrated his 55th birthday. This photograph was taken on that occasion and shows him receiving the congratulations of his military friends. The officer in the centre of the picture, with white lapels to his greatcoat, is Arthur Phleps, an SS General. (Photograph supplied by the Heeresgeschichtliches Museum in Vienna and reproduced by kind permission of the Rendulic family.)

Soviet attacks continued with the aim of first isolating 9th Army and then going on to encircle the whole Army Group. Aware of the weakness of his forces, Model demanded that fresh troops be airlifted in to protect the vast supply depots in Orel. On 20 July Hitler's order forbad 2nd Panzer Army to undertake any withdrawals. Model protested so energetically that the directive was revoked, and 2nd Army moved back to positions which Model had prepared against such an eventuality. Hitler's demand that Orel be held to the last could not be carried out, and Model asked Kluge to advise the Fuehrer of that fact. He then put his whole energies into saving as much as possible from the Orel area, and thanks to him more than 20,000 wounded, together with 53,000 tons of supplies, were taken out. Model himself was among the last to leave the abandoned sector. Russian attacks began to die away, and defensive fighting marked the months until the beginning of November.

On the 5th of that month Model left 9th Army and was placed in the Fuehrer Reserve of senior commanders. He was not long inactive, and on 29 January 1944 took over Army Group North, where his brusque attitude created difficulties with his headquarters staff as well as with the Luftwaffe. He demanded to know why the Stukas were not flying, and upon being told that it was not flying weather flew into a rage, stating that if the infantry had to fight in all weathers, then the Luftwaffe should at least make an effort to support them. On 4 February Model regrouped Army Group North into Army Group Narva and gave it the task of preventing a Soviet breakthrough to the Baltic. He and his Command were so successful that they totally dominated the enemy formations opposite them.

For that success Model was promoted on 30 March 1944 to the rank of generalfeldmarschall, the youngest in German military history, and sent to command Army Group South, later renamed Army Group North Ukraine. That Army Group was being forced back under the pressure of heavy Russian attacks, and when Model reached his new headquarters on 2 April his first orders were that the approaches to the Carpathian mountains had to be held at all costs. Army Group South had a great number of foreign contingents in its Order of Battle, and Model's manner created problems with those allies; particularly with the Hungarians. Deeply conscious of the shortage of men in his Command, Model used his usual 'combing' methods to create a reserve of formations. These small groups could be used against the Soviet Fronts which were preparing to batter a way through the Carpathians and invade Hungary.

The Red Army opened its offensives on 22 June 1944, not against Army Group South, but against Army Group Centre, as OKH had anticipated. The weight of the Russian attacks was so severe that Hitler ordered Model to take on the burden of commanding that Army Group as well as his own. He first pinpointed the weaknesses in the German battle line, then moved units to support those understrength sectors. By this time he had brought his Army Group North

Ukraine to a high combat level, and was able to move the 4th Panzer and the 28th Jaeger from that Army Group to support 2nd Panzer Army. He then began to take Army Group Centre in hand, but soon realised that it was burned out. Energetically he galvanised the Staffs into feverish action, while he himself went among his troops in the field and had soon inspired them with new confidence.

Morale in Army Group Centre was soon restored, and it was time to deal with the breach that the Russians had smashed between 4th Army and 3rd Panzer Army. To Model it was obvious that there were not enough men on the ground to seal the gap, and even though he had soon created a counterattack formation made up of Army and SS units he knew that he had insufficient soldiers and demanded more. These were not so much required to fight back the Soviet assaults as to keep open the supply routes along which the Army was nourished. He oversaw the operations to ensure that the convoys got through by flying over the battle zone every day in a Fieseler Storch. The Soviets were well aware of Model and his reputation, and one morning they mounted an air raid aimed at killing him. At the start of the raid someone gave the order to take cover, but Model retorted that only those officers with red stripes on their breeches should do this. He remained seated because his trousers did not carry a general's red stripes.

The fury of the Red Army's attacks did not lessen, and 4th Army began to break under its blows. Model flew to the threatened sector and had soon restored the situation, but, as usual, his proposals for a withdrawal to shorten the line forward of the German frontier were rejected by Hitler. The Fuehrer ordered a counterattack in the Memel area of East Prussia; this completely ignored the situation further south, where the Red Army was advancing upon Warsaw. At the height of this critical situation Hitler ordered Model to leave the Eastern Front and take over as Supreme Commander West. Despite his strongest representations to be allowed to stay on the Eastern Front, Hitler was adamant. Model had to accept the posting, and not only took over the supreme commander's post in France but also that of Commander in Chief of Army Group 'B'.

On 16 August, the day on which Model was appointed to the new posts, Hitler awarded him the Diamonds to the Knight's Cross. When the new Supreme Commander West flew to Paris and took over from von Kluge, he found a catastrophic situation. In the south-west of France Allied forces were driving the 1st and 19th German armies back towards Germany, while in northern France Anglo-US armies were exploding across Belgium and advancing towards the Siegfried Line. Parts of 7th Army and 5th Panzer Army (the former Panzer Group West) were trapped in the Falaise pocket, and 15th Army, holding the Channel coast, was in danger of being cut off. Also, across the whole region there was an active, highly co-ordinated and well armed partisan force.

Model did not come to the Western Front as an angel of salvation, but rather as a whirlwind. It cannot be denied that he had always treated his Staff officers badly, so badly in fact that on one occasion a whole group had asked to be sent to other duties rather than serve under him. He, himself, had not wanted to move to the Western Front, for he considered himself to be an Eastern Front specialist. Reports that he had taken over command in north-west Europe circulated quickly, usually bearing the news that 'the terror machine has arrived'. When Bayerlein, commanding the Panzer Lehr Division, asked that his Division be withdrawn from the line for rest and recuperation, Model's answer was: 'On the Eastern Front we rest and recuperate IN the front line. In future it will be like that here in the West. Your units will stay where they are.' Model's next meeting was to discuss with Eberbach, Dietrich's Chief of Staff, and SS General Hausser how they were to break the ring around Falaise, which had grown to become a massive encirclement 36km long and 18km deep.

In view of Hitler's demand that Paris be defended, Model drew up plans for a defence along the lines of the Dives and Toucques rivers, and for urban warfare in the suburbs of the city, but he then found that he lacked the military strength. When he inspected his Divisions he found them to be exhausted fragments of units, and promptly demanded from OKW no fewer than 30 fresh ones, knowing full well that he would not get even half that number. Certainly, von Choltitz, the Army commander of Paris, could not supply men from his own force to help Model. He did not have sufficient men even to put down the Maquis uprising which had begun in the French capital. Hitler's order that Paris was to be burned was relayed to Model, who passed it on to Choltitz. Model was as astonished as Hitler to learn that the order had not been carried out. To him Paris meant nothing. He had more important things to concern him than bricks and mortar, however historic they might be. His chief task was to set up defensive lines to the north and east of the city, on the Marne and the Somme.

Von Salmuth, commanding 15th Army, advised Model to take his whole force back across the Seine, otherwise he would lose all his armour and heavy weapons and the greater part of his infantry force. The Supreme Commander West refused to countenance such an action, but shortly after Hausser was wounded on 21 August the Command situation in north-west Europe deteriorated. Realising the worth of von Salmuth's advice, Model took action against the Allied advance towards the French capital. Conscious that time was running out and that his plans to hold northern France and Belgium were unlikely to succeed because he lacked the necessary troops, Model ordered work to begin on defence lines along the Maas and Mosel. If he could not stop the Allies taking France, he was determined to prevent them advancing into western Germany.

At the beginning of September 1944 German losses in the West had been so great that many of the Panzer divisions had been reduced to fewer than 2,000 men, 25 vehicles and just over 50 pieces of artillery. The advance of the Allied armies seemed unstoppable, and their armour was moving with such speed that General Eberbach, who believed himself to be in a safe area, found he was not and was taken prisoner. The scale of losses alarmed Model, who reported to Fuehrer Headquarters that the strength of his Army Group was sufficient for it only to hold a defensive line running from the Maas to the approaches to the Siegfried Line. There could be no question of Army Group 'B' undertaking any offensive operations. He demanded a reinforcement of 25 new infantry Divisions and five panzer Divisions. Although he knew such a demand could not be met, he was determined to show Fuehrer Headquarters the seriousness of the situation. What he actually received were two Panzer Grenadier Divisions and two Panzer Brigades.

When the British advanced into Belgium, Model ordered 15th Army to pull back to the Lower Scheldt. He was aware that the Allies needed Antwerp as a supply base because their supply routes from Normandy were overstretched. Even if the city of Antwerp were to be captured, he could prevent the Allies using the dock installations by holding the approaches to the city on the seaward side. He ordered that the approaches to Antwerp be held, confidently believing that although his Army Group could not stop the Allied advance, a petrol famine might. During the first week of September the burden of Supreme Commander was lifted from his shoulders when Hitler recalled von Rundstedt to that post. In the pause in the fighting brought about by the Allied fuel shortage, Model regrouped his forces. These were in a poor state, but he was determined to bring order out of chaos, and soon his methods had created the beginning of a defensive line; weak but continuous. His name and reputation for establishing order had been sufficient to bring about that result.

Two further crises arose at this time. The Americans reached Aachen, just inside Germany, and Operation Market Garden, the airborne assault, was launched. On 17 September, D-Day for the operation, the staff of Army Group was lunching in the Park Hotel in Hartenstein when a rain of bombs fell, to be followed by the airborne landings. Model was convinced that he was the target of the Allied air drop; to his mind there was no other objective close to the drop zone. The Arnhem bridge was 10km distant and, logically, no drop would be made so far from its objective. He and his staff moved to Terbourg, and from there he drove to Bittrich's II SS Panzer Corps headquarters at Doetinchen. Model gave orders for the Rhine bridges to be held and for a counterattack group to be formed. He also ordered that the undamaged bridges were not to be blown, even though those across the Maas at Greve and Eindhoven, which had not been destroyed, had both been seized by the Allies.

Model directed the German counterattacks which prevented a link-up between British XXX Corps and the paratroops in Arnhem, and on 18 September he personally led the assaults which went in between Oosterbeek and Wolfsberg. Although the British airborne assault failed to gain its objectives, it left a blunt salient in the German line at Nijmegen which Army Group was unable to take out. A new call had been made upon its strength when US 1st Army opened a major offensive to break through the Siegfried Line. The fighting on that sector lasted until the second week of October, and Model showed his character in forbidding the troops fighting in Aachen to break out. His signal concluded with the words: 'You will hold to the last man'. He knew that every day they held out won time for Germany.

In the middle weeks of the month he gave an appreciation of the Allies' three chief options. These were: first, an attack to liberate Holland; second, a pincer attack from the Reichswald and Aachen to gain the Rhine; and third, an advance through the valley of the Mosel to reach the Saar. Once again he demanded men and supplies; 200 panzers and SPs, 200 armoured personnel carriers and 20,000 men. During a seminar held on 2 November with the commanders and staffs of 5th Panzer Army and 5th Army, Model was discussing the possibility that the Americans might launch an attack along the seam of those armies. Suddenly the Chief of Staff of LVIIIV Corps telephoned with the news that the operation under discussion was actually taking place, and asked for reinforcements. Model's response was simply to send the commander of LVIIIV Corps back to his headquarters and then continue with the seminar. The American offensive died in the staunchness of the German defences. Model had knitted the front together again.

During that period of crisis, Hitler had been planning a new offensive in the west with the intention of separating and destroying the Allied armies in an operation which has become known as the Battle of the Bulge. The Chiefs of Staff of the Supreme Commander West and of Army Group 'B' were briefed by the Fuehrer and ordered to obtain the opinions of their respective superiors. Model's first reaction was to condemn Hitler's plan and prepare an alternative in conjunction with the other senior commanders – the so-called 'small solution', an offensive with limited objectives which would take out the US salient at Aachen. Hitler turned down the plan produced by his most senior field commanders and insisted that they carry out the 'big solution'. This was his plan for the German forces to drive for and reach Antwerp, splitting the British from the Americans, then go on to destroy each in detail. Army Group 'B' with the 6th Panzer Army (later to be named 6th SS Panzer Army), the 5th Panzer Army and both 7th and 15th infantry armies under its command was to carry out the operation, starting from the Eifel area. A fresh Army Group, 'H', was created to hold the Maas front.

There were continuing arguments about the wisdom of the forthcoming offensive. Model insisted that the 'big solution' could only succeed if all the armour was grouped in a massive fist. Hitler rejected that tactic in favour of the panzers being spread out across the whole battlefront. The arguments came to a head when, in a telephone conversation with Jodl, Model categorically refused to obey an order given to him by OKW. At a final conference in Berlin on 2 December, Model once again pressed for the 'small solution' and Hitler once again refused, although he did concede that if the 'big solution' showed signs of failing, then the 'small' one would be implemented. Model was not alone in expressing doubts that the Luftwaffe could give continuous cover to the advancing columns. Hitler promised an air umbrella of 4,000 fighter aircraft. Despite the Fuehrer's promises, only ten of the fourteen Panzer Divisions intended for the attack were available, and only eleven of the fourteen infantry Divisions. Of the promised four Paratroop Divisions two were available, and of the Army troops to support the assault only 60 per cent could be supplied. In the matter of fuel, Model's Army Group was almost in a state of famine.

Nevertheless, when the operation opened on 16 December it made good initial progress. Despite the most strenuous efforts, the closest that any German unit reached to Antwerp was Dinant, a long way east of the Maas. When the advance of 6th Panzer Army was decisively slowed, Model, acting in his usual decisive fashion, swung Army Group's main effort from the 6th Panzer Army in the north to Manteuffel's 5th Panzer Army in the south. That switch might have stood a chance of success had there not been a fateful change in the weather. The skies, which had been overcast since the offensive opened, cleared, allowing the Allied air forces to attack the German armour. A combination of Allied ground and air strength halted the German advance. Hitler ordered the 'small solution' to open on 27 December, but it was too late. The Battle of the Bulge had been lost, and a retreat back into Germany by the German forces which had taken part was inevitable.

Throughout the battle Model had usually been found in the fighting zone, encouraging, inspiring and, where necessary, bullying his subordinates in order to bring the attack forward. It was reported by one officer that he saw Model, '... a small, undistinguished-looking man with a monocle in his eye ...', directing traffic near St Vith. That story may be apocryphal, but it was the sort of gesture Model would make to speed the pace of the advance. When it became clear even to Hitler that the Ardennes offensive was at an end, and that Army Group 'B' had to pull back, Model tried in vain to convince the Fuehrer that Germany's defence in the west must be based along the river barrier of the Rhine and not along the Siegfried Line.

His Army Group's task was impossible. It had to hold back the overwhelming weight of the Allied (predominantly American) forces, and by March 1945 those forces had not only closed up to the Rhine but had crossed it in places. Hitler brought Kesselring from Italy to restore the situation, and the Luftwaffe Field Marshal reached his new area of responsibility confident that he could carry out the Fuehrer's directive to save the Ruhr. Kesselring and Model met, and when the Luftwaffe commander mentioned OKW's poor opinion of Army Group 'B', Model, almost incoherent with rage, denounced the High Commander and the Supreme Commander in the bitterest terms.

The Americans continued to advance towards the Ruhr, and the two huge pincer arms of 1st and 9th US Armies met in the area of Lippstadt, trapping Model's Army Group. Hitler refused to let Army Group 'B' withdraw so that they could escape the American encirclement. Hitler ordered the total destruction of all the Ruhr industrial complexes, to deny them to the Allies, but this was an order that Model had no intention of carrying out. With the support of Albert Speer, the Reichs Armaments Supremo, he saved the factories of the Ruhr from destruction. On 29 March Model issued orders to General Bayerlein, commanding LIII Panzer Corps, that he was to group the remnants of the Panzer Lehr Division, 9th Panzer, 3rd Panzer Grenadier Division and 3rd Fallschirmjaeger divisions. That mass of units was to strike eastwards, break out of the encirclement and gain touch with units of Army Group 'G'.

Bayerlein's old Division, Panzer Lehr, led the breakout operation, the last major German offensive in the west. The attacking units struck, but were stopped by the fire of superior American armoured formations. Bayerlein, leading Panzer Lehr in person, renewed the attack and broke through the opposition. It seemed as if the attack might yet succeed. Then the rain which had fallen almost continuously for days cleared, and with the return of fine weather Allied fighter-bombers swooped down and their first attacks halted the advance. A second air strike destroyed the last armoured fighting vehicles of the breakout group. The 3rd Paratroop Division attack had also opened well, but it too was struck by Allied aircraft, which fragmented it into small battlegroups. The survivors of Bayerlein's LIII Corps pulled back to their start lines on 2 April, by which time 1st and 9th US Armies had drawn the ring tight around the Army Group.

The fighting of the next few days reduced the Panzer Lehr Division to a strength of twenty panzer and ten other tracked vehicles, a state that was symptomatic of all the Divisions contained in the encirclement. The end of the Ruhr pocket was close, and when it was split during the second week of April, Model, on his own initiative, dissolved his Army Group, sending home immediately the men of the oldest and youngest age groups after issuing them with the necessary demobilisation papers. Model rejected the offers of surrendering with honour sent by General Ridgeway, answering that not only had he sworn a personal oath of allegiance to Hitler, but his own sense of honour prevented him from even considering such a course of action. Model was determined to find death on the battlefield, but that release was denied him.

Obsessed with thoughts that he had failed in his duty, he asked his Chief of Staff whether he had done everything possible to justify his actions in the light of history, and was assured that he had. On 17 April he set out on his last journey. In a three-vehicle convoy he drove to a point east of Dusseldorf, crossed the autobahn near Ratingen and entered the nearby woods. For several days Model brooded on the fate of Germany and her Army. Then, on 21 April, after shaking hands with the officers of his escort, he entered a thicket of trees and shot himself. He was buried, as he had requested, on the spot where he fell, under a huge and spreading oak tree. For years his last resting place was unmarked. Then, in 1955, his remains were disinterred and Field Marshal Walter Model was reburied in a military cemetery in the Huertgen forest.

Panzer Theoretician and Practitioner

General der Panzertruppe Walther K. Nehring

Born on 15 August 1892 in the West Prussian province of Stretzin, Walter Kurt Josef Nehring was descended from a Dutch family which had fled religious persecution in the 17th century and settled in Germany. While he was still a child, his family moved first to Zoppot and then to Danzig. The young Nehring was surrounded by military influences from his earliest days, so it was no surprise when he resolved to become a soldier.

In the German Army of imperial days a commission was gained either through a cadet school or by virtue of educational qualifications. It was through the latter channel that Walter Nehring entered the Army in 1911, an entry aided by his father's contacts with the 152nd Regiment. Although that formation bore the title of the Deutsch Orden (the Teutonic Knights' Order), it was a military fiction because the regiment had been raised only in 1897 and could not trace its ancestry directly back to medieval times. However, the German Army maintained that fiction, and the Colour which the 152nd carried bore on one side the Insignia of the Teutonic Knights, not the Prussian eagle.

Within two years of entering the Service as an Ensign in the 152nd, Nehring was commissioned as a second lieutenant and was posted to the regiment's No. 8 Company. Prussian training had always been based on the theory that sweat in training during peacetime saved blood on the battlefield in war. Thus it was that his first years with the 152nd were hard and exhausting, with a constant need for thrift because an officer's pay was low. Nehring was later to write that officers served their King and Country more or less at their own expense.

The first years of the 20th century saw Europe's slow drift to war, and the German Army's units in the Prussian provinces were reinforced by newly raised formations. The Army's XX Corps was added to the establishment of the forces in west Prussia, 152nd Regiment in the 41st Division forming part of that Corps. Upon the outbreak of war in August 1914, XX Corps advanced slowly eastwards to confront the oncoming pincers of the Tsarist Army. The enemy force was made up of two huge bodies. In the north, General Rennenkampf's 1st Army formed one pincer, while 2nd Russian Army, commanded by General Samsonov, made up the southern pincer. Faced with overwhelming numerical superiority, the German commander ordered a retreat and the Russian forces swept into Prussia.

The hesitant German commander was replaced by two new commanders, Hindenburg and Ludendorff, who not only halted the withdrawal but determined to convert it into an offensive operation striking into the flank of Samsonov's southern host. Their plan to convert a retreat into an attack could only succeed if one of the German Corps stood fast and held its ground. That Corps would have to act aggressively, attracting the whole attention and weight of attacks by 2nd Russian Army, and also acting as a shield behind which the rest of the German Army on the Eastern Front wheeled to attack Samsonov.

The task fell upon XX Corps, and it committed its 41st Division to an attack Waplitz, a village south of the Muehlensee which had been captured by Tsarist forces. The 152nd Regiment had its 1st and 3rd Battalions 'up', leaving 2nd Battalion, with which Nehring was serving, in reserve. The relative quietness of the reserve area was shattered when the Russians, sweeping through a breach in the German line, over-rolled 2nd Battalion, which had not deployed for battle. The order was given for the platoons and Companies to fight their way out of the Russian encirclement and to regroup in the village of Seythen. Nehring's platoon was among the last to leave, and was unable to make the rendezvous at Seythen. Instead it attacked the nearby village of Muehlen. The defending Russians were not only driven out, but some were taken prisoner. Late in the afternoon Nehring and his men made contact with a battalion of the German 37th Division, and days later learned that their action had made a contribution to a victory; the defeat of Samsonov's army.

With one Russian Army defeated, Hindenburg swung his forces northwards to engage and eventually defeat General Rennenkampf's force. The threat to the Prussian provinces was lifted. It was during the latter fighting against Rennenkampf's 1st Russian Army that Nehring was wounded in the head and also shot through the throat. He returned from convalescence to take up the appointment of acting Company commander in the replacement battalion until he was fit once again for active duties. He was then posted to 141st Regiment and served as adjutant to its 2nd Battalion until he returned to front-line duty. When he did so he was wounded for a second time, shot through the calf of the right leg. At the end of January 1915, even though his wound was not completely healed, Nehring was back in action with his original regiment, the 152nd, where he was given command of a Company. He had also been awarded the Iron Cross Second Class in addition to the wound badge in black.

The war on the Eastern Front, which had begun as a conflict of mobile operations, descended into trench warfare, and Nehring, wishing for a more active fighting role, volunteered for the air force. On 6 June 1916, the day on which he was promoted full lieutenant, he entered the flying school for what was to be but a brief adventure. Only two weeks after he had started training, the aircraft in which he was flying as observer crashed, and he sustained a broken jaw. He returned to the infantry, and in the first week of December 1916 was posted to the Western Front to take command of 22nd Regiment's No. 1 Machine-gun Company.

Nehring spent the remainder of the war on the Western Front. During that time he was wounded for a third time, shot through the stomach in the fighting for Mount Kemmel in Flanders. This third injury brought him the wound badge in silver to add to the Iron Cross First Class which he had been awarded on 19 November. Upon discharge from hospital on 27 September 1918, just before the armistice, Nehring was posted to the replacement Machine-gun Company of XX Corps, and within a week of the end of hostilities had been promoted Adjutant of the Corps' replacement machine-gun troops.

On 16 November 1918 the Reich government authorised the raising of volunteer units to enter southern Russia and bring out those German Army formations which had been stationed in the Ukraine and the Caucasus when the armistice came. The units which would undertake the operation had to be volunteers because Germany, as a defeated nation, was forbidden to deploy Regular Army troops for such a purpose. Even had the Allies permitted the use of Regular troops, it would have been a difficult task for the German Army to undertake because the regiments of the standing Army were no longer at full strength. A too-rapid demobilisation had reduced most of them to cadres.

The fate of the men in the Ukraine and the Crimea was not the only crisis facing the German government. There was also a need to find soldiers to man and hold the eastern frontier against incursions by the Poles. Lieutenant Nehring was given the task of recruiting men for units of the 'Volunteer Frontier Defence Force' and, as early as the end of December 1918, units of that Force were in action against Polish regular and irregular troops. The XX Corps quickly raised 'Brigade No. 37', but its strength of 400 officers and more than 10,000 rank and file was above establishment. The supernumeraries were posted to 'Volunteer Infantry Division No. 41', to which Nehring was posted on 1 April 1919 in the dual role of machine-gun Company commander and reconnaissance officer. In time, political and diplomatic activity brought stability to Germany's eastern provinces. The government ordered that the Frontier Defence Force be disbanded, but the Army set up commissariats to liaise with the civil authorities should the need arise to reactivate the Force. Nehring was one of the commissars in that liaison scheme. To ensure that he had the formal and legal military authority to carry out that duty he was officially sworn in as an officer of the Regular Army, being appointed adjutant in the 20th Brigade.

Throughout the early years of the decade 1920-30, Nehring studied to improve his prospects of promotion in the Reichsheer, the army of the Weimar Republic. That force was made up of two distinctly different types of unit. The first consisted of former Imperial regiments using the old-fashioned command structure and discipline. The second type was formed out of formations of the 'Volunteer' or 'Freikorps' type, with more modern and less formal methods. The task of welding those various units into a united and potent national force was fraught with difficulties, but Nehring succeeded so well that in 1923 he was promoted to the rank of captain. He was then eligible to apply to sit for the Army examination which, if he passed, would take him into the hierarchy of the General Staff. He passed the entrance examination with an excellent result. It has previously been explained that under the terms of the Treaty of Versailles Germany was forbidden to have a General Staff organisation, but that that body was in fact kept active by being given a bland, deceptive title.

In 1923 Nehring married the youngest daughter of an East Prussian landowner. Two years later, in October 1925, after a spell of duty as adjutant with 2nd Regiment, he was posted temporarily to the combined Services (Reichswehr) headquarters in Berlin. In his research for the examinations he was about to sit, Nehring made himself familiar with the weapons and tactics of arms of Service other than those of the infantry in which he had served during the Great War. He first trained with the artillery and, when that period of secondment ended, he took up another Staff post in the Reichswehr Ministry. A new series of examinations at General Staff level brought him a transfer to the Mobilisation and Planning Department, and there, in accordance with the edict that officers of the General Staff must become proficient in a specialist subject, Nehring chose as his discipline the employment of motorised units. His choice was influenced by the arrival in the Department of Major Guderian, with whom he developed a strong friendship based upon a common belief in the effectiveness of motorised/tank action.

A return to regimental soldiering came in 1929, when duties in the 6th battalion of the Vehicle Training Command gave him the opportunity to practise the theories on motorised operations which he had formulated. He found that secret work within that unit had resulted in the creation of a panzer Company, and also a motorcycle infantry Company and a panzer reconnaissance Company. Nehring's tactical principles were tried out during the autumn manoeuvres of 1929, and proved so successful that the Reichswehr authorities ordered the Army's other lorried battalions to be trained along the same lines.

The retirement of the Inspector of Motorised Units in 1930 brought as his replacement General Lutz, who can be considered the creator of Germany's panzer arm. He strongly supported the work of his two principal subordinates, Nehring and Guderian, both of whom had written papers on the employment of armoured forces in a future war. Nehring foresaw that mobile operations had to be based upon the employment of vehicles which combined high mobility and strong firepower. This concept became the founding principle of the panzer arm. To allow Nehring to work unhindered on theoretic planning, Guderian obtained a transfer for him to serve as his own Chief of Staff. In December 1933, less than a year after Hitler came to power, the restrictions of the Treaty of Versailles were abolished, and Germany was able not only to increase the size of her Army but also to build her own armoured fighting vehicles; the nucleus of a panzer force.

In 1933 Nehring went on an exchange visit to the Italian Army, and studied its tank force. Upon his return to Germany he was posted to the first panzer unit, and there met officers who had trained illegally in the Soviet Union, as well as others who had served in the Army's motorised battalions. In October 1935, when 5th Panzer Regiment was created, Nehring was working on the reorganisation of Germany's expanding Army. He proposed that it should include Panzer Divisions as well as the standard infantry divisional types. His ideas on armoured warfare were not confined to theory but ranged into the practical, and he advocated the introduction of special tank-destroyer units.

From his extensive reading Nehring became aware of the very high peacetime output of tractors from Soviet factories. If they were converted to tank production, the factories would have the capacity to turn out more than a thousand armoured fighting vehicles each month. Guderian advised Hitler of the predicted output and was mocked as a scaremonger; something the Fuehrer would later regret. On 1 September 1934 Nehring was promoted to lieutenant colonel in the General Staff and, together with Guderian, sought to overcome the hostile attitudes of senior commanders who thought of a 'defensive' Germany and who, therefore, saw no need for a panzer arm. Chief among those opponents was General Beck, Chief of the General Staff, who believed that tanks should not be employed as divisions in their own right but should be tied to infantry formations for use in a support role; a complete negation of Nehring's 'blitzkrieg' concepts.

On 2 July 1936 Nehring was selected to take a one-year course in the 'Wehrmachtakademie fuer hoehere Fuehreranwaerter', to which were posted officers destined for the highest echelons of command. Before he could enter the academy, however, an order was received that he was to undertake the organisation of the flow of volunteers, guns and tanks to General Franco's army in Spain. That secondment lasted until October, when he was free to enter the Wehrmachtakademie. On 1 March 1937 Nehring was promoted to the rank of colonel and, because of his reputation as an armoured warfare theorist and military author, was invited to lecture to the Swiss Army. He returned to Germany to attend the autumn manoeuvres of 1937, the climax of which was an attack by 800 armoured fighting vehicles operating with strong Luftwaffe support. The event proved to be a poor debut for the Panzer Arm. During the vast operation some tanks fell out through mechanical failure and others from fuel shortages or other reasons. Enough reached the target, however, and Hitler was impressed. Nehring returned to regimental duties, and on 13 October took command of 5th Panzer Regiment, one of the formations of Geyr von Schweppenburg's 3rd Panzer

Division in X Panzer Corps. His subsequent return to General Staff duties brought him the task of raising the XIX (motorised) Corps, of which he became Chief of Staff on 1 July 1939.

Immediately before the outbreak of war, Guderian and Nehring, together with their staffs, went to check on the strength of the defences of Silesia in the event of a pre-emptive Polish attack. XIX Corps was part of von Kluge's 4th Army, whose task in the war with Poland was to thrust for the Vistula and there to cut off and annihilate the enemy forces in the Polish corridor. The war, which began in 1939, was to be the first in which radio communications between commanders and front-line units, as well as between individual AFVs, were to play a prominent part. In the course of operations, Nehring discovered that orders issued to panzer and motorised formations enabled commanders to change targets or objectives or even to alter a unit's thrust line. But there were difficulties with the infantry Division, which was also on Corps establishment. Tied to a foot-marching speed, it could not keep pace with the panzer/motorised echelons. The Army Group commander, von Bock, recognised the inhibiting effect of slow-marching infantry upon fast-driving motorised formations and regrouped his armour and motorised Divisions to create a 'fast group' out of 3rd and 10th Panzer and 2nd and 20th (motorised) Divisions. He ordered that group to advance and take Brest-Litovsk. Although the war with Poland was only weeks old, combat experience had demonstrated that in armoured warfare senior commanders had to be as far forward as possible, and during the battle of Brest-Litovsk both the Corps commander and his chief of staff were usually to be found in the front-line echelons.

The Soviet invasion of Poland served only to hasten the end of a war which was already won, and at the military parade to mark the conclusion of that war Nehring met and was impressed by the Russian tank specialist, Korovshin. However, he could not assess the Russian armoured forces because he saw no tanks. For the parade the Red Army deployed only armoured reconnaissance machines. During the winter of 1939-40 Nehring was busy planning the campaign in the west, in which the panzer Divisions, grouped into a mighty fist, were to punch through the Ardennes and across the Maas. On 9 May 1940 an urgent signal recalled him from leave to rejoin XIX Corps, composed of 1st, 2nd and 10th Panzer Divisions as well as the élite infantry regiment 'Grossdeutschland'. The War in the West was about to begin. The advance of the German Army's powerful panzer fist was covered and brought forward by dive bombers. The use of such aircraft as a rolling artillery barrage was another of Nehring's innovations. He had foreseen that dive bombers could carry out precision attacks upon individual targets instead of area bombing, which was the standard form of air attack.

As the panzer host swept across northern France, Guderian suggested that his Corps should advance to the mouth of the Somme and thereby cut deep into the rear of the French army. Von Kleist, his superior, rejected the proposal, but gave Guderian a day in which to regroup and reorganise his Corps. Guderian did not waste that day regrouping, but continued to advance using plans worked out by Nehring. Within that allotted 24 hours Corps had captured Ribemount on the Oise, and it continued its forward move on 17 May, beating down French counterattacks. To master those assaults, Nehring, who unusually was not forward with the front-line units but was at Corps TAC headquarters, deployed the follow-up 10 Panzer Division, and sent it in to deal with the threatening situation. On 19 May OKH accepted Guderian's plan which Kleist had rejected, and soon XIX Corps had crossed the Somme and reached the Channel coast. High Command then swung it northwards towards Flanders, where a British/French force around Dunkirk was trapped with its back to the sea.

On 20 May Hitler ordered Guderian to set up a panzer Group composed of XIX, XXXIX and XLI Corps, with Nehring as its Chief of Staff, and further directed that his force was to cross the Aisne canal and reach the plateau of Langres. This was accomplished by 15 June, and only two days later the Swiss frontier was reached. The campaign in the west was now in its final stages, and with its end came Nehring's promotion to major general. One other announcement was the OKW order, issued at the end of September, converting certain Divisions to Panzer and/or Panzer Grenadier status. When those formations named had completed their conversion, there remained a number of units which had no formal attachment to a parent body. By combining those remnants it was possible to create two additional panzer Divisions; the 18th and 20th. On 25 October Nehring was given command of 18th Panzer Division, but found this lacked proper weapons, vehicles or equipment. He complained that he had not been given a fully equipped, well established formation, and his representations did not go unheeded, for within weeks he was able to take on charge the 18th Panzer Brigade. This was a first-class formation which had been stood down after the cancellation of the proposed invasion of the United Kingdom. It seemed at first that Nehring's command of 18th Division might be of short duration, for orders came for him to join Rommel's Afrika Korps. That order was rescinded, however, and Nehring spent the next few months carrying out inspections of the units of his Division, as well as training his men for the role they would play in Operation Barbarossa, the attack upon the Soviet Union.

During March 1941 the 18th Panzer Division concentrated near Prague, where it was very slowly fleshed out with new units. Although OKH must have known of the Division's weakness in men and vehicles, it nevertheless ordered it to be prepared to take the field by 10 June. At the beginning of that month the officers of the Division travelled to Paris, where they took over the mass of French tanks with which the Division was expected to fight the coming war. The French machines were completely unsuited to the Soviet Union's difficult terrain and harsh climate. There was little time to familiarise the crews with their new mounts, and soon the Division was undertaking the long drive to the jump-off areas in eastern Europe. Aware of the strain that a succession of long drives would impose on both men and machines, Nehring ordered that they were not to make for the concentration area designated by OKW. Instead they were to carry on to the start line, which had been laid out to the east of Warsaw.

For the Russian campaign his formation was to spearhead XXXXVII Panzer Corps, which was itself to be the cutting edge of Guderian's 2nd Panzer Group. In his usual fashion Nehring was in the lead vehicle from the very start of the new war, and remained so as 18th moved into the Ukraine, where it played its part in closing the ring of armour around the forces defending Kiev. The optimism felt by the German Army at this time was understandable. Their Russian opponents seemed to be in dissolution, and for panzer theoretician Nehring it must have been gratifying to see his ideas of mobile warfare, the Blitzkrieg, proving themselves on the steppes of the Ukraine.

As an example of the confidence that was felt, Guderian sent Nehring's Division to head 2nd Panzer Group's advance to Trubchevsk, even though the 18th Division was isolated, was more than 30km ahead of the other units of the Group and therefore unsupported, and was under constant attack. One dangerous incident during that drive occurred during the afternoon of 31st August, when a Russian cavalry brigade attacked and all but encircled an infantry regiment which Nehring was visiting. Heavy attacks mounted by other Soviet units supporting the Red cavalry threatened the whole Division with total destruction. To make the decisions which would master these crises, it was vital that Nehring return to his divisional headquarters, but this was not possible. He was isolated with the cut-off infantry regiment. He grouped his panzer TAC headquarters and broke through the enemy cavalry to reach his headquarters, bringing in some prisoners of war and an anti-tank gun as booty.

On 5 October 18th Panzer Division was sent on a panzer raid, one of the tactical phenomena of the war on the Eastern Front. The aim was to drive from Karachev, cover a distance of more than 150km, and strike into the flank of the Red Army formations which were being encircled around Bryansk. Nehring's Division reached Karachev, and he sent out battlegroups to throw a ring around 50th Red Army, but a sudden emergency then caused Guderian to order 18th Panzer to pull out and to drive at top speed to Fatesh. Heavy rain had turned the ground to a quagmire which was holding fast the vehicles of 9th Panzer Division. Nehring deployed a rescue group and completed the mission of recovering the vehicles of the 9th within two days. The glutinous mud produced by the first winter snow showers, which had trapped the 9th's machines, was a warning to the German Army of the difficulties it would face if it did not win the war in the East quickly and decisively.

The manpower casualty figures were high, but the losses of vehicles of all sorts were catastrophic. As a consequence the panzer forces had been weakened to the extent that Guderian was forced to commandeer and concentrate all his Group's available 'runners' before he had sufficient AFVs under command to attack Tula. Nehring's panzers were taken from him for that mission, leaving his unit immobile, and it was not until the AFVs were returned that his Division was able to operate again. By 23 November 18th Panzer was active and roared into battle, reaching and capturing the town of Skopin. Indicative of the drain upon the strength of the tank forces was the fact that the combat strength of the 18th had been reduced by 70 per cent.

On 7 January 1942 Nehring was advised that his Division was to be reinforced so that it could carry out yet another rescue operation; this time to bring the 216th Infantry Division out of the Russian encirclement at Ssuchinitshy. The operation began on the bitter cold morning of 16 January, and deep snow drifts so hampered the advance that, according to Nehring, the tenacity of the Russian soldiers was less of a problem than the climatic conditions. Within days the Soviet ring was broken and the 216th, together with a thousand wounded men, had been brought out. That mission ended Nehring's association with the 18th Panzer, for on 1 February 1942 he handed over his Division and took command of the Afrika Korps with the rank of lieutenant general.

The situation in Africa, as Nehring found it, was that the opposing armies, drawn up along a line running inland from the sea to a point deep in the desert, were protected by deep and extensive minefields. The positions were known to the British as the Gazala Line. Both sides were preparing for new offensives, but the German/Italian forces struck first. Their battle plan had two objectives; firstly, to capture the strategically important port of Tobruk and, secondly, to seize Egypt's principal cities and the Suez canal.

The operation to capture Tobruk had two phases. A vast armada of Axis armoured fighting vehicles was to drive by night down the British front and turn Eighth Army's southern flank at the desert strongpoint of Bir Hachim. The panzer mass would then wheel northwards, back towards the sea. The success of that wheeling movement would bring the main Axis host east of the British line – that is to say behind it. Meanwhile, a smaller Italo/German group would make feint 'Chinese' attacks against the western front of the British line. Rommel's plan was based on the expectation that the British would come out from behind their minefields to engage the 'Chinese' attacks, leaving themselves vulnerable to the stab in the back which would be made by the mass of the Axis forces. That stab in the back would force Eighth Army to retreat, leaving Tobruk virtually undefended. The port would then be captured and the fleeing, disorganised British would be pursued, brought to battle and destroyed.

Nehring was worried by the fact that during the second phase of the operation, the wheel northwards to the sea, Afrika Korps would be cut off from its supplies. It would be east of the British minefields with its supplies to the west of those fields. His doubts about the wisdom of Rommel's plan were proved to be justified when a critical shortage of fuel and ammunition developed. To resolve that crisis Nehring planned an operation to smash a way through the British minefields. The plan was for an attack to go in from east of the fields while, simultaneously, the 'Chinese' group would begin mine lifting from the west. The plan worked. A gap was created and the urgently needed supplies began to move. Without waiting to see that his plan had been successful, Nehring rode out eastwards with 15th Panzer Division to engage Eighth Army's armour while the mass of Panzer Army Africa swung back westwards towards Tobruk and captured it. Promotion to the rank of General of Panzer Troops was Nehring's reward for his part in the successful operation. Ahead lay the second part of the summer offensive; the advance towards Cairo. During the last week of August preparations were completed and 200 panzers stood ready.

On the last day of August the Battle of Alam Halfa opened. As was his custom, Nehring rode with the leading panzer echelon; this time the vehicles of 21st Panzer. British Eighth Army had made careful preparations to meet the new assault, and launched wave after wave of bombers against it. During one of the raids Nehring was wounded in the head and body, and had to be flown out to a rear hospital and from there to Germany. Although a wound in his arm did not respond to treatment, he reported himself fit to take up his duties and on 9 November was ordered to return to Africa. Not to the deserts of Libya this time, but to Tunisia, where a new front had opened. An Anglo-American force had invaded the French North African colonies and was racing to capture Tunis. If the Allies succeeded in capturing the Tunisian capital, they would be positioned to strike into the back of Rommel's desert army.

Kesselring, the Supreme Commander South, realised the danger to the Axis forces, and upon Hitler's order to 'send everything possible' ordered 5th Fallschirmjaeger regiment to be flown in. The High Command in Berlin, aware of German military weakness in the area, ordered that a Staff Officer 'with red stripes on his breeches' be sent to Tunis. OKW was confident the Allies would be bluffed into believing that such a distinguished officer MUST have an army at his disposal, and Nehring was selected as that officer. It was a calculated risk by OKW, because German strength in Tunisia at that time was estimated to be less than 300 men.

The first German detachments began to land on Tunis airfield during the 11th, by which time the Supreme Commander South had briefed Nehring on his new duties. These were to create a bridgehead perimeter in Tunisia large enough to accommodate the entire Panzer Army Africa, which would retreat into it. To form that perimeter, and also to carry out the orders he had been given, the force immediately available to Nehring consisted of the advance parties of 5th Fallschirmjaeger regiment. These were being deployed across Tunisia, in penny packets, to guard airfields, protect bridges and carry out patrols in western Tunisia. Nehring had few troops and no military infrastructure. All that was available to him were the services of a civilian taxi and the hotel telephone, although within a few days of his arrival he was able to use a direct telephone line from Tunis main post office to Kesselring in Rome.

Nehring ordered Colonel Lederer, acting commander of German troops in the Tunisian bridgehead, to expand the perimeter westwards. Reinforcements began to arrive from the European mainland, and soon the Axis force included two battalions of 5th Fallschirmjaeger regiment, a Fallschirm Engineer battalion, four pieces of artillery, an armoured car Company, two battalions of Italian Marines, two more companies of the élite Italian 'Superga' Division and, most important of all, a high-powered wireless set. It was a small body, but strong enough to halt the weak Allied armour/infantry group, 'Blade Force', advancing towards the capital. One political success gained by Nehring in those first critical days was the assurance of a French admiral that the men under his command would remain neutral and would undertake no hostile action against the Germans.

By the end of November Nehring had also been able to extend his bridgehead southwards, and had gained touch with Rommel's forces coming up out of Libya. The German formations in the Tunisian bridgehead were formally grouped under the title of XC Corps, and while in charge of that formation Nehring planned an operation at Tebourba which was so brilliant a tactical success that the Allied formations were dominated, ensuring that the front was quiet for several weeks. On 9 December he was ordered to hand over XC Corps to General von Arnim, and flew back to Europe.

Once more in Germany, Nehring was given command of XXIV Panzer Corps, a body which had been reduced to a remnant in the fierce winter battles. He built up the fragments until they were once again able to hold the Corps bridgehead on the east bank of the Dnieper river. The Red Army's 1942/43 winter offensive had exhausted itself. The limited scale of military operations which then followed on XXIV Corps' sector was due not only to that exhaustion but also to the early spring thaw, which restricted the movement of both sides. The Red Army needed to regroup and rebuild its strength, while on the German side the welcome inaction allowed Army Group South to prepare for a new summer offensive, Unternehmen Zitadelle. This large-scale offensive was planned to pinch out the huge Russian salient centred around Kursk, and the role of Nehring's Corps was to exploit the breakthrough by Manstein's Army Group South. The battle plan foresaw that when that breakthrough happened, Nehring's Corps would drive rapidly upwards to meet the swift southward thrust of Model's 9th Army.

Unternehmen Zitadelle opened on 5 July, and Nehring deployed XXIV Corps but no breakthrough occurred. Instead, a crisis developed in the south and XXIV Corps was forced to change the direction of its front to face Soviet attacks coming across the Mius river. During the course of these battles Nehring was wounded for the fifth time. The situation in which Army Group South found itself was precarious. Having destroyed Zitadelle, the Russians did not halt to regroup, but moved without pause into counteroffensives which struck Army Group hard. Nehring's Corps was used as a fire brigade, and on the 18th a mission was undertaken to re-form the broken battle line; a task which was accomplished within a week. Corps was then sent northwards to close the gap between VII and XXXVII Panzer Corps.

At the beginning of September, immediately preceding the autumn rains, the German battle line in the south began a slow retreat to the Dnieper under constant pressure from Red Army units. The Russians were determined to cut off the German formations before they could reach the safety of the river and establish themselves on the western bank. The Soviet tank units succeeded in their intention, and advanced so rapidly that at some places they had crossed the Dnieper before the Germans could bring the river's western bank to a fit state of defensive preparedness. One such Soviet operation was the air drop of two Guards Paratroop Brigades behind the west bank of the river. In the fighting of that autumn Nehring was proud of the fact that, although the major formations on either flank frequently failed to hold the Russian assaults, the front of XXIV Corps remained unbroken. The tempo of the fighting then died down, and there was a phase of aggressive/defensive warfare on the German side and active preparation to resume the offensive by the Soviets.

Nehring's reputation for sealing a broken front grew, and to aid him in this duty, which became more and more frequently demanded, XXIV Corps was reinforced. A number of minor but bloody engagements brought to a halt the Red Army's attempts to expand one of their west-bank bridgeheads and, taking advantage of that brief quiet period, Nehring was able to go on leave, returning shortly before Christmas 1943. Not long after his return the Soviet offensive opened against 4th Panzer Army, and in the fury of that assault the huge supply depot at Kasatin was lost on 28 December. So severe had been the Red Army's blow, and so shattering its consequences, that a 20km-wide gap had been torn in the German line. Nehring grouped detachments of the 18th Artillery Division, one of his Corps formations, and created a counterattack force to put in against the Red Army's armour, which was determined to exploit the massive breach. His counterattack group struck the Russian tank units so hard that they were flung southwards in confusion. The task which Nehring had been set, to halt the Russian penetration and to reseal the battle line, had been carried out, and for that success he was awarded the Oak Leaf to the Knight's Cross on 8 February 1944.

The Russian offensive in March of that year made such progress that by the 23rd 1st Panzer Army was surrounded and had to be rescued, a mission undertaken chiefly by Nehring's Corps. He was next posted to Galicia, to the area of Model's Army Group North Ukraine, where he took over temporary command of 4th Panzer Army. The greater number of Divisions he controlled were infantry, because the panzer formations which had been in his battle line had been taken away to master the situation brought about by the disastrous collapse of Army Group Centre. Russian Intelligence soon learned that the panzer Divisions had been withdrawn from 4th Panzer Army, and 1st Ukrainian Front was flung against the junction of that Army and 1st Panzer Army. Using his infantry forces, Nehring mastered that Soviet offensive, but late in August 1944 he was ordered to leave 4th Army and resume command of XXIV Panzer Corps. Sickness prevented him taking up his new post at that time, and it was not until the middle of October that he felt fit enough to return to his Corps, now located in Bardiyev, in Slovakia.

Although the front of 1st Panzer Army was quiet at this time, the Soviets were known to be preparing a new offensive. This opened on 12 January 1945, against the Baranov bridgehead on the Oder river. Nehring's XXIV Corps was in reserve behind what was considered to be the firm front of 4th Panzer Army. But the front was not firm, and when the Soviets attacked it ruptured.

The fault was Hitler's, for he had ordered the reserve formations of the Army Group 'A' to be moved close to the combat zone. Colonel General Harpe, the commander, had intended to place them farther back to escape the fury of the first Soviet assaults. When the enemy offensive opened with a massive bombardment, the hail of artillery fire smashed the German reserve forces. They reeled in shock, trying desperately to re-form and counterattack the Red forces. Along the entire front of Army Group 'A' the Soviets broke through. Nehring's Corps, together with other major formations, was cut off and surrounded.

The few panzers which escaped encirclement were grouped under Nehring's command and formed into a 'wandering pocket', and together with a number of infantry units the armour began to fight a way back to the main German battle line. The fact that the pocket succeeded was due not only to Nehring's firm grasp of the formations under his command, but also to the confidence he inspired in his men. The 'wandering pocket' was located in eastern Poland, and its march line was initially east-north-east from the city of Kracow, striking for the city of Lodz. Stavka, aware of the pocket and its direction, moved troops to block the escape route. Remembering a standing bridge over the Pilica river, Nehring changed the march line from north to west to reach it. The change of direction and the desperation of the German attacks flung the Soviets off balance, and the wandering pocket smashed the Red encirclement. Once his formations were clear of the Soviet ring, Nehring changed the thrust line again, once again going northwards towards Lodz. That 250km march, lasting eleven days, was carried out in the depths of winter through dense and gloomy forests and during nights in which dense fog caused men and units to lose contact with each other.

On 22 January the leading elements of the pocket gained touch with 'Grossdeutschland' units. Nehring's order of the day, issued during the evening of 22 January, records in a few sentences the strain, the difficulties and the horror of that march: '... little or no rest coupled with shortages of ammunition and fuel but with frost and snow in abundance, along frozen roads, against a stronger and more speedy enemy, traversing difficult country and crossing rivers which had no bridges ... none of these could stop our determination to succeed and to defeat the enemy wherever he was met. All these things were made possible by our cohesion and solidarity ...' For his leadership in commanding 'Nehring's Wandering Pocket', he was awarded the Swords to the Oak Leaf of the Iron Cross.

The military situation in a Germany facing imminent defeat did not allow units or their commanders time to rest. On 25 January, two days after the end of the 'pocket' episode, Nehring and the headquarters group of 16th Panzer Division was sent to Gloggau on the Oder to prepare the city's defences against the advancing Russians. The drive to Gloggau was not without incident, and included being shot at by Red Army tanks which had broken through and were roaming the countryside. The sector which Nehring's XXIV Panzer Corps had to defend ran along the Oder from Steinau to Neusalz. Among the units now attached to his Corps was 'Grossdeutschland', which was holding an important bridgehead on the eastern bank of the river.

Nehring faced another difficult task. The great mass of vehicles belonging to 'Grossdeutschland', together with the units of that Panzer Corps, had to be brought back across a river which by this time was spanned by only a few bridges. Despite the difficulties, Nehring accomplished the seemingly impossible task by the beginning of February. At one place the retreat was changed to attack when a newly created panzer group, consisting of the XXXIX and LVII Panzer Corps together with a number of infantry Divisions, was placed under Nehring's command. He had received orders to recapture Lauban and reopen the strategically important railway line. For this, one of the last offensives carried out by German panzer units during the Second World War, the Divisions thrust along both sides of the objective. Their advance trapped the Russian forces holding the town in an encirclement, and after a short but intense battle destroyed them.

Then the whole Group was moved to Upper Silesia, where 1st Panzer Army was fighting under great difficulties. Nehring took command of that force on 21 March. In this post, with the war lost, Nehring saw that he had a dual-purpose task. He had to ensure that as many of his soldiers as possible became prisoners of the western Allies, rather than of the Red Army. Concurrent with that duty was the mission to protect the civilians who were seeking to escape the onward-sweeping Russian hosts. Nehring visited as many units as possible to let his men see him, and to encourage them in their battles. In addition to the strain of the military burden, he had to endure the personal fear which affected all German soldiers whose family homes lay in areas already under Soviet domination, or would soon do so. In Nehring's case his home had been destroyed in an air raid and his family had become refugees.

His intention at the beginning of May 1945, to bring 1st Panzer Army through Czechoslovakia into Germany, could not be realised. The war ended before the formation could reach US lines. Nehring was in Deutsch Brod, Czechoslovakia, when the surrender came into force, and moved his Army to Tabor, where he surrendered it to the Americans. In 1947, after two years of imprisonment, he was released and returned home.

Marine Soldier to Paratroop General

General Hermann Ramcke

Hermann Bernhard Ramcke was the scion of a family which had farmed for generations in the Schleswig province of north Germany. Born in 1889, Hermann eventually decided not to follow the family tradition but to go to sea. Although he was not physically robust, the training he underwent on the German Navy's training ships built up his strength, and when he passed from cadet status into active service he was physically fit and remained so throughout his life. Shortly after the outbreak of the First World War the German Imperial Navy raised a Division of marine-infantrymen, and it was with that formation that Ramcke fought on the Western Front. The sector which his unit held was on the extreme right of the German battle line in Flanders, on the Channel coast.

He quickly gained a reputation as a first-class fighting man, and as early as 1916 had been awarded the Second and First Classes of the Iron Cross, together with the Prussian Military Service Cross. The considerable bravery he showed in action also brought him promotion to the rank of second lieutenant. The Marine-Infantry Division was transferred from Flanders to the Eastern Front, and took part in the invasion of the Baltic island of Oesel. For his work in that campaign Ramcke was promoted to the rank of full lieutenant. At the end of the Great War, as he was considered to have been a soldier rather than a sailor, he was kept on in the 100,000-man Army of the Weimar Republic. Over the years he rose slowly but steadily through the military hierarchy until he reached the rank of lieutenant colonel and was appointed commandant of the Pomeranian military training area of Gross-Born.

In 1940, at the age of 51, Ramcke, now a colonel, volunteered for the paratroop arm of service, and he first came to prominence as a result of his actions during the fighting in Crete in May 1941. Until then he had been serving in the Paratroop Replacement Battalion, where he had spent many difficult months trying to obtain heavy weapons for the airborne units. Once promoted and given command of the battalion, he used his newly acquired rank and authority to obtain the equipment and weapons he had formerly been unable to procure.

On 2 May 1941 he was ordered to accompany General Student on an advisory mission to General Ringl's 5th Gebirgs (Mountain) Division. That formation had been detailed to replace 22nd Division and act as the airlanding component of Student's Paratroop Corps in the Crete operation, but neither the commanders nor the men of Ringl's Division had knowledge of what such tasks involved. Before the two paratroop commanders met Ringl they had discussions in Salonika with General Sussmann, commanding the 7th Paratroop Division. It was he who would direct the ground fighting on Crete until the mountain troops landed in strength and Ringl assumed command. Student and Ramcke then flew to discuss with the Mountain Division's commander the employment of his soldiers in the forthcoming campaign. Talks on boarding and deplaning from the Junkers Ju 52 aircraft and other techniques used by the airlanding component lasted several days, but when the two officers left Ringl they were confident that he would quickly train his mountaineers in the tasks they had to achieve.

The aerial bombardment of the Allied garrison on Crete by the fighters and Stukas of Richthofen's Fliegerkorps opened on 14 May and continued for nearly a week. The first paratroop drops and glider landings were made during the early morning of the 20th, and during those early hours the glider carrying Sussmann, the Airborne Division's commander, crashed, killing all on board. A crisis of major proportions loomed.

The situation at the end of the first day of battle was confused. Reports coming in to Para headquarters in Greece showed that the drops over the eastern end of the island had been largely unsuccessful and had met considerable opposition. Small pockets of Fallschirmjaeger were, however, holding out in the east of the island as well as around Canea, in the central drop zone. In the western part of Crete, where the main Para effort had been made, the Assault regiment had only gained part of the airfield at Maleme. That area, its airfield and Hill 107, were the keys to the whole Crete operation. Despite several attacks the tactically important Hill 107 was still in New Zealand hands. It dominated the airfield, and possession of it was vital for the development of Corps' battle plan, which had foreseen waves of reinforcements being brought in by Ju 52s and landed on the runway. The whole operation was in jeopardy until those reinforcements arrived, but the aircraft could not be expected to land under artillery fire being directed from observation posts on the crest of Hill 107. In an effort to gain the hill, the paratroop groups launched a number of attacks, but they were uncoordinated. With Sussmann dead there was no central control on the Maleme sector, and other senior airborne officers who could have retrieved the situation had been either killed or wounded.

Back in his headquarters in Greece, Student realised that what was needed at Maleme was a strong, determined and aggressive commander; one who would co-ordinate operations in the several bridgeheads. He knew that Ramcke was immediately available, and selected him to take charge of the ground operations until the 5th Gebirgs landed. The next task was to find a reinforcement group to accompany Ramcke and replace the losses which had been suffered in the Maleme sector. Every unit of 7th Paratroop Division had been committed to the mission, and there were no paratroop replacements immediately to hand.

Ramcke received Student's orders and was briefed on the situation in Crete. He intended to fly to Maleme with the first wave of Gebirgsjaeger during the early morning of the 21st, and spent the evening before his departure helping the mountain troops load the transport aircraft. When that task was completed they emplaned and waited for the order to fly out. They all knew that there could be no take-off until the airfield at Maleme had been captured, but hoped not to be kept waiting too long. While Ramcke was seated, waiting, a stream of paratroop officers came up to discuss the situation with him. Some of them had already collected and grouped men; those who had not been able to fly out on the first day because of unserviceable aircraft or for other reasons. Those paratroops who had been disappointed at being left behind on D-Day hoped to fly in with the second wave. One officer brought in two Companies, and others brought smaller detachments. In a short time Ramcke was able to advise Student that there was now a reinforcement group of 500 Fallschirmjaeger ready and waiting for orders to take off.

Student issued the executive order, and within an hour of its receipt Ramcke and his battlegroup of paratroops were en route to Crete. Their drop zone was to the west of Maleme, and there they would go in to support the attacks intended to gain the still uncaptured objectives of the first day. The Gebirgsjaeger, sitting patiently in the Ju 52s, had been ordered out of the machines and their places had been taken by the paratroops. Ramcke wrote in his post-battle report that, as a result of the frantic preparations, there had been no time to think about his own requirements, so he had at first neither a parachute nor jump equipment. He was wearing riding boots, not jump boots, and he had neither knee protectors nor a steel helmet. He was standing in the doorway of the aircraft long before the drop zone was reached, and when the machine was throttled back he knew that the time to jump had arrived. The machine flew at the lowest possible height for a jump, so that the paratroops could reach the ground quickly and give the Anzac defenders less chance of killing them in the air.

Ramcke landed and swiftly released his parachute harness. His first action was to draw his pistol to arm himself. He took a quick look round. There was no sign of the enemy, but he could hear sounds of battle. Some of his soldiers were in action, and he joined them. While his group was concentrating, a Para Intelligence officer came in with a report on the current situation. General Meindl, who had been badly wounded, had been evacuated by air; one battalion commander had been killed, another had been wounded and a great number of officers had fallen. On the positive side, the Maleme airfield had at last been captured, Gericke's battlegroup was fighting a successful defensive battle, another battalion battlegroup was ready to carry out the assault against Point 107 and aeroplanes carrying the first Gebirgsjaeger had begun to land under fire on the airport runway. Within minutes Ramcke issued his first battle orders, but he then learned that not all of his group of 500 Jaeger had landed with him. For a number of technical reasons half of the Ju 52s carrying the paratroop replacements had been unable to take off, and Ramcke's battlegroup had shrunk from 500 to fewer than a couple of hundred men. He amended his battle orders accordingly.

At his tactical headquarters, set up in an olive grove, he planned an attack at last light to drive back the enemy batteries so far that they could not fire on the airfield, and then sent replacements to the depleted battlegroups. More detailed orders were issued at the O Group which was held that night, the most important detail being that Ringl's Gebirgsjaeger were to carry out a march through the mountains to outflank the British positions. While the mountain troops were marching through the mountains, two paratroop battlegroups were to attack eastwards from Maleme and bring the advance forward until the German units holding out in Canea were relieved. Two disappointments marked the night. The attack by the Paratroop battlegroup Gericke was beaten back, and the convoy of ships bringing in the bulk of the Gebirgsjaeger Division and all the heavy weapons was intercepted by the Royal Navy and sunk.

During the morning of the third day of fighting Ramcke had a battlefield O Group with his two subordinate commanders, then returned to the airfield, where he found one of his officers using a British light tank to drag crashed aircraft from the runway. A path was soon cleared, and the Ju 52s, some of them loaded with light artillery pieces, were able to land in quick succession. The battle for Crete was now swinging in favour of the Germans, and when Ringl landed on 22 May Ramcke was able to hand over conduct of the ground operations in the western part of the island. He then returned to his battlegroups to direct the operations to capture the Platania ridge, which dominated the island's northern coastal strip. The battle was hard and there were heavy losses as the paratroops advanced through artillery and infantry fire and across minefields to fight their way uphill towards the village located on the crest of the ridge.

Late that morning General Student arrived from the mainland and was briefed on the situation. During the night of the 24/25th battlegroup Heidrich, which had been holding out in Galatos, was relieved, but the advance could make no further gain. The New Zealand defenders at Galatos had set up a new defence line, and this was not broken until the Stukas came in and bombed a way clear for the attacking paratroops. When the Galatos defence line fell, it became clear to Ramcke that the enemy was weakening. The paratroops could now go into the pursuit stage of the battle to take Canea. That objective fell at 1500 on 27 May, and more than 1,000 prisoners and 400 guns were taken.

Ramcke wrote scathingly, not only of the use by the New Zealand Army of Maori troops, whom he considered savages, but also of the brutalities and mutilations practised upon his wounded men by the Cretan population. He admitted that he carried out reprisals against those villages in which mutilated bodies of paratroops had been found. He had the offending villages razed to the ground, but justified his actions by saying that against the brutalities carried out by the civilians there had to be ruthlessness. On 2 June the campaign ended on the southern coast of Crete with the capture of 10,000 Allied soldiers. In total, 12,245 British and 5,255 Greeks had been taken prisoner. Five thousand Allied soldiers had been killed, and no fewer than 136 guns and 30 tanks had been taken.

On 18 June Ramcke returned to his old unit to instruct paratroop schools and replacement units on the lessons learnt from the Crete operation. On 1 August 1941 he was promoted to generalmajor, and wrote delightedly of the surprise which Colonel Heidrich had prepared for him. Shortly before midday on the 2nd Heidrich called to collect him, and led him to the front of the Braunschweig barracks. In front of the building stood the regimental band with a guard of honour at the present arms, together with all the officers of the training school. There was also a Cretan donkey carrying a shield round its neck with the legend 'Canea', and one final surprise, his wife, waiting to greet him. On 23 August Ramcke and some NCOs were ordered to fly to Goering's headquarters, where they were presented with Knight's Crosses. In the spring of 1942 Ramcke was posted to serve with the Italian Army, but was soon called back to Berlin and given a new task.

Shortly before the invasion of Crete, Germany had taken the war out of continental Europe when detachments of the Africa Korps were disembarked in the Italian colonial city of Tripoli. Rommel, the commander of Panzer Army Africa, had tried but had failed to capture the vitally important port of Tobruk during his 1941 spring offensive, and had built up his forces, determined to take it during the following year. In the early summer of 1942 Rommel asked OKW for reinforcements. Paratroop General Student was ordered to despatch a battlegroup of Fallschirmjaeger in approximately Brigade strength to reinforce the Afrika Korps, and selected Ramcke to command that unit. Some battalions of Ramcke's Brigade were veterans of the fighting on the Eastern Front, while others were in newly trained Companies lacking any sort of battle experience. Kroh's 1st Battalion of 2nd Regiment and Hubner's 2nd Battalion of 5th regiment had both served in Russia, while battlegroups Burkhardt and von der Heydte were made up of men under training whose ranks were stiffened by a number of veteran officers and NCOs.

Ramcke soon grasped that the conditions in the Western Desert were similar to those in the Russian steppes; vast, mainly empty spaces. He realised that the tactics and operational practices used on the Eastern Front could apply in Africa. To cover his Brigade's sector of the Axis front Ramcke dispersed it in independent battalion-sized groups. All the battalions of Ramcke's Brigade were, of course, fighting an infantry war, and were supported by 2nd Battalion of 7th Airborne Artillery regiment, together with a paratroop anti-tank Company, Engineers and Signallers. It had been projected that Ramcke's formation, acting as an élite assault group, would exploit the anticipated breakthrough of the British line. The commanders of Panzer Army Africa had confidently predicted that the breakthrough would come when the fast-moving panzer formations went into the pursuit stage of the battle of Gazala and drove Eighth Army before them up to the El Alamein positions. Ramcke's Brigade would then smash through the Alamein line and reach the Suez canal.

As a result of the German/Italian offensive at Gazala, British Eighth Army had indeed been forced to retreat to Alamein, but there it had stood fast and prevented a German breakthrough. Montgomery's counteroffensive opened in October 1942, its main effort being made in the northern, coastal sector. Ramcke's Brigade, positioned in the centre of the Italo-German battle line, between Ruweisat Ridge and the Quattara Depression, faced the formations of British XXX Corps; notably the 50th (Tyne and Tees) Division. The paratroops were not involved in really heavy fighting, as Montgomery's main effort had gone in on the northern, coastal, sector. When the British offensive developed it smashed the Axis line and isolated Ramcke's Brigade, threatening to outflank and destroy it.

To avoid that fate, Ramcke decided that his unit had to march, because there was insufficient transport to carry all the men. The retreat from the positions which had been held since June began on 2 November, and should have entailed a march of about 25km to the nearest German positions. The distance was increased when a British tank attack on 3 November broke through the Italian sector and caused a retreat of the Panzerarmee battle line. Threatened once again with being cut off, the battlegroup was forced to undertake another long march. The orders were that Brigade was to reach the area of the Fuka Pass and there take up positions on either side of the coast road leading to Bir Fuka. That meant that the men of Ramcke's Brigade now had to carry out a 120km march across territory occupied by British Eighth Army. It was a choice of march or captivity, and the retreat began towards the Axis lines, initially on a westerly bearing. Then Ramcke changed direction and his Brigade marched northwards to reach the Via Balbia, the main desert road. On 6 November the paratroops hiding along that main highway intercepted and captured an Eighth Army supply column and drove the trucks, loaded with food, drink and NAAFI supplies, through the British lines. They gained touch with Afrika Korps on the following day.

No record exists of Ramcke's remarks to the Staff of Panzer Army Africa, who had done little or nothing to help his Brigade, but the Paratroop General had a sharp tongue and would have condemned in soldiers' terms the officers who had failed him and his men. Shortly after his Brigade rejoined the Axis forces, Ramcke was posted back to Germany to carry out Staff duties within the Paratroop organisation. He then took command of 2nd Fallschirmjaeger Division. At that time he was awarded the Oak Leaf to the Knight's Cross for his work on Crete. The 2nd Paratroop Division was in the process of being raised in the

Vannes region of Brittany, around a cadre of convalescents from the Ramcke Brigade in Africa, other members of that formation who had escaped before the campaign's end, and remnants of units which had fought on the Eastern Front. The divisional order of battle was 2nd, 6th and 7th Fallschirmjaeger regiments, an artillery regiment and battalions of Service units. The Division formed part of 7th Army until May 1943, when it was sent to southern France as an element of General Student's XI Airborne Corps. When the western Allies landed in Sicily during July 1943, Ramcke's Division was immediately alerted and sent to Ostia, southeast of Rome, where it was to act in a defensive role.

The capitulation of Italy in September 1943 was a political crisis, and Berlin sent orders for the German Army Group in Italy to master the situation. The German Army Group commander directed Student's Corps to disarm the Italian forces in and around Rome, and Student passed the order to Ramcke, who carried out an air drop on 9 September. On that day, too, Gericke's 2nd Battalion of 6th Regiment dropped over the Italian Army headquarters at Monterotondo, captured it and compelled the surrender of the commanding general. Another unit of Ramcke's Division, Major Mors' 1st (Training) Battalion of 7th regiment, carried out the operation which rescued Mussolini on 12 September, and Hubner's 3rd Battalion of 7th regiment dropped over the island of Elba and captured it by 17 September. It had always been Ramcke's policy to act swiftly and decisively, and the prompt actions of his Division removed the threat of any counter-action by Germany's disaffected former ally. With that threat eliminated, 2nd Paratroop Division moved to carry out coastal defence duties in the area between Citavecchia and Genoa. In the late autumn of 1943 British forces landed on the islands of Kos and Leros in the Dodecanese, posing a threat to the German forces in the Balkans, and Ramcke's Division was ordered to remove that threat. The 1st Battalion of 2nd Regiment took part in a combined operation; an air- and seaborne invasion that recaptured the islands by the end of November. But Ramcke's Division was not to remain intact for long. The need to reinforce the fighting line to the south of Rome led to some of its units being taken *en bloc* and split up to be employed as infantry in battlegroup detachments.

When the 2nd moved to the Eastern Front a number of its divisional formations were used in the bitter fighting to the west of Kiev during the winter of 1943-44. Throughout the weeks of battle in the East, Ramcke spent much of his time visiting his men in their front-line positions. The losses suffered by the Division were heavy, and Ramcke felt them keenly, for he knew most of the men personally. He left his Division for two brief periods, and although he returned when the Red Army's offensive opened in March 1944, he was not to remain long leading the 2nd in battle. He was posted back to Berlin and then given the task of retraining his old Division, which had been taken out of the line and was being reinforced after the frightening losses it had suffered. He resumed operational

125

command of the 2nd when it reached its training area outside Cologne, at the end of May 1944.

On 13 June 2nd Para was ordered to leave for active service in Brittany, where it was to defend that area against possible Allied airlandings or paratroop drops. Upon receipt of OKW's order, Ramcke sent an advance party. Then the whole Division was ordered to move and place itself under the command of XXV Corps of 7th Army. Although the advance parties had arrived quite quickly, the follow-up fighting echelons endured long and difficult journeys which often ended in long foot marches. A combination of Allied bombing and French sabotage action delayed and sometimes halted entirely the movement of all German formations to the combat zone, and 2nd Para suffered with the rest. Nor were the men of the advance parties spared during this time. They had to be on duty day and night, ready to go into action against possible Allied airborne landings, and were also in action fighting US armoured Divisions and attacks by French partisans.

On 3 August parts of Ramcke's Division marching towards the beachhead at Avranches were struck by American tank formations. The hastily formed Paratroop battlegroup Rolshevski was put into an immediate counterattack, and after hard fighting forced the US tank men to withdraw. The battlegroup's prompt action and speedy victory prevented the capture of Dinant. Finding that they could not capture the town by direct assault, the US units then bypassed it and began to probe a breach that had been made lower down in the German line. Subjected to pressure from the flank, Rolshevski's battlegroup was forced to pull back to St Malo, leaving the mass of the Division still trying to make its way to the beachhead. All of the divisional transport was still in the concentration area, and in order to move his men quickly Ramcke took the only course open to him and commandeered French civilian vehicles. However, there were so few of these that Division had to be divided into groups marching up the line and miscellaneous vehicle detachments.

On 5 August the divisional reconnaissance battalion was attacked to the west of Gouarec, and after a hard fight was totally destroyed. The 7th Paratroop Regiment was another formation which had been attacked by an overwhelming mass of American armoured vehicles at Huelgoat. The paratroops sought to escape into the dense forests around the village, but almost immediately partisan groups attacked the regiment, inflicting heavy losses. Only a part of 7th Regiment's 2nd Battalion was able to break out of the woods and escape. Although the Division was neither completely concentrated nor properly grouped, it held the line for two days, and was only forced to pull back to the heights of Mont d'Areem through the failure of the 266th Division, its left-flank neighbour, to hold firm. That necessitated a new withdrawal which took it into the outworks of the fortress of Brest. Under fresh and very heavy attacks the unfortunate 266th was almost destroyed in the subsequent fighting, and only two battalions made good their escape into the Brest citadel.

By 8 August the American forces had reached Buipavas aerodrome, to the north-west of Brest, and General Middleton, the US Commander, demanded the surrender of the fortress. Colonel von der Mosel, the Commandant of Brest, rejected the demand. When Ramcke's Division pulled back into the fortress he, as the senior officer, took command of all the troops in the area – remnants of 2nd Paratroop Division, 143rd Infantry and formations of the naval commandant. Facing those understrength and exhausted men were three US armoured divisions, enjoying air superiority. The withdrawal of 2nd Para into Brest was not only carried out under the pressure of American forces, but also under attacks by the Maquis, who had infiltrated the area in great strength. To illustrate the seriousness of the fighting against the partisan forces, in the period from the middle weeks of June to 12 August 2nd Para lost 50 killed, 100 missing and 200 wounded. Although the Division was holding an essentially defensive position, its units continued to make attacks and counterattacks to pre-empt the assaults of the US forces and hold the enemy at bay. In the Brest area, large numbers of French civilians were being subjected to all the rigours of the siege. Ramcke wanted to evacuate 40,000 people from the battle area, and with General Middleton's agreement brought most of them to safety during four successive days. Some 7,000 civilians refused to leave; it was the firm conviction of 2nd Para that these belonged to the Resistance and intended to continue partisan operations.

Fresh US assaults came in on 20 August. The Para Division was now carrying almost the full burden of the defence, and held out undefeated until 1 September. On that day the whole fortress area was surrounded and cut off. Compressed into an ever-smaller area, the paratroop regiments fought on, gaining time, as they thought, for Germany. On 13 September General Middleton again offered the garrison the chance to surrender with honour, pointing out that its position was hopeless and that further resistance could only lead to further loss of life. Ramcke's reply was a brief, one-sentence rejection: 'General, I reject your offer'. Three days later, on 16 September, Ramcke was forced to move his headquarters to the La Crozon peninsula, and on the 18th American attacks finally broke into the fort. Bitter fighting ensued until the afternoon of the 19th, when infantry of US 8th Division reached Ramcke's bunker at Pointe de Capucins. The official history of that Division recorded the final act in the following words:

A German doctor, speaking perfect English, said that General Ramcke was in his headquarters and wished to discuss the conditions of surrender with an American officer. Brigadier General Cannam, acting second-in-command of the Eighth Division, then arrived together with some officers and soldiers. They were escorted into the deep dugout where General Ramcke was waiting for them. He spoke to the Brigadier through an interpreter. "I have to surrender

to you. May I see your credentials?" Cannam pointed to the bayonets of his soldiers. "These are my credentials," he replied. At 8pm
in the early evening of the 19 September, resistance ended.

Ramcke was then taken to General Middleton's headquarters, and at the end of
the meeting the American commander asked if there was anything he could do
for his captive. The Paratroop General responded with the only answer that the
years of his service could have produced: 'Make sure that my soldiers are treated
well as prisoners of war'.

Two days later Ramcke learned that he had been awarded the Diamonds
to the Knight's Cross. His plea to General Middleton had little effect. The German Paratroops were treated very shabbily in the United States, for it was widely
accepted that men who had fought so well must be dedicated Nazis. Just before
Christmas 1945, while in a prison camp in America, Ramcke read that two US
senators were in favour of a just settlement of the German problem. Ramcke
wrote them a letter, complaining of the conditions under which his men were
being held. He knew that because all mail was censored the senators would be
unlikely to receive his letter, and so, determined to make contact, he escaped
through the camp perimeter wire and posted it in a civilian mail box. The politicians received the letter, and responded by demanding action to deal with the
complaints made by Ramcke.

The General was transferred to another camp and then passed through a
succession of camps in America and England until, finally, he was held in France,
where he was reviled as the 'Butcher of Brest'. He escaped from his French prison
camp, but then returned voluntarily. For that escapade he was sentenced to a
further five years imprisonment, but on appeal the sentence was overturned.
Ramcke was then released and returned to Germany. His action in escaping and
returning to prison had achieved the intended result; German prisoners of war
held in France were released. Ramcke had always been called 'Papa' by his men.
His action in drawing a vindictive prison sentence upon himself in order to help
his soldiers showed that the title was no empty one. Ramcke had truly been the
father of his men.

Hitler's Austrian Fireman

Generaloberst Dr Lothar Rendulic

The man who became known as 'The Fuehrer's Austrian Fireman', began his military career in the service of the Imperial Army of Austria-Hungary. Born in Wiener Neustadt on 23 October 1887, Lothar Rendulic read law at university before entering the Maria Theresa Military Academy in Wiener Neustadt in 1907. Three years later, on 18 August 1910, he graduated and was gazetted a second lieutenant in the 99th Imperial and Royal Infantry Regiment. Four years later he passed the entrance examination for the War College as top candidate, but upon the outbreak of the First World War he abandoned his academic studies and rejoined his regiment. It was with the 99th kuk Infantry Regiment that he marched out to fight on the Eastern Front.

The opening battles of that war caused heavy casualties on both sides, and it soon fell to the young subaltern officer to take over the post of regimental adjutant of the 99th when the incumbent fell in action. Another distinction was the medal bestowed upon him for bravery displayed in the fighting at Stary Zamsc. During the 1914 campaign in Poland, Rendulic received the first of several wounds he was to suffer. Early in the morning of 23 October, while carrying out a reconnaissance to check crossing points along the river San, he was caught in a Russian artillery barrage. A piece of shell casing tore a five-inch gash his skull, and the wounded officer fell unconscious from his horse into a shallow tributary of the river. He was in danger of drowning when his batman pulled him from the water and brought him, weak from loss of blood, into the regimental aid post.

The High Command in Vienna did not return him to regimental duties after convalescence, but posted him to serve on the staff of 14th Division, in action in the Carpathian mountains. He was later transferred to the Italian theatre of operations, where he was wounded for a second time when the horse-drawn cart in which he was travelling smashed into a rock. The force of the impact flung Rendulic from the cart and broke his arm. Before his injured arm was completely healed he discharged himself prematurely from hospital and returned to the Division. By the middle of 1918 it was clear that the offensive powers of Austria-Hungary and her ally, Germany, were exhausted, and at the war's end Rendulic returned to Vienna with his wife and infant son. By this time promoted to the rank of captain, he was retained in the army of the Austrian Republic and served in the Administration Department. Late in 1920 he graduated as a Doctor of Law, and during the following year taught the disciplines of organisation and tactics in the Army College. He was transferred from that institution during the autumn of 1923 and entered the General Staff Academy, from which he graduated in 1925 with the rank of Major. His next assignment was the command of a battalion of 4th Infantry Regiment, formerly the 'Hoch und Deutschmeister', Vienna's own regiment.

Promotion in peacetime is slow in every army, and it was not until 1933 that Rendulic was promoted colonel in the General Staff. While holding that rank he served as Austria's military attaché in London until his retirement in February 1936. He then devoted his energies to the study of law and politics, but was not long inactive in the military sense. When the Third Reich annexed Austria in 1938, Rendulic was offered the post of Chief of Staff in the German Army's newly-raised XVII Army Corps. On 3 August that Corps was posted to Silesia and came on to the strength of List's 14th Army. Rendulic fought in the Polish campaign of 1939, but was taken ill at its end. During his convalescence he was promoted to the rank of major general.

In June 1940 he took over command of 14th Infantry Division, which had been selected to take part in the French campaign, but the campaign in western Europe ended before Rendulic could lead his formation in action. He was then cross-transferred from 14th Division to command the 52nd, which had been selected to be one of the second-wave formations for Operation Barbarossa, the invasion of the Soviet Union. The 52nd was concentrated round Lodz in Poland, and when Germany opened hostilities against Russia on 22 June it made ready to take part in the new campaign. The first action it fought was on the line of the river Drut, a tributary of the Dnieper. This was the first time that Rendulic had led a Division in action, and it was also the first major operation undertaken by the 52nd in Russia. Both commander and men acquitted themselves so well in that first mission that it deserves to be covered in some detail.

The Division advanced into the Soviet Union on 26 June, but it was not until 15 July that it engaged the enemy. As part of LIII Corps its task was to protect Corps' left flank as it closed up to the Dnieper. The main body of Corps struck Russian opposition between Bobruisk and Rogachev, immediately to the west of the Drut. Under heavy pressure, Corps ordered Rendulic to march southwards and to bring his Division to Oserany, where it would contact the main body of Corps and thus strengthen the Corps' defence. When that order came, the 52nd was preparing for a day's rest after the strain of marching throughout the past weeks. It should be realised that the lack of railways in western Russia meant that the German Army's infantry Divisions had to march from eastern Poland and, because of the shortage of all-weather roads in the Soviet Union, they were forced to march across country. The orders from Corps faced the tired

Division with a night march of between 20 and 25km through dense woods. Once Rendulic's formation reached Oserany it would have to cross the Drut and strike down the river's eastern bank to seize Rogachev, which lay some 25km beyond Oserany.

Rendulic was unable to obtain any further details of the orders he had received, as his Division's wireless link with Corps then malfunctioned. Acting upon his own initiative, he decided that when his formation reached Oserany it would not turn east and cross the Druth, as ordered, but would maintain its southwards drive. He had it in mind to seize intact the bridges at Rogachev. Such an enterprise carried with it the risk that the Red Army might strike into Division's left flank as it marched southwards, but there was, on the other hand, the probability that Rendulic's thrust would take in flank the contesting Russians Corps' advance. Were he to achieve that intention, it would halt the attacks the Red Army was making out of Rogachev. The Division's first blooding was imminent, but each unit of the Division faced this major operation in Russia with the same confidence as did the commander.

At Oserany the primeval woods through which the Division had forced their way with such difficulty began to thin and then petered out, giving way to a terrain of open and cultivated land. Division's task was to advance across that gently rolling ground against an enemy of unknown but certainly superior strength who was holding well sited and prepared positions. On a hot Sunday afternoon the first units crossed their start lines, covered by a 'shoot' fired by every gun the Division could muster. The élan of Rendulic's infantry brought them forward 10km into the Soviet front, but there the advance was brought to a halt, pinned down by enemy artillery and machine-gun fire. The Russians were firing a curtain barrage to protect a strip of ground on the west bank of the Druth. The Red Army was determined to hold that area as a sort of bridgehead when their own counterattack went in. Rendulic's men could make no headway, and the reason for their failure was soon made plain.

From intelligence reports it soon became clear that the advance of the 52nd was being contested by three Soviet infantry Divisions. In addition, the key position to the whole Russian defence of the sector was a strongpoint on 52nd's left flank. That ulcer had to be taken out, but the first German attack to take the position was beaten off. Division regrouped and mounted a second assault which went in under a concentration of artillery fire. The attack was successful and the strongpoint was taken. Rendulic wrote in his account of the battle that many of the enemy wounded had committed suicide by slitting their throats. Other Russian infantrymen, too badly wounded to kill themselves, had had their throats cut by the commissars. The few enemy prisoners taken alive were shaking with fear; they had been told that the Germans murdered those whom they captured, but the treatment they received showed that the commissars had lied. At last light the fury of battle died away, allowing Rendulic to regroup his units once again.

The attack by the 52nd was resumed on the morning of 16 July. Despite the bitter and at times fanatical opposition of the Red Army Divisions, now increased to four, not only was the threat to Corps' left flank smashed but the Soviets had been driven back almost to the Dnieper. Rendulic wrote movingly of the courage of his men and the leadership of their officers in this first battle. He and his men did not know at that time that it was on their sector that the Red Army's major counteroffensive was to be made. This was to result in a battle which was to endure without pause or let-up for more than a fortnight. Stavka, the Soviet High Command, had ordered the massive operation because German LIII Corps formed the link between German Army Groups South and Centre. If the Red Army could smash a way through Corps' front and pour sufficient soldiers through the gaps, then the great strategic gain might be achieved of rolling up the inner flanks of one, or both, of the German Army Groups.

At the height of the battle no fewer than five Red Army Divisions attacked the 52nd Division's 16km-wide front. Wave after wave of Russian infantrymen marched into the assault, advancing in lines extending across the entire divisional sector, but each attack was held and flung back. The Division held even though it received no reinforcements or replacements for the whole period of the Soviet offensive. Rendulic's men stood firm, even though they were heavily outnumbered throughout the weeks of fighting. Because no support from the higher echelons was forthcoming, the most important priority within the Division was to find soldiers to man the battle line. As an example of the losses suffered, two batteries of the artillery regiment were reduced to a single gun, and the men of another battery which had fallen silent were discovered to be fast asleep, totally exhausted by the strain of battle.

The crisis in the Soviet counteroffensive came during the fourteenth day. The fighting was so bitter and the Red Army attacks followed each other at such close intervals that it was obvious the Russians were making their supreme effort. Under the terrible pressure it was feared that the Red Army might break through. The Corps commander reached Rendulic's headquarters and told him in great confidence that if the enemy breakthrough did happen, the Division could be withdrawn to form a bridgehead around Bobruisk. The decision as to whether or not to pull back was his. Rendulic was surprised at being asked to make such a decision. The action of the Corps' commander was militarily wrong; he was attempting to unload the responsibility upon his subordinate – Rendulic. After long and serious consideration of the advantages and disadvantages of accepting the offer, the divisional commander turned it down. It was, in his opinion, a question of morale.

His men were exhausted, but they were still willing to fight. He must show the same strength of character as his subordinates. The 52nd would stand fast and fight. Reorganisations within the battalions and their sub-units, literally the final combing out, produced a few groups of men, ten or twelve at the most, who would form counterattack units which could be moved quickly from one threatened sector to another. The morning of the fifteenth day of fighting opened with the usual barrage followed by an infantry attack of unusual strength. It seemed that the previous day's battle had not been the climax. This day's was. The soldiers of the Red Army advanced in six waves across the torn countryside. Prisoners taken were found to belong to the five different Divisions which had been put in in a vast effort to crush the 52nd.

During the sixteenth night came a pause, and with it a chance to rest. What could this unusual silence on the enemy's part betoken? The morning brought an artillery barrage, but no infantry attack. The Russian counteroffensive had run its course and had achieved nothing. Fighting on the sector held by Rendulic's Division then diminished to a sort of positional warfare, with a chance to rest, repair and reorganise. But it was a respite of short duration. Ahead lay a new objective; the town of Ssusnitche. There, Rendulic's formation was attacked by a Red cavalry division, and as the horsemen swept through the lines the divisional commander ordered his men to take up all-round defence. For his leadership of the 52nd during those early operations Rendulic was promoted to the rank of lieutenant general. There then followed hard fighting at Aserovo, where the 52nd spent Christmas 1941, and then at Yucknov, where Rendulic fought at the head of the advance, leading in his men . During the winter of 1941-42, frostbite casualties reduced the strength of the Division to just over 1,000 men, but it fought on and destroyed the Soviet forces which had broken through its lines. Rendulic was awarded the Knight's Cross of the Iron Cross, and as a reward for the successes he achieved during July 1942 was appointed to command XXXV Corps, whose order of battle contained the 34th, 56th, 262nd and 299th Infantry Divisions.

By the spring of 1943 the German armies on the Eastern Front had been pushed back to approximately the line they had held in the summer of 1942. The situation forced Hitler to consider the strategic options open to him in 1943. He decided on a campaign aimed at weakening the Red Army to such an extent that it would be unable to launch major offensives either in the summer or in the winter of that year. That breathing space would leave Germany free to deal with the Allied invasions of France or Sicily, which could be expected now that the Axis Powers had lost the war in Africa. The operation upon which Hitler finally decided, Unternehmen Zitadelle, was designed to pinch out a vast bulge, more than 500km long and over 200km wide, which had been created during the 1942/43 Russian winter campaign.

Zitadelle was to be carried out by Model's 9th Army of Army Group Centre striking down from the north, and 4th Panzer Army of Army Group South driving up from the south. The 2nd Army (Army Group Centre) on the left of 9th Army was so weak that its role was basically defensive. According to its commander, General Weichs, not one of its seven Divisions was up to strength in either men or arms, and it had neither Luftwaffe nor panzer support. The line which 2nd Army had to defend was more than 160km long, and Weichs foresaw that once the German Army was committed to Zitadelle, the Soviets with their greater manpower resources would immediately counterattack in the Orel sector of his army's front. Were that Soviet operation to succeed, 2nd Army and Model's 9th Army would be cut off and the cohesion of Army Group Centre would be shattered.

It was accepted by both sides that Zitadelle would be an armoured operation, and although the Germans could muster 2,000 tanks (Army Group South with 1,137 and Army Group Centre with 878), the Red Army could field 6,000 and had the capacity to reinforce them continually and replace the losses its regiments would suffer.

The battle opened on 5 July 1943, and as early as the 11th of that month the Russians had made their counter-moves against 2nd Army in the Orel bend. There, Rendulic's XXXV Corps was deployed in an arc to the east of the town. Within a day the Red Army probes, initially weak but growing in strength, had developed into a full-scale counteroffensive mounted chiefly by 3rd Guards Tank Army. The Soviets made such considerable gains that 9th Army was forced to release its 20th and 36th Divisions to protect its rear. It had to be accepted that by detaching those formations 9th Army's attack in Zitadelle would be gravely weakened.

Shortly after daybreak on 12 July six Red Army Divisions, supported by a vast fleet of tank regiments, attacked Rendulic's Corps. The Russian armada advanced to the banks of the Ssush river, intending to cross the wooden emergency bridges which Soviet engineer detachments had erected. A German artillery barrage opened, strong by the German standards of 1943, but weak when compared with those the Red Army could put up. The Russian armour passed through the Corps' long-range defensive shellfire almost unscathed and entered the close-defence artillery zone, where it came under the direct fire of batteries of 88mm guns and standard pak. Sixty Russian tanks soon lay knocked out or burning. Dominated by the German fire which then fell upon them, the Soviet infantry, following closely behind the armour, broke and ran. On the next day the regrouped Soviet forces came on again and were smashed again. This time 40 enemy tanks were left either shattered on the battlefield or burning in the bright sunlight.

Aware that Rendulic's Corps held a sector of great strategic importance, and even more aware that the Soviets would make every effort to capture it, Model decided to reinforce Rendulic's Corps with 30 SP guns and eight tank-destroyer vehicles. It was a timely move, for Corps was soon under attack by eight Red Army infantry Divisions and 250 armoured fighting vehicles. The weight and fury of the Soviet assault brought the Red formations storming across the Ssush river and into XXXV Corps' forward positions. As the T 34s and KVs passed over the German trenches, Rendulic's Grenadiers rose up and fought the Russian armour at close quarters, flinging Teller mines under the tank tracks or placing high-explosive charges on the outsides of the vehicles. The Russian break-through attempts were thwarted by the desperate defence of the battered Corps, and the Red commanders pulled back their tank formations under cover of a massive smokescreen, leaving the abandoned infantry to be shot down by the German Grenadiers. The slaughter of the Russian footsoldiers was prodigious although, proportionately, the tanks had suffered more heavily. Almost a half of the attacking force, 120 armoured fighting vehicles, had been destroyed.

In his usual fashion Rendulic had been forward with his own hard-pressed infantry, and he noted that the Soviet attacks had been destroyed because of weaknesses in the enemy's tactics and through a lack of initiative on the part of the Red infantry. Years later, when he was a prisoner of war in American hands, he wrote a paper entitled 'The fighting qualities of the Russian soldier', based upon the vast fund of knowledge accumulated in his years of campaigning. Two extracts from that paper illustrate some of his conclusions.

> ... Combat demands initiative [by the soldiers of the fighting arms of Service] ... even if only on a limited scale ... Because of his pas-sive nature the Russian soldier is not given to offensive and indi-vidual combat. In the many battles and engagements in which I took part in Russia in positions of authority ranging from divisional commander to Commander in Chief of Army Groups, I do not know of one [battle or engagement] that was decided by the superior ini-tiative and fighting spirit of the Russian infantry. In an attack, even in mobile warfare, the Russian soldier was only able to succeed when he had overwhelming all-arms superiority along the entire attacking front or at those points in our battle line against which his main attack was being directed...
>
> The Russian High Command recognised very early the poor offensive quality of its infantry. It attempted to make up for this deficiency by a vast increase in artillery. ... The Soviet infantry depended upon the props of massive artillery and armour...

On the battlefield of July 1943, Soviet attempts to break XXXV Corps continued at the same intensity. Model was deeply concerned at the losses being sustained by the 432nd Grenadier Regiment of 262nd Infantry Division, and ordered it to be withdrawn and rested. Its place in Corps' battle line was taken by 36th Divi-sion, and it was against this fresh formation that the new Red Army attacks were launched on 16 July. For these assaults Stavka committed eight new infantry Divi-sions supported by 300 AFVs. The huge force struck the 36th Division, which had the support of just twenty panzers. The fighting rose to a climax on the following day, when, determined to break XXXV Corps, the Soviets sent in a further ten Divisions and 400 tanks. Under that enormous pressure 36th Division began to give ground. Then the 252nd came under direct attack and was forced back. Finally, 56th Division, which had been struck in its turn by the bulk of the enemy's armoured force, began to waver.

Rendulic drove to the TAC headquarters of 36th Division to discuss with General Gollnick, its commander, the measures to be taken to prevent the enemy breaking through. While he was there news was received that the Corps on Rendulic's left flank was being pushed back, and that there was a danger that his own left wing would be opened and might be turned. The Corps commander drove back to his own headquarters. During the journey he had evidence of the depth to which the Soviet tanks had reached in Corps front, as well as the confusion which the Red armour was creating, when his car, theoretically in the German rear area, was fired at by a troop of Russian vehicles. By the evening of that day of crises and alarms Rendulic's measures had to a great extent stabilised the situation along Corps front, and 56th Division's evening SITREP reported that its units had destroyed more than 50 Russian machines; the entire enemy force which had created the gap between 36th and 252nd Divisions.

But the enemy High Command was preparing to exploit that sector of the gap which had still not been closed. The force which was used was a fresh infantry grouping supported by 100 tanks. Rendulic realised that the objective on his Corps' sector, which the enemy was fighting to gain, was the supply depot and the important rail junction in Archangelskoye, and ordered the SPs and a tank battalion of 2nd Panzer Division to move at best possible speed to the threatened area. It was a calculated risk. If he was wrong and the Red Army attacked on other sectors, the infantry formations holding the line in those places, now without panzer protection, would be overrun and crushed.

The decisive day was 18 July, when Stavka made a desperate attempt to achieve the breakthrough victory that had eluded it until now. It deployed along a 120km battle line no fewer than 400 armoured machines, and that number excluded the 100 positioned in the front of the gap. The armoured mass rolled into the attack supported by waves of infantry taken from 42 Divisions belonging to, among others, 4Eighth and 63rd Red Armies. The man whom Rendulic had appointed to command Corps' limited armoured force was Colonel Gaedke, his Chief of Staff. Gaedke's panzers drove back the first Soviet tank assault, inflicting upon the enemy a loss of 43 vehicles. The remainder retreated from the field, regrouped and then came on again. For a second time the armada was driven off. Again it regrouped and launched a third attack, but that charge, too, and all the subsequent assaults, were to no avail; the Soviets could not smash through Rendulic's defence. The evidence of the Soviets' determined attacks lay immobile on the battlefield. The shattered hulks of nearly 300 tanks covered the ground and the bodies of the Russian infantry lay in swathes across the steppes.

Another mass attack on the 19th was held when reinforcements were rushed forward to support Rendulic's Corps. With the help of those replacements the areas into which the Red Army troops had penetrated were sealed off. By 20 July it was clear that the enemy attacks were weakening. The battle for Orel was ending. Stavka had been forced to redeploy its forces in the hope of finding sectors where the defence was less resolute than that of Rendulic's Corps. That force, which eventually numbered seven Divisions, had been under continual attack by 22 Soviet Divisions supported by 1,500 armoured fighting vehicles, and had destroyed 819 of them.

Rendulic's next Command was announced during the first week of August 1943, when he reported to Hitler's field headquarters at Rastenburg in East Prussia. There he was informed that he was to be given command of an Army which was being raised in the western Balkans. Hitler's orders were that the new Army was to crush Tito's partisan force and disarm the unreliable Italian Army of Occupation which was holding the coastal areas of Yugoslavia. Hitler went on to say that once that latter task had been accomplished, Rendulic's Army was to occupy the areas formerly held by the Italians; Albania, Dalmatia and Montenegro. It was not an easy task, for many units of the Italian Army of Occupation had abandoned their weapons and left the arms dumps to be pillaged by the partisans. A few formations had chosen to resist the Germans, resulting in casualties on both sides. That resistance was shortlived. Within days the last fighting by 9th Italian Army had been overcome and its commander had signed the instrument of surrender. More than a quarter of a million of his men then passed into captivity.

Hitler was pleased with Rendulic's swift and decisive action, and on 15 September recalled him to Rastenburg to be decorated with the Oak Leaf to the Knight's Cross. He then sent the Army commander back into Yugoslavia with orders to wage all-out war against Tito's guerrilla forces. Hitler was, perhaps, unaware that the partisans were no longer a scattered band of irregulars but had grown to become the Yugoslav Army of National Liberation (YANL), lavishly supplied with arms by the British government. Instead of ill-armed bands of dispirited soldiers, Rendulic faced a modern, well equipped and highly organised national army ready and willing to meet the Germans in set-piece battles. As a means of supporting partisan land operations, as well as to open new supply lines from Italy to Yugoslavia, British Eighth Army, fighting its way up the Adriatic side of Italy, carried out assault landings on the islands of Lissa and Brac. Rendulic, who had become aware of Italian laxness in the matter of coastal defence, took immediate steps to improve those defences, and when British seaborne commando assaults were repeated they were met and beaten back with heavy loss. It was a small but a significant victory. That success made it clear to the British that they could no longer raid the Yugoslav coast with impunity.

In the Balkan theatre of operations, perhaps more than in any other, the success of military operations depended upon intelligence gathered from local sources. Playing skilfully upon regional, religious and racial divisions among the Yugoslav peoples, the German authorities gained a great deal of information as a result of betrayals. It was by such means that 'Brandenburg', Germany's equivalent of Britain's SAS formations, learned where Tito had set up his new headquarters. Under German pressure he had repeatedly been forced to change its location, and in May 1944 he had located it in a steep, narrow valley in western Bosnia. For as long as his headquarters was forced to keep moving, Tito had been unable to exercise the close control over the YANL that was required. As a result the scale of its activity had had to be reduced. Rendulic, now advised of the location of his enemy's headquarters and aware of the reduction in YANL operations, determined to exploit the advantage afforded him by destroying Tito and his Command staff in a single operation. The XV Gebirgs Corps, to which he passed the order to carry out the operation, issued its own battle orders on 21 May. The first paragraph of the Corps directive stated: 'The Communist Supreme Command headquarters is located in Drvar, western Bosnia ... [and] in nearby Petrovac there is a supply centre and an aerodrome. In the whole area there are about 12,000 men with heavy weapons, including artillery and anti-tank guns, as well as, possibly, a few armoured fighting vehicles held in the Petrovac area ...'

The gathering of intelligence details was not a German prerogative, and YANL soon learned that an operation was to be launched on 25 May, Tito's birthday, which was intended to surprise and destroy him. With adequate time to prepare defences and strengthen positions, the partisan formations met and fought off Rendulic's challenge. Tito and the Supreme Command were not captured, and the main body of the partisan force melted into the hills and filtered through the German encirclement.

Rendulic had been unable to carry out the Fuehrer's order to crush the enemy, but there was no time for recriminations, or for him to plan another offensive. A new appointment was given him; a post which was to take him from the Balkans to the Arctic Circle. The former commander of 20th Gebirgs Army in Lapland, General Dietl, had been killed in an air crash, and Hitler chose Rendulic to take over the vacant post. He flew from Yugoslavia to Berchtesgaden, where he was briefed on his new assignment. Hitler repeatedly stressed that Germany's only source of the strategically important mineral nickel was the Kolosyoki mine in northern Lapland. The role of 20th Gebirgs Army, which Rendulic was now to command, had less to do with offensive military operations in Finland than defensive ones, ensuring that the nickel mines were not captured by the Red Army. The Order of Battle of Rendulic's new Command was three Corps, the XVIII with 6th SS Gebirgs Division 'Nord', the Krautler Divisional Group and 7th Gebirgs Division. The XXXVI Corps was composed of two infantry Divisions, the 163rd and the 169th, while on the strength of XIX Corps were 2nd Gebirgs, 6th Gebirgs and 210th Infantry Divisions.

Up to this time Finland had been Germany's staunchest ally in the war against the Soviet Union, holding firmly to the alliance despite Russian efforts to separate her from the Reich. But the Finnish army had suffered terrible losses, and called upon Germany to make a greater military contribution to meet the manpower crisis. It was to be briefed by Hitler on this matter that Dietl had flown to the Fuehrer's headquarters, and his aeroplane had crashed during the return flight. As the new GOC 20th Gebirgs Army, Rendulic was as determined as his predecessor to do his utmost to prevent the collapse of his country's ally. He flew to the headquarters of Marshal Mannerheim, Finland's national hero, to discuss the political and military situation. It needed only a few minutes for Rendulic to appreciate that the Finnish leader had already decided to withdraw from the war. In an effort to influence the Marshal, Rendulic pointed out that his soldiers and those of the Finnish army were first-class warriors. If they were forced to fight against each other, the losses might be as high as 90 per cent. In the course of the discussion Mannerheim asked the direct question: 'Why are you still in Lapland?', to which Rendulic could only reply that the decision to stay was not his, but was that of OKW, and that he as a soldier had to obey the orders which that body gave him.

On the way back to his headquarters Rendulic heard over the radio that the Finns had sought an armistice with the Russians, that they had accepted the Soviet demand to break off relations with Germany by 3 September, and that the Finnish government had demanded from the Reich government that the German forces be evacuated from Finnish territory by that date; within fourteen days. Such a deadline could not be met. It might be possible to remove by ship those German formations which were garrisoning the south-western parts of the country, but those in the central sectors and in the high north could not be taken out within so short a space of time. Those areas were difficult to evacuate because there was no road network capable of carrying Rendulic's force of nearly a quarter of a million men, together with all their weapons and stores. It was clear to him that the Soviets had fixed that inflexible deadline in order to bring about armed conflict between the forces of Finland and the Third Reich.

In a letter to Hitler, Marshal Mannerheim had expressed the hope that he would not to have to use force of arms against German troops, but that he was compelled by the terms of the armistice to do so if they were still on Finnish territory when the deadline expired. As sort of apologia for his surrender, he went on to point out to the German Fuehrer that if the Reich were to be defeated in the war, then her manpower resources would allow her to rise again. The Finnish nation, however, had so small a population that she faced the threat of total extermination. For the sake of her national existence Finland had no choice but to withdraw from the war and abide by the terms, admittedly harsh, imposed by the Soviets.

Faced with the evacuation problems and a tight deadline, Rendulic, together with his capable staff, had soon worked out a timetable for the withdrawal. His predecessor, Dietl, had drawn up contingency plans for such an eventuality, but these had been based on 20th Gebirgs Army being given longer to evacuate Finnish territory. The evacuation operation was given two names; 'Birch Tree' for the first part, and 'Northern Lights' for the second. The withdrawal was to become one of the most dramatic defensive victories of the Second World War. It has already been stated that the road network was poor. From Rovaniemi, where the German headquarters was located, a road led eastwards towards the combat area at Kandalakscha. The northward road from Rovaniemi to Kirkenes, known as the Arctic Sea road, branched at Jualo, and that branch led to Lakselv. The north-westerly road out of Rovaniemi, known as the Finland road, ran towards and then along the frontier with Sweden. In the far north, connecting Kirkenes and Lakselv, ran the east-west Reichsstrasse 50, built by the German forces in Finland.

The task facing Rendulic was to evacuate his army along those few roads and over tremendous distances in what would soon be deep winter conditions. And this had to be achieved within fourteen days, or he would face the additional problem of fighting against the forces of his former allies and those of the Red enemy. The key to the problem was Rovaniemi, for that town controlled the several evacuation roads. He was also under orders to hold the nickel mine for as long as possible. Clearly, both Rovaniemi and the Kolosyoki mine area would have to be garrisoned until the last moment. That meant that when the time came for them to pull out, the garrisons of those places would have to undertake forced marches. Otherwise they would not gain touch with the main of the Gebirgs Armee nor keep ahead of their pursuing enemies. The withdrawal plan foresaw that Army's Divisions in the southernmost part of Finland would begin to move first, swinging in a reverse arc and moving northwards. When all three Corps had concentrated they would march out of northern Finland to reach positions in west Lapland. Once 20th Army reached Norway it would no longer be pursued by Finnish forces, and could then move at a slower pace from the high north of Norway to the southern areas of that country.

The logistical problems of moving the Army and all of its equipment were enormous, and the distances which the troops had to march were prodigious. The 6th SS Gebirgs Division 'Nord', for example, had first to march 800km from its battle area to reach Rovaniemi, and would then have to cover the long distance to the frontier area. The movement of Rendulic's troops was made more difficult when Finnish units attacked their former allies as they marched through the sopping wet, dark and gloomy Lapland forests. The meeting place for the three Corps was set as the border area of Karaguendo, just north-east of the Swedish-Lapland frontier, and XVIII Corps had been ordered to stand there as a rearguard to protect the withdrawal of the rest of 20th Army. To add to the misery of the day-long marches, the autumn of 1944 was exceptionally wet and cold and the soldiers usually slept in the open air. Added to those problems was the additional one that the Red Army had opened a series of major offensives to take Rovaniemi and cut the few roads. If it succeeded, a major part of Rendulic's army would be trapped.

On 3 September OKW ordered Operation Birch Tree to begin, and the march continued until the last weeks of December. Rendulic reported to Hitler on 17 January 1945, and during the interview was awarded the Swords to the Oak Leaf. His real reward was to be told by the Fuehrer: 'You have saved Germany's best Army. To be honest, I did not think that such a feat as you have carried out could be accomplished.' But Hitler gave his commander no time to rest. On the Western Front the Allies were fighting inside Germany, in Italy they were nearing the Po, in the Balkans the Loehr's Army Group was withdrawing from Greece into Yugoslavia, and on the Eastern Front the Soviet winter offensive had brought the Red Army almost to the river Oder. At this time of deep crisis for Germany, Rendulic flew to Courland, where, on 27 January 1945, he took over command of Army Group North, with orders to hold the Russian assaults.

The forces under his command carried out their given task although they faced an enemy who outnumbered them in infantry by five to one and who had a superiority in guns and armour that rose to double figures. Hitler's confidence in his 'Austrian Fireman' remained undiminished. On 12 March he named Reundulic Supreme Commander in Courland, but it was a post he would not hold for long. Within weeks came the order to fly to Berlin and report to Hitler in the Fuehrerbunker under the Chancellery. During the evening of 6 April 1945 Rendulic saw the Fuehrer for the last time, and noted no sign of the physical decline that other people had reported. Hitler's body was, indeed, bowed, his left leg dragged slightly and he supported his left arm in his right hand, but these were probably the effects of the assassination attempt of July 20. What impressed Rendulic most was that Hitler's eyes were still clear and very lively; there was no evidence of mental degeneration there.

In the centre of the small conference room stood a table covered with maps, and Hitler spoke with his usual clarity and determination. He dealt first with Rendulic's new appointment as General Officer Commanding Army Group South, explaining to the new commander that he must stop the withdrawal of his Army Group and thus prevent a Russian penetration of the Danube valley. Vienna was to be held by every means possible. There was uncertainty about the situation along certain sectors of the Army Group, and when the conference with Hitler had been concluded Rendulic asked OKW for details of his new Command. That Army Group, whose forces had only a few years before advanced with high hope as far as Stalingrad, was now only a remnant, and was fighting along the borders of Austria. The battle line held by Rendulic's formations extended from southern Czechoslovakia to northern Yugoslavia, and to man it he had four

141

armies. From north to south, these were Eighth, 6th SS Panzer, 6th and 2nd Panzer armies. The state of his Command can be gauged if one takes 6th SS Panzer Army as an example; there was not one fully operational unit in its order of battle. An OKW assessment evaluated 1st SS Panzer Division as 'burnt out'. The 2nd SS Panzer Division was considered to be of only average strength, the 3rd SS was made up of fragments of units, the 6th SS Division was weak and the 12th SS Panzer Division was seriously weakened.

The most crucial sector of Army Group South was the Steiermark, which was held by 6th Army. In its instructions to Rendulic the OKW directed that it was essential for 6th Army to hold its front because this would be 'decisive to the fate of the Reich'. The explanation for that demand was that Field Marshal Loehr's Army Group was pulling out of the Balkans. If 6th Army broke, the full flood of Tolbhukin's 3rd Ukrainian Front would rush in and cut off not only 2nd Panzer Army, but also the half-a-million men under Loehr's command. The Russian 3rd Ukrainian Front disposed seven armies, three of which were Guards formations. Against that great host 6th Army could put up only units of low numerical strength. The 13th Panzer Division, for example, numbered only 1,013 all ranks. The Army Group's left flank army, the Eighth, was in western Slovakia as well as in that part of Austria to the north of the Danube river known as the Marchfeld.

It was obvious to Rendulic that the Soviet main effort would be first to capture Vienna and then go on to thrust as deeply as possible into central Austria. The Foreign Armies (East) Department of OKW advised him that the Russians had one tank and two motorised armies as well as an infantry Army all advancing on Vienna, and that the defence of that city hung upon two badly weakened German panzer divisions. Most worrying was the problem of the Danube bridges, particularly that at Hainburg, which nourished the Red Army bridgehead on the river's northern bank.

The terrain of Army Group's front was generally hilly or mountainous. On the Semmering sector of 6th Army there were high mountains, and as the battle line ran down towards Yugoslavia the peaks scaled down so that in the south, where 6th Army's right wing brushed the left wing of 2nd Panzer Army, the ground was rolling and good going for armour. Rather surprisingly, the main thrust of Tolbhukin's offensives were not made to reach that better terrain, but came in against the mountainous Semmering sector. The Soviet assaults were heavy and frequent, but with Rendulic to inspire them the men of Army Group South held their positions and carried out their given task of holding the German Army's right flank. But outside Vienna there were too few troops and no defences, and there was no time to dig trenches.

Although he could not defend the city, Rendulic appreciated that he could not give up the Austrian capital without a fight. Firstly, it would be against Hitler's direct order; secondly, such an evacuation would prejudice the position of Eighth Army. What he could do, however, was order the Eighth Army to pull back to a stronger defensive line. Once that move had been made, 6th SS Panzer Army could be directed to withdraw from the Austrian capital. The weakest-held sector of the battlefront was at the junction of 6th SS Panzer and Eighth Army. It would only be possible to cover the shortage of men on that sector by withdrawing units from the Vienna garrison. Rendulic had made his first decisions as commander of Army Group South while driving to reach his new Command area, and having ordered the necessary regroupings he directed that all explosives be taken from the bridges in his area and also halted the blowing of bridges. He specifically forbad the destruction of bridges on those areas towards which the US Armies were driving.

At the time Rendulic made no mention of the reason for that decision, but it may very well have been due to a propaganda story spread by Goebbels. The Propaganda Minister disseminated the lie that the armies of the western Allies were about to join forces with the German Army, and that together the Anglo-US-German forces would drive back the Red Army and win the war. Only a lie of such proportions coming from such a senior source could have influenced the actions which Rendulic carried out, which will be described later in this chapter. A great many other German senior commanders also believed that propaganda story. In their opinion it was the logical step which Britain and America had to make if they were not to stand idly by as Europe passed under communist hegemony. Such a *volte face* on the Allied part may have been seen to be logical to the senior German commanders, but it was not so to the western leaders, who saw the alliance with Russia as an enduring political necessity.

Vienna and the whole of the southern bank of the Danube was evacuated by 6th SS Panzer Army during the second week of April, a move delayed until all the wounded in the city's hospitals had been carried away. Russian pressure, and the weakness of Army Group's front between the Danube and the foothills of the Alps, forced the Army Group commander to move troops from his central front in the Steiermark, a regrouping that he carried out while the Russians were fighting to seize Vienna. The battle in eastern Austria reached its climax when 3rd Ukrainian Front changed its point of maximum effort from 6th Army's sector to that held by Eighth Army. The Ukrainian offensive had a two-fold purpose. Firstly, to capture the oil refineries at Zisterdorf and, secondly, to turn Eighth Army's right wing and separate that Army from the forces fighting inside Czechoslovakia. Along the rest of the front Rendulic's deployment of units and the courage of the men of those units prevented a Soviet breakthrough, although the Russians did make several deep penetrations in the Semmering area.

During the second week of April, fighting along Army Group's front diminished in intensity, due in Rendulic's opinion to the total exhaustion of the enemy forces. He utilised the welcome pause to knit together his battle line. Aerial reconnaissance photographs taken at this time showed the recent construction of a defence system some 20km deep behind the Soviet front line. Its purpose could not be understood by the Staff of Army Group South because the Soviets knew full well that the Army Group was in no position to mount a major offensive. The reason for the complex of trenches became known in the final days of April, when Russian loudspeaker vans announced 'the greatest betrayal in the history of the world is about to occur'. The Soviets, too, had accepted Goebbels' lie that the western Allies were about to join with Germany and turn against their Russian ally.

Another lie spread about at this time reported that the Reich was building an Alpine Fortress, inside which élite units would be concentrated and from which those formations would erupt to win the war for Germany. This lie was accepted by the Americans, who diverted the thrust of their armies in Germany to take out that supposed last bastion of Nazi militarism. Although Rendulic dismissed that story as nonsense, he continued to believe the lie of a split between the victorious Allies.

Then another peculiar situation arose, underlining the fact that Rendulic had accepted Goebbels' propaganda. At Lambach in the Salzburg area Army Group had a vast ration dump, and Rendulic learned that not only were his troops drawing supplies from that source, but US Divisions were also using it. Lorried columns of both sides were using the Salzburg-Linz autobahn and were not firing a shot at each other. It was a ludicrous situation, and the more Rendulic pondered on it the more convinced he became that there was substance in Goebbels' 'split' story. The Americans were not firing at the German columns because they would soon be allies. But that hoped-for solution had not yet come about, and until it did there was a danger of Army Group being trapped between the advancing Americans in the west and the Soviets in the east. Rendulic transferred several Divisions from 6th Army to confront the American formations along a line between the city of Linz and the Enns river and delay them. The arms factories in Linz turned out sufficient armoured fighting vehicles to equip each of the three transferred Panzer divisions with 65 Tigers or Panthers, and sufficient men were found to flesh out the depleted Divisions.

The announcement of Hitler's death in some way reinforced the fiction that the Western Powers would ally themselves with Germany, and Rendulic allowed himself to be convinced of this. He sent General Gaedke, Chief of Staff of 6th Army, to meet Patton, the commander of American 3rd Army. The letter which the Army Group Commander entrusted to Gaedke, and which was addressed to Patton, requested that German medical supplies held in the west should be released and transported through the American lines to replenish the reduced stocks of Army Group South. It also asked that German units in the west should be sluiced through the US lines to reinforce the Eastern Front. Patton's telephoned reply was: 'What makes you think that I should pass troops from my front to fight against the troops of my ally?"

Upon receipt of that refusal, Rendulic decided to end his Army Group's war. He was out of touch with Supreme Command and did not know what was

Left: General Rendulic coming forward to greet guests at his birthday party. (Photograph supplied by the Heeresgeschichtliches Museum, Vienna and reproduced by kind permission of the Rendulic family.)

ght: A formal portrait of ndulic after the award of e Swords to the Oak Leaf the Knight's Cross.

Above: Rommel, here seen as commanding general of 7th Panzer Division, with his Corp commander, Hoth, in France, 1940.

Opposite page, top: Rommel, here seen as GOC of 7th Panzer Division in St Valéry, France, 1940. This picture was taken after his division had captured the town and he had accepted the surrender of the Allied units there.

Opposite page, bottom: Rommel enjoying an *al fresco* meal in his command car, Libya, 1941.

Left: A formal portrait of Rommel showing him wearing the Knight's Cross with Oak Leaf and Swords. Under the Knight's Cross can be seen the Pour le Mérite which he won during the First World War.

Left: A formal portrait of Rommel taken late in 1942

Right: Oberst Graf von Strachwitz.

Right: A snapshot of Hyazinth von Strachwitz, taken during the time he was serving in the panzer regiment of 'Gross-Deutschland' Division.

Left: A formal portrait of von Strachwitz, showing h[im] wearing the Oak Leaf to t[he] Knight's Cross of the Iron Cross.

Below: At the conclusion [of] the campaign in Belgium, Student paid a visit to Koch's Assault Battalion t[o] thank the men of that formation. He is the office[r] wearing a greatcoat. Immediately behind him is Koch, the battalion commander, and behind him Rudolf Witzig, who captured Eben Emael.

Kurt Student, Generaloberst

formal, signed photograph of Colonel General Kurt Student, here seen wearing the Oak Leaf to the Knight's Cross of the Iron Cross.

Left: A snapshot of Gener Student in an aircraft en route to Crete, 1941.

Right: General Student (right) and General Ringl, GOC 5th Gebirgs Division, (left) planning a new atta Crete, 1941.

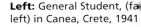

Left: General Student, (fa left) in Canea, Crete, 1941

Right: General Student (right) and Colonel Brauer (centre) during a tour of t island of Crete at the clos of the campaign, 1941.

Left: A studio portrait of Otto Weidinger, showing him wearing the Knight's Cross of the Iron Cross, the German Cross in Gold (right breast) and the Close Combat award (above his medal ribbons.)

Right: A formal photograph of Otto Weidinger.

Below: Otto Weidinger and the Command group of his battle group posing outside the trucks that took them from the Eastern Front to southern France, spring 1944. Weidinger is the central figure (seventh from the left).

Left: A formal photograph of Otto Weidinger taken during a parade, summer 1944.

Below: A snapshot of Otto Weidinger (central figure) taken during the fighting for Vienna, April 1945. The officer standing on the right is General Bunau, commanding the troops in the Austrian captial.

Above: Michael Wittmann and his Tiger crew in Normandy shortly after the victory at Villers Bocage, June 1944.

Right: As a result of his success at Villers Bocage in Normandy during June 1944, the German Propaganda Ministry mounted a publicity campaign to make Michael Wittmann more widely known to the German public. This is one of the publicity pictures taken at that time.

Above: Another propaganda picture of Michael Wittmann during the summer of 1944, showing him wearing on his breast the Iron Cross 1st Class, the Panzer Assault badge and the Wound Badge in black. Around his neck is the Knight's Cross with Oak Leaf.

Above right: A studio photograph of Rudolf Witzig taken shortly after Hitler bestowed upon him the Knight's Cross of the Iron Cross, May 1940.

Below: Panzer 007 in which Michael Wittmann was 'mounted' when he was killed on 8 August 1944. The force of the explosion blew off the Tiger's turret and it landed upside down on the grass, some 40 feet from the chassis.

Above: During the Tunisian campaign of 1942/43, Major Witzig was commanding the Para Engineer battalion. Here he is seen presenting the Iron Cross 1st Class to Corporal Becker. The officer on the right of the picture is Hardt, the commander of No 4 Company in which Corporal Becker was serving.

Below: Witzig, here seen making the funeral oration for Oberleutnant Hardt, Tunisia, 1943.

Above: Witzig, here seen as commander of 8th Para Regiment, on the Western Front after the unit's return from fighting in Lithuania.

Below: This picture, taken during a post-war reunion of the German Para organisation, shows Colonel Witzig (on the left), Rudi Hambuch, an officer of the Para ex-Services Association and the author (on the right) wearing the Service Cross of the Austrian ex-Services Association which had just been bestowed upon him. Kassel, Germany, June 1983

happening either politically or militarily. He issued his last orders. The units of Army Group South which were fighting against the Americans were to cease hostilities at 0800 on 7 May, while those embattled against the Red Army were to hold out and were to disengage and withdraw westwards at last light on the same day. All of the German forces were directed to reach the river Enns by midday on the Eighth, for those who did not do so would become prisoners of war of the Russians.

Thanks to Rendulic's careful planning, more than 600,000 men of his Army Group passed into American captivity. During the early afternoon of 7 May he drove into the American lines to carry out the formalities of surrender. From divisional headquarters he was taken to US XX Corps headquarters where he and Walker, the commanding General, discussed Rendulic's letter to Patton. The Army Group Commander was clearly surprised that the Americans did not appreciate the threat which communism represented. At the end of their discussion he warned the US General: 'Together we can fling the exhausted Russians back across their own frontiers. If in future there are problems [with the Soviet Union] you will have a very difficult task, particularly if you disarm Germany. You will remember my words, one day.'

Rendulic was passed from camp to camp, and in September 1946 was sent to Nuremberg for trial as a war criminal. The court which tried him contained three civilian judges, and he was sentenced to 20 years' imprisonment for crimes which, as it turned out, could not be proven. He was released in September 1951, after 6,000 Austrian officers, including 18 generals, petitioned President Truman for his release. By this time he was too old to practice, and turned to authorship, producing a number of books on military matters. The Colonel General died in January 1971 at the age of 83.

The Desert Fox

Generalfeldmarschall Erwin Rommel

Erwin Rommel was born on 15 November 1891 at Weidenheim ner Ulm, in the kingdom of Württemberg, one of the five children of a teacher of mathematics. He was poor in health and small in stature, but from his earliest years showed a determination to succeed in whatever he undertook. In July 1910 he applied to join the Imperial German Army's 124th Infantry Regiment (also known as the 6th Württemberg), and was accepted as a cadet in that unit. He passed through the courses for corporal and sergeant grade and was finally commissioned in March 1911.

At the outbreak of the First World War Rommel left the Field Artillery Regiment to which he had been attached and returned to his parent regiment, the 124th, which was in action on the Western Front. There he won the Iron Cross Second Class for bravery in the field. Military action had shown that he was a natural warrior. He was wounded during one attack, and upon returning to active service in January 1915 took over command of a Company and fought first in the Argonne sector and later in the Vosges mountains. In the autumn of 1915 he was transferred to the newly created Württemberg Gebirgs Battalion, which had a war establishment of six rifle Companies and six machine-gun platoons. That battalion first went into action in the High Vosges mountains and in August 1916, and saw service in Romania before returning to the Western Front in May 1917. During the latter part of 1917 the firepower of the Rifle Companies in the battalion was supplemented by the issue of lighter, air-cooled weapons, although the battalion's machine-gun platoons still retained the heavier Maxim machine-guns. Then another reorganisation of the Gebirgs Battalion divided it into detachments. One of these, No. 1 Detachment, made up of three rifle Companies and a machine-gun Company, was placed under Rommel's command. That reorganisation was part of the preparation for an offensive in Italy, and it was during that operation that Rommel won Imperial Germany's highest award for bravery; the Pour le Mérite.

Since 1915 the forces of Austria-Hungary and Italy had been fighting in the high mountains of the Alps. The Italians were striving to break eastwards through the mountain barrier to reach the Llubljana Gap, while the Austrians aimed to strike south-westwards to reach the plain of Lombardy. Successive offensives to achieve these military objectives, all of which were known as the battles of the Isonzo, had been fought without either side achieving the breakthrough.

The German Army, which had been fighting on both the Western and the Eastern Fronts, had not been an active participant in the war in Italy, but in 1918 that situation changed. When the Treaty of Brest-Litovsk took Russia out of the war, it became possible to withdraw from the Eastern Front a great many Divisions and Corps which were no longer needed to man the battle line. The High Command was able to put more troops into the fighting on the Southern Front, and the formations were posted to Italy to take part in a new offensive which it was hoped would gain the victory which had so far eluded the Central Powers.

The sector on which the High Command had chosen to launch the offensive was that held by German 14th Army. One of its formations was the Alpen Korps, in whose Württemberg Gebirgs battalion Rommel was serving. The battle plan was for the Alpen Korps to strike through the mountains and gain the three seemingly impregnable mountains, Monte Stol, Matajur and Kolovrat, which blocked the western side of the Isono between Zaga and Tolmein. Their capture was essential to the success of the offensive. In addition to the three mountains, there were other areas of high ground which had tactical significance. Of these, Monte Hevnik and Monte Kuk were the most important. If all of these objectives could be taken quickly, the way into the Italian plain would have been opened. If not, the Army advance would be stuck in the bottleneck of the valley of the Isonzo. After the peaks had been captured, the Alpen Korps was to cut the track leading from the village of Luico, at the head of the pass, and go on to take Monte Mrzli. The Italian positions in the area the Korps had to assault were well sited, laid out in depth and so strong that the Italian High Command considered them impregnable.

The Austro-German offensive was timed to start at 0200 on 24 October with a violent artillery barrage whose projectiles would include gas shells. According to Anton Wagner's *Truppendienst Taschenbuch*, which summarised the multi-volume Austrian official history of the Great War, Czech and Romanian deserters betrayed details of the forthcoming offensive to the enemy. Despite the Italian High Command's foreknowledge, when Rommel's detachment moved off at 0800 it quickly overran the Italian forward positions on the mountains of the Tolmein area and carried the advance forward to the Krn, another mountain peak. On other sectors of the front the pace of the advance was slower because it met strong Italian opposition.

Rommel planned to bypass the Italian defences which were holding up the attack by the neighbouring unit, and set two of his Companies climbing the steep mountain slopes. Although the attack was carried out in pouring rain, the defenders soon became aware of the attackers' presence and poured down a destructive fire upon them. Rommel decided to amend his plan of action. He

147

ordered the leading Sections of the two Companies to remain where they were and return the Italian fire while he, using a narrow ravine as an approach route, led the remainder of the detachment in an effort to work round the flank of the Italians. On reaching the summit he found that the enemy had left the open trenches they were supposed to be defending and were sheltering in nearby dugouts. They were all taken prisoner.

In the battle orders he had been given Rommel had had it impressed upon him that the prime need was for his formation to make ground. With no pause for rest he led his men on, but the rate of the advance was governed by the pace of the machine-gun Company, whose men had to porter on their backs the heavy load of weapons and ammunition. Although slow, the assault moved smoothly enough and resulted in the capture of a succession of enemy positions, including an artillery post holding a battery of guns. So decisive had been the attack by Rommel's unit that the point of maximum effort on that sector had altered. His men were no longer attacking the enemy in a frontal assault. They had passed through the enemy front and were attacking the enemy from the rear, and the assault from that direction threw the Italians into confusion. In Rommel's own words: 'The deeper we penetrated into the enemy's defences the less ready they were [to confront us] and consequently the fighting became less intense'.

By late morning he and his detachment had reached a dominant ridge to the east of Monte Hevnik, and they pushed on until they stood on its crest. The group's advance went on until it took out the enemy's positions between Monte Hevnik and Foni. By last light Rommel had set up his TAC headquarters and was planning the following day's battle. He decided that the Kolovrat ridge was to be the next objective. At dawn the detachment resumed its attack and quickly overran an Italian outpost position, in which the garrison was sound asleep. The fighting had shown that although the enemy positions and garrisons were prepared and sited to meet an assault coming out of the Isonzo valley, no preparation seemed to have been made for one coming from any other direction, and certainly not from where his detachment was attacking. The assaults launched by his unit had not only overrun the enemy main defensive position, but had also penetrated into the second-line sector. During their advance Rommel's men had captured a battery of guns and taken nearly a thousand prisoners. Confused fighting followed, but by mid-morning his unit had taken another important ridge.

Anticipating a major counterattack against him, Rommel decided to pre-empt the blow, and his surprise assault threw the enemy so completely off balance that many of them fled as his detachment approached. Soon the young lieutenant was faced with the problem of whether he should attack Monte Kuk or advance and capture the village stipulated in his battle orders. If he took the latter option he could open the valley pass for the rest of his Division. A third option was to cut a mountain road and thereby trap the Italians in an encirclement. He decided on the third option, reached the road, cut the telephone wires connecting the garrison in a nearby village with its headquarters, and deployed his small force in an ambush.

The Italians reacted as Rommel had anticipated. Groups of men came out to find the break in the telephone line and were captured. Other infantry or vehicle groups moving up to the front line entered the ambush area and were taken. Finally, a column of Bersaglieri leaving the line marched out of the village. The Bersaglieri were intercepted, fired upon and the whole detachment taken prisoner. Rommel's commanding officer then ordered the group to capture Monte Cragonza. During this attack the young lieutenant was surprised when he came upon an Italian force holding a trench line. Without hesitation he demanded the surrender of the enemy troops and, thinking themselves surrounded, they gave themselves up. A total of 37 officers and 1,000 men was added to the numbers he and his group had already taken prisoner.

Rommel then swung his small force in the direction of Monte Matajeur and encountered, en route, a sight he had not seen before. In his march along the mountain crest he saw a large body of the enemy engaged in violent argument, and called upon them to surrender, whereupon the Italian rank and file ran towards him and hoisted him on their shoulders with shouts of 'Viva Germania'. The argument he had witnessed had been between the officers and the other ranks of the Italian unit as to whether or not they should lay down their arms. Rommel's group had captured the 1st Regiment of the Salerno Brigade. The advance towards the peak of Monte Matajeur was no less rewarding in terms of prisoners taken, and another 1,200 men surrendered to him. At 1140 Rommel fired the flare signal to show that the crest of Matajeur was in German hands. He had captured thousands of the enemy, 80 pieces of artillery and a great mass of transport. The losses to his detachment during the 2½-day battle were six dead and 30 wounded. The attack by German 14th Army had shattered the Italians, but it was a victory that was not exploited. Inexplicably the offensive which might have taken the armies of the Central Powers into the Po valley was called off by the High Command.

Rommel went on a brief period of leave after being decorated with the Pour le Mérite, and during that time he was posted away from the fighting. He was serving as a Staff officer when the war came to an end in November 1918. He was not demobilised, but was retained on the strength of 124th Infantry regiment. An officer with his gifts of leadership and proven courage would be an asset in the post-war republican Army. In those immediate post-bellum years he had neither a chance to serve on the Staff nor opportunity for quick promotion. He carried out his regimental duties conscientiously, including one period of eleven years as a Company commander in 13th Infantry regiment. On 1 October 1929 he was posted as an instructor to the Infantry School in Dresden, and during this period wrote an account of his front-line experiences, adding the conclusions he had drawn from active service life: His book *Infantry Attacks* was not only a best seller; more importantly it brought him to the notice of Adolf Hitler.

There then followed a further term of regimental service and, in 1933, he commanded 3rd battalion of 17th Infantry Regiment before being posted two years later to be an instructor at the War College in Potsdam. In 1938, holding the rank of colonel, Rommel was appointed Director of the War College at Wiener Neustadt, but was in the post only a short time before being seconded to command Hitler's personal military security unit, the Fuehrer Begleit battalion. He accompanied Hitler during the Munich crisis of September 1938, and during the occupation of Prague in March 1939. Because he was still on the Fuehrer's staff he took no active part in the Polish campaign. At the end of the war against Poland, Hitler, who liked Rommel because he was brave, efficient and, more importantly, because he was not an aristocrat, asked him what unit he would like to command. He received the reply: 'A panzer Division', and on 15 February 1940, at the age of 48 and in the rank of major general, Rommel took over command of 7th Panzer. He was determined not only to impress his personality upon his new Command but also to master the concepts of the 'blitzkrieg' method of warfare which he had observed in action during the Polish campaign. The climacterics of Rommel's military career were the campaign in France in 1940, the war in the North African desert and his period as Army Group Commander on the Western Front in 1944. The war in France and Flanders during the spring of 1940 demonstrated how well and how quickly he had mastered the techniques of mobile warfare, and that demonstration of Rommel's mastery of the battlefield will now be dealt with at length. The other climaxes of Africa and Normandy are less closely detailed.

FRANCE AND FLANDERS

Until he assumed command, Rommel's new unit had been a 'Light' or motorised infantry formation. Upon its upgrading to Panzer status it took on strength several units essential to its new role, including a panzer regiment made up of 218 vehicles. The Division had the standard two infantry regiments combined into an infantry brigade, a reconnaissance, a machine-gun and an anti-tank battalion, together with three battalions of field artillery. This was the formation which Rommel was to lead as part of Hoth's Panzer Corps during Unternehmen Gelb (Operation Yellow), the opening campaign in the west. The role which OKW had envisaged for Hoth's Corps was for it to protect the flank of the formations which were making the principal thrust. It was the way in which Rommel handled his Division that raised it from the low-profile role it had been given and made it the spearhead of the armoured strike which decided the campaign in the west.

The OKW plan was for Army Group A, the central Army group, to make the main effort, by bursting through the Allied line and driving for the Channel coast. That panzer drive would bisect and separate the Allied armies. The left wing of Army Group A would then regroup in preparation for a drive south-wards into France, while the right wing, including Hoth's Corps, would swing northwards to envelop the flank of the Franco-British armies in northern France and Belgium.

When Unternehmen Gelb opened at 0535 on 10 May 1940, the men of 7th Division's infantry Brigade advanced swiftly, taking the high ground at Maspelt before moving on to take the line Espeler–Dorler. A group of AFVs and the motorcycle battalion passed through the infantry in a leap-frogging operation and quickly smashed Belgian resistance at Mont Le Ban. Despite immediate and determined attacks by a French tank formation which had come forward to aid the Belgians, the 7th maintained the pace of its advance, and by the evening of that first day of the campaign its leading elements had reached the objectives Rommel had set them. Behind those leading formations the rest of the division lay like a series of links extending back to the German frontier. The most easterly unit was made up of the bulk of 25th Panzer Regiment. To the west of the armour lay 7th Rifle Regiment, one of the components of the infantry brigade, together with the flak units. Farther still to the west and forming the central group was divisional headquarters and the panzer reconnaissance battalion. The units for-ward of those were 6th Rifle Regiment, the motorcycle battalion and the engi-neers. In the far west, and in touch with the enemy, was a battlegroup composed of tanks and artillery.

Rommel could be well pleased with what he had achieved at the end of that opening day of a campaign in which he was directing a panzer Division in action for the first time. The 7th was so far in advance of the sister divisions on either flank that there was only wireless contact between them. He realised that his Command, with both flanks uncovered and forming a shallow salient in the Allied front, might be attacked and destroyed, but it was a calculated risk and one he was prepared to take. Corps laid down as divisional objective for the sec-ond day of Gelb the crossing of the Ourthe river. Rommel ordered the engineers to erect a bridge at Hotton, and by 0400 this had been built and the first vehi-cles were moving over it. The crossing was not restricted to that single place; a ford and several intact bridges provided additional points from which the advance was pressed forward.

Several crises arose during the morning. The probability that a Franco-Bel-gian force would move against the divisional salient was realised in the early hours of the morning, when the left-flank units came under attack. To counter the threat Rommel brought the panzer regiment forward to the threatened area and ordered an infantry attack to comb the deep woods which are a feature of that region. An hour or two later French artillery fire blanketed with a hurricane of fire the sector across which the rifle regiment was advancing. Rommel moved forward to accompany the infantry and saw waves of French tanks moving for-ward out of the woods. His infantry units came under an attack by the French armour, and to cover the Rifles he ordered the divisional gunners to lay a strong curtain barrage between the first and second waves of enemy tanks. The second line of French AFVs refused to face the explosions and turned tail, leaving the first wave to advance without support. The German gunners then switched targets and opened fire on those vehicles. Soon five of them had been destroyed, forcing the survivors to vacate the field. The infantry advance resumed.

The events and successes of the first two days' campaigning set the pattern for the subsequent days and weeks. On 13 May, according to the divisional war diary, '... the Maas was crossed between Houx and Dinant by 7th Rifle Regiment'. Those bare and sober words cover a spectacular military feat. They announced that in a single day Rommel had gained and was holding a bridgehead across one of the great rivers of Europe. The French High Command had been confident that the Maas, the first major obstacle barring the way to the Channel, could be held for at least a week. Events proved that it could not, but it was not just Rommel's skilful generalship that inspired his men, but also the example he set. At a pontoon bridge site the Engineers came under a long and sustained artillery barrage as well accurate sniper fire. Rommel drove to the site and set to work hauling baulks of timber with the sappers, working up to his waist in water, and by personal example brought the work forward. To conceal the bridging site from French artillery observers he gave orders to set fire to houses close to the bridge. Soon, huge smoke clouds covered the area. The sniper fire still presented a problem, and his solution was to line up a panzer group along the edge of the river. The fire from their main armament and machine-guns soon silenced the French.

Rommel had been told years earlier by General Beck, one of his superiors, that the task of a divisional commander was to plan attacks using maps and a telephone; there was no need to move out of his divisional headquarters. But that was not Rommel's style.

The line of the Maas river had been defended by formations from two French Divisions backed by strong artillery. That strong defence was further enforced when the Allied High Command massed tanks and guns, determined to destroy the 7th Division's bridgehead. To confuse the Allied defence plans, Rommel frequently changed the divisional thrust line so that his panzer thrusts out of the bridgeheads often overran French artillery units which believed themselves to be safe behind their own front line. Behind the thrusting panzers were small pockets of French and Belgian infantry bypassed by the speed of the 7th's advance. They were left by the panzers and mopped up by the follow-up infantry regiments.

Unternehmen Gelb was proving a brilliant success, despite the fierce and at times fanatical defence put up by the Allied formations. Although all the panzer Divisions were making great progress, the advance by the 7th was so successful that the Corps commander placed under Rommel's command those elements of 5th Panzer which had at last come across the Maas. Hoth also set new and distant objectives which the amalgamated panzer force was to achieve. Allied tank formations, some units fielding 32-ton monsters, advanced into action to destroy the Maas bridgehead, but Rommel ordered Stuka strikes. The dive bombers swept down, breaking the cohesion of the Allied armoured assaults and knocking out a number of tanks. On the ground it was a different matter. The pak gunners of the 7th quickly realised that the shells of the standard 3.7cm anti-tank gun could not penetrate the thick armour of the French vehicles, so they fired at their wheels and tracks, crippling those machines they were unable to 'kill'. It was at this time that Rommel was wounded. The panzer in which he was riding to reach his forward units had come under fire and had been crippled.

With the defeat of the Allied tank attacks against the Maas perimeter, 7th Panzer Division broke out of the restricting bridgehead. Rapid thrusts and the sudden appearance of its panzers miles behind the Allied front led to it being given the name 'Ghost Division'. Up to the Maas breakout, the campaign in the west had been fought conventionally, though at a very fast pace. From the time of the breakout the full tactical exposition of the 'blitzkrieg' technique was employed, and the speed confounded the Allies. For the operations of 14 May Rommel divided his Division and led the right-hand column in person. The 7th struck into the French 9th Army, causing its commander deep concern. General Georges, worried that his flanks were not sufficiently protected, ordered his Army to withdraw, and that retrograde movement opened a gap between it and the neighbouring 2nd Army. Quick to exploit the opportunity, Guderian poured his panzer forces into the breach in the Allied line. The chance to achieve a complete breakthrough had come and had been taken.

The 7th met heavy fighting in the Philippeville area, including attacks by French heavy armour. These were repulsed. All along 7th Panzer's line of advance there was heavy fighting as the strung-out divisional column was attacked by French units which, bypassed by the spearhead formations, debouched from the woods around Vedeces. Rommel raced from his position with the leading panzer group back to the Vedeces, and having put in a battlegroup against the French infantry, then spent time effecting a junction between his leading and follow-up formations. This was badly needed, for 7th Panzer's next objective was a set-piece attack; to capture and pass through an extension of the Maginot Line defences.

The divisional reconnaissance battalion, leading the advance, was struck by French tank attacks but beat them off and closed up on the outworks of the French defensive line. Rommel spent time disposing his units. The divisional objective was the town of Avesnes, to the west of Sivry, behind the Maginot Line. It would therefore be necessary to fight a way through the Line before the objective could be gained. The battle to take out the defences and capture the town demonstrated Rommel's ability to fight a conventional operation equally as well as those involving fast, mobile advances through strongly-held enemy territory. Using a First World War artillery technique, the divisional artillery fired a long and heavy barrage to seal off the 'walls' of the sector which was to be attacked. The barrage then switched to the ground across which the attack was to be made. Shortly before 1800, the time set for the panzer assault, the gunners fired smoke shells to create a screen. Covered by that dense cloud, the panzer formations had to cover 4km of open ground before they reached the permanent defences of the Maginot Line.

The AFVs, with Rommel in a command tank, made their way slowly forward through the smoke. The Assault Pioneers, leading the assault on foot, attacked cupolas and individual forts and cut passages through the belts of barbed wire and mines, creating gaps through which the panzers rolled forward. As the AFVs rumbled past the forts they opened fire at cupolas and into embrasures, while the follow-up infantry finished off the dazed and confused enemy troops inside them. Late in the evening the point units of the panzer regiment were close to a breakthrough. At 2300 the divisional machine-gun battalion and the panzer reconnaissance battalion, with Rommel still in the lead vehicle, went into the final assault. For this panzer charge Rommel ordered his vehicles to advance at best possible speed with all guns firing; contrary to standard operational procedure, in which AFVs halted to fire their main armament.

The force of the German attack and the unusual use of armour were irresistible, and when the panzers reached the Avesnes road Rommel knew they had broken through and had gained the objective. They were now free to open the pursuit stage of the battle. This carried the 7th to Landrecies, where its vehicles crossed the bridge over the Sambre and were ready to push on to Le Cateau when Rommel ordered them to halt. The Division was in a 48km-long salient, was dangerously over-extended and was being attacked along most of the length of that salient. The capture of the Sambre bridge at Berlimont brought up 5th Panzer, still under Rommel's command, to form line with the 7th. That evening, Rommel's satisfaction at the advances made was increased when a signal was received announcing the award to him of the Knight's Cross of the Iron Cross. He could be well pleased with his Division's accomplishments. In ten days' campaigning it had advanced more than 300km, including one spectacular night drive of more than 90km. This was a rare operation; in those days it was unusual for armour to drive or fight by night.

Bitter battles marked the next few days, and the 7th was held along the line of the Canal du Nord. The attack to carry the Division across the canal opened at 0140 on 20 May. Once again, Rommel formed his panzer regiment into two columns and rode into battle heading one of these. During the advance his men met for the first time soldiers of the BEF who were defending Arras. Rommel, who had already escaped capture once, faced that danger a second time when French tanks attacked his escort group and cut it off from the main body of the Division. Only when the vehicles of the panzer regiment raced to the scene was the situation restored and the commander rescued.

As the Allies were pushed back towards the Channel coast their resistance stiffened and their counterattacks against the 7th, once again strung out along a thin, unprotected salient, became fiercer. At Arras, for example, a British attack by 4th Royal Tank Regiment (RTR) struck so hard that fearful reverberations of this reverse were felt up to OKW level. In a conversation at the end of the campaign Hitler remarked to Rommel: 'We were very worried about you'. The cause of that worry had been real enough. The attack by 4th RTR struck Rommel's lorried infantry, and when the pak gunners tried to engage the British tanks they found that their armour, like that of the French AFVs, was proof against the standard German anti-tank-gun shell. Just when it seemed that the charge by the RTR would fragment the division (the tanks had already overrun a battalion of 6th Rifles), an improvised anti-tank gun screen of 10.5cm weapons was wheeled into line and within minutes had destroyed twenty of the British machines.

Rommel was in the front line throughout that long day, and during one British charge he personally directed the fire of each artillery piece. The determined resistance of the British force was an unpleasant shock to 7th Panzer, which lost six Panzer III and three Panzer IV in the fighting, as well as nearly 400 men killed in action. At first light on 22 May the British assaults were renewed, but Rommel countered them and put the leading elements of his Division across the Scarpe river. Once again he headed in person a column of armour and infantry.

The advance reached the La Bassée canal, but then came Hitler's order halting the advance of the panzer Divisions closing in on Dunkirk. A few days later the order was rescinded, and Rommel was advised that, for the operations planned to seize the heights to the west of Lille, 5th Panzer Brigade had been placed under his command. This meant that he was now directing the armoured spearhead of Army Group 'A'. Working pragmatically and reinforcing the successes gained by Hoth's Corps, OKW had changed the point of maximum effort of Army Group to the sector on which Rommel was operating.

The speed at which he moved that spearhead was bewildering to the Allies. The 7th overran French units on the roads and created confusion in the Allied rear areas. There was worse confusion to come. At 1800 on 27 May the three panzer regiments under Rommel's command struck like a single steel fist into the French positions. The impetus of that thrust convinced many enemy soldiers that their army was fighting a foe who could not be defeated. Demoralised in morale and defeated in spirit, they began to surrender in their hundreds. Shortly after midnight on 27/28 May the 7th cut the main Lille–Armentières road and pushed the advance forward, fighting down the Allied counterattacks launched against it. During the 28th, Rommel's Division, which had been fighting without pause for eighteen days, was taken out of the line and 5th Panzer Brigade passed out of his control. Around Dunkirk the British Army was beginning to take ship for the United Kingdom, and the whole area behind the Channel coast was in German hands. The battle for Flanders was at an end.

The 7th Panzer Division went back into the line to take part in the battle for France which followed the campaign in Flanders. The so-called Weygand line, set up to defend the heart of France, was soon penetrated, and with Rommel's Division in the van the German advance swept southwards, 'bouncing' the great rivers of France. Then the 7th's thrust line was altered and it was directed to strike for St Valéry and the Channel coast. The offensive to gain the new objectives opened at 0430 on 10 June, and so quickly brushed aside the opposition that by mid-afternoon the advance guard had reached the sea. The War Diary entry for 11 June records that the 7th '... gained the high ground to the west of St Valéry', and that the divisional artillery had opened fire on shipping trying to take off the 51st Highland Division.

Rommel sent a written demand for the garrison of St Valéry to surrender, but his ultimatum was rejected. The war diary paid tribute to the hard fighting qualities of the British troops, and specifically the Highland Division. The British formations were under French command and had to comply with the orders given by their ally. The French GOC decided to fight no longer, and the result of his decision is shown in the diary entry for 12 June, which states: '[The Division] forced the unconditional surrender of the English [sic] and the French troops in and to the south of St Valéry'.

That victory was followed by a non-stop 240km drive, completed in a single day and led by Rommel in a Command tank. The objective was the great naval base at Cherbourg, and its capture was the last major operation carried out by 7th Division in France during 1940. The French capitulation then brought to an end the fighting in the west, during which Rommel had demonstrated his mastery of armoured warfare. His Division had taken nearly 100,000 prisoners and more than 470 tanks. As a result of those achievements, Rommel had become a familiar name to both the German Army and the German public. Despite this, his next promotion to the rank of lieutenant general did not come for a further six months, and with it came command of a Corps and the posting to another theatre of operations, North Africa, where he was to win international fame.

NORTH AFRICA

An incompetently mounted and poorly executed offensive by Italian 10th Army during September 1940 had been flung back by Wavell's Army of the Nile. The British counteroffensive, opening on 9 December, advanced so quickly that within a few months it threatened to capture Tripoli, the capital city of the Fascist North African colony. Hitler feared that, if the Italian Army in Africa was defeated, Mussolini would sue for peace. That would leave exposed to British attack the whole southern flank of Nazi occupied Europe. To prevent his Axis partner's collapse, a small German ground and Luftwaffe force would be sent to Libya; not merely to bolster Italian morale, but also to block a further British advance towards Tripoli. Hitler accepted OKW's advice that a single panzer Corps would be sufficient for the task, and the Afrika Korps was created. Rommel was chosen to command Afrika Korps, and the directive he was given stated that he was to hold Tripolitania at all costs.

On 6 February 1941 OKW issued instructions for Unternehmen Sonnen-blume to begin, and the first transport of German units sailed, disembarking in Tripoli five days later. Rommel paid a lightning visit to his new Command area, and at a subsequent meeting with Hitler laid out his intended strategy. He planned to set up a blocking line, along which he would dispose the two Divi-sions of his Corps; the 5th Light and 15th Panzer, once these had come across from the Italian mainland and disembarked in Tripoli. Together with two Italian Divisions, he would then operate against the British Army of the Nile in a series of swift aggressive/defensive actions.

If we anticipate the events which took place during the spring of 1941, we can see that Rommel's first mini-offensive ran more smoothly than the German commander could have anticipated. This was because Churchill had decided to aid the Greeks in their war against the Axis powers. To do so he had been obliged to withdraw a major part of Wavell's army from Africa and deploy it in Greece. Left behind in the desert was a reduced British contingent, just sufficient to gar-rison the conquered Italian territories and observe Gariboldi's 10th Army.

Rommel's methods of conducting warfare in the deserts of North Africa owed more to naval operations than to conventional land battles. The desert, like the great oceans, was a vast and almost featureless wilderness which, in the words of one German senior officer, was 'a tactician's paradise but a quarter-master's hell'. Rommel's first operation erupted into action not long after the first elements of his Corps had disembarked, and the speed with which he moved against the British force not only brought him quick military victories, but also introduced into the German language the new verb 'to rommeln'; to overwhelm and to confound an opponent through fast and decisive action.

So successful was Rommel that one British general found it necessary to mount a campaign pointing out that the German GOC was no superman, but merely a commander who had had a lot of luck. He was not entirely correct in his judgement. Rommel was not only a leader who could produce victories; he also had a charisma which made him immediately popular with the soldiers of both sides. He was less popular with his superiors in OKW. They considered that his method of being forward and leading from the front might be excusable in a divi-sional commander, but was wrong for a man who was leading a Corps. It was Rommel's good fortune that he had a succession of Chiefs of Staff who thought as he did and acted as he would have done.

It was his misfortune that the African theatre of operation, which had held the whole attention of the German nation in the spring of 1941, was relegated to the status of a sideshow by the summer of that year. The war against the Soviet Union took all the headlines. Because of that reduction in importance from a major to a minor theatre of war, at least so far as the Supreme Command was concerned, Africa and Rommel's force had a low degree of priority in the matter of supplies. This was particularly true of fuel oil, with the result that the panzers of the Afrika Korps were frequently immobilised. Rommel knew that the British were more lavishly equipped than his Corps, and advised those who came with lists of demands that they should take what was needed from the enemy.

On 13 February 1941 Rommel sent 3rd Reconnaissance Battalion to establish how close Wavell's Army had advanced towards Tripoli, while he disposed the arrangement of the units of the blocking force. The reconnaissance battalion reported, among other details, that the British units were not deployed for battle. This was welcome news indeed, and Rommel decided to mount a preemptive strike. It was to be a classic pincer attack, and although it was not successful in all its particulars it exposed British tactical weaknesses and demonstrated that German soldiers were capable of fighting in North Africa's tropical conditions. Although he was directly subordinate to the Italian GOC, Rommel bypassed all the layers of authority and on his own initiative undertook an offensive which, by capturing the Agedabia wells, opened the way for an advance into Cyrenaica.

During the Agedabia battle he re-used the tactic which had proved itself in France. Faced with superior British armoured forces, he set up lines of 88mm guns and induced the tank regiments to charge them, killing the British machines in a rain of armour-piercing shells. Rommel knew that just pushing Wavell's Army back into Egypt would not produce the victory that was needed. He had to destroy completely the British host and the British presence in North Africa. All his battles from the spring of 1941 to the early autumn of the following year were intended to achieve that final solution on the battlefield. This was denied him.

Following on from the initial success at Agedabia, the battle for Mechili was fought on 8 April 1941, and a few days later, with the British in retreat, the Axis armies struck for Tobruk. The capture of that deep-sea port was vital to future Axis strategy, but it did not fall at that time. Thwarted but not disheartened by the failure to capture Tobruk, Rommel drove eastwards and seized both Bardia and Sollum. The British retreat to the gateway to Egypt was eventually halted, and Wavell's army regrouped. Towards the middle of the year, in June 1941, Rommel decided to build up his forces in the eastern outpost; those around Halfaya. In his planning for future battles he needed to carry out this operation to build a strong jump-off point, even though the armoured strength of his Corps had been reduced to less than a hundred 'runners'.

Corps headquarters ordered a long-range penetration to reach Halfaya via Sidi Rezegh. Rommel divided his force. Leaving a containing group around Tobruk, he led a 'dash to the wire', stressing to his subordinate commanders that there was to be no halt to fight; the priority was to reach Halfaya pass. The 15th Panzer Division, with 5th Light on its left flank and the Italian 'Ariete' Division in support, drove eastwards. The appearance of German and Italian armour so deep in the British rear areas created alarm among Eighth Army's 'tail' units. Exploiting that insecurity, Rommel and his Corps advanced into Egypt.

British countermeasures to meet the German thrust included the order for Eighth Army to recapture the Halfaya area. Wavell's counteroffensive opened, but was quickly broken off with a heavy loss of armour. Rommel sent an order to 15th Panzer Division: 'Halfaya will be held and the enemy beaten'. At that place a short line of 88mm guns, backed by some vehicles of Eighth Panzer regiment, destroyed more than 60 attacking British tanks. Two days of inconclusive fighting followed, and then, on 16 June, Rommel took a calculated risk and ordered a general assault to destroy the British around Halfaya. The battle ended with the loss to Western Desert Force of 200 tanks.

On 5 August 1941 the German contingent in Africa was expanded to the strength of a Panzer Group, and Rommel, despite shortages of fuel and men, prepared another attack to take out Tobruk. His offensive was pre-empted by the British host, now renamed Eighth Army, which intended to break the German ring and raise the siege of the port. The clash of armour at Sidi Rezegh resulted in the partial defeat of British 7th Armoured Division. After a short period to retrain and to regroup, Eighth Army was ready to attack once again.

Faced with the prospect of a strong new enemy offensive, Rommel pulled back the Axis forces to prepared positions at Gazala, leaving Tobruk still uncaptured. He decided to mount a summer offensive in 1942. This would erupt out of the Gazala positions and have the double aim of taking the port and destroying Eighth Army in the field. The operation opened, and part of Rommel's Italo-German host mounted diversionary attacks against the western wall of the British positions and held the attention of part of Eighth Army. Rommel then swung the main Axis force around the British flank at Bir Hachim, and in a clash of armour destroyed most of the opposing tank formations. Leaving just a holding force to confront Eighth Army, he swung back from the Gazala positions, attacked Tobruk and captured it by *coup de main*. Without pause, he then returned to the Gazala battlefield and opened a race to the ultimate objective; the Suez canal.

The Panzer Armee's advance was held in front of the El Alamein position, and in an attempt to outflank Eighth Army Rommel repeated the tactic that had proved so successful at Gazala. This time, however, it failed. Then Eighth Army opened its own offensive at El Alamein on 23 October 1942. Rommel, by this time promoted to the rank of feldmarschall, was on sick leave in Austria. Although not fully recovered, he returned to North Africa. Despite his personal intervention the Axis hosts were involved in an unequal battle, the outcome of which was decided by the flow of supplies and the numbers of soldiers. In the words of General Stumme, who had led the Panzer Army while Rommel was on sick leave: 'We stop one hole only to tear another one open'.

Within a few days the AFV strength of 15th Panzer Division had diminished to 39 'runners', while the 21st Panzer was a little better off with 98 machines. By 27 October the entire armoured strength of the Afrika Korps contingent of the Panzer Armee was just 114 machines. The Italians had 206 tanks. Faced with the prospect that his armoured force would be destroyed, Rommel requested permission to pull back, and was told by Hitler that his units were not to take one step back. It was, in the Fuehrer's words, a matter of victory or death. On 8 November Anglo-American formations landed in Algeria and Tunisia. Rommel now faced the prospect of being caught between the nutcracker jaws of Eighth Army in front of him and the Anglo-Americans behind. To add to his growing dissatisfaction with Hitler, he saw men and materials that were denied him in the days when a victory in the desert might have been gained being sent to Tunisia, where, at best, only a defensive perimeter could be held.

Slowly, Panzer Army Africa conducted a fighting retreat out of the Italian colonies and into Tunisia. During that withdrawal Afrika Korps turned at bay to fight off the British Imperial forces which pressed too closely, or mounted successful but minor offensives against the unskilled US forces. Despite those local triumphs, the Axis armies were contained in a perimeter whose area reduced with every passing week. Rommel accepted the true situation when he addressed a conference in Tunisia. Without supplies, he said, no bridgehead could be held, and even if the Axis forces, now known as Army Group Africa, held the best possible defensive positions, the life of the Army Group was a matter of months. Rommel was worn out by years of frustration and by the heavy responsibility he had borne, and his deteriorating health required that he undergo medical treatment in Germany. He flew out of Tunisia at the end of February 1943, three years after he had arrived in the African continent.

With the war in Africa lost, the prospect confronting the Axis Powers in the spring of 1943 was that the Allies could strike at any point they chose along the southern coasts of Europe. The Anglo-Americans invaded Sicily, and when that island fell they followed the victory with landings on the Italian mainland. Rommel's prediction that Mussolini was finished soon became fact. On the matter of the defence of Italy, Hitler's initial opinion was that the German Army could not hold the whole length of the Italian peninsula. Accepting that, he was prepared to evacuate the south and defend just the agriculturally fruitful and industrially rich northern provinces. The troops needed for that role in the north were formed into Army Group B, and Rommel was given command of it. The OKW directive was that, in the event of an Italian surrender, his Army Group was to seize and hold all the passes, railways and important installations in the north while Kesselring's army in the south of the country carried out a fighting retreat. When Kesselring's formations reached the northern Italian provinces Rommel would assume command of all the German forces.

On 15 August 1943 he sent Army Group B into action, and his units acted to such good effect that they soon controlled the whole of northern Italy. Rommel, fearful of Allied seaborne landings along the length of the peninsula, argued that the German forces below Rome should evacuate the southern provinces without delay and retreat into the defended northern area. Hitler, impressed by Kesselring's successful operations which were holding the Allied armies to the south of Rome, did not agree. How well Kesselring succeeded is shown by the fact that his soldiers held the Allies confined to the south for nearly nine months.

WESTERN FRONT

On 6 November 1943 Kesselring was appointed GOC in all Italy and Rommel was posted to north-west Europe, where an imminent Allied invasion was expected. He toured the length of the western seaboard from Denmark to southern France, improving the defences of the whole area. In June the strength of Army Group B, which he commanded, was bolstered when both 7th Army and 15th Army came on Army Group B's establishment. Nominally, Rommel now controlled the German forces in the west, but he was in fact subordinate to Field Marshal von Rundstedt, the Supreme Commander West. There was a conflict of opinion between the two men as to how operations were to be conducted once the Allied invasion had come in. Rommel planned to defeat the invaders at the water's edge, before they had established a bridgehead and while they were still disorganised. Rundstedt's plan was to let the Allies come ashore and then defeat them in set-piece battles.

When the Allies landed on 6 June 1944 Rommel was on leave in Germany, but he returned immediately to Normandy. He still hoped to seal off the beachheads and to destroy them, but Allied air power denied this, and he then proposed a withdrawal from Normandy. At a battlefield conference with von Rundstedt and Hitler on 17 June, both field marshals demanded freedom of action to move their forces as they saw fit. That demand was rejected by the Fuehrer, who not only criticised their handling of past operations, but uttered his usual demands for fighting to the last man and ordered a counterattack at Bayeux. On 29 June Rommel and von Rundstedt met Hitler again. The situation in Normandy had become critical, and when confronted with the facts the Fuehrer repeated the demand for his soldiers to fight to the last man. He also rejected their demands for a withdrawal.

Von Rundstedt was replaced by von Kluge, who, beginning optimistically, soon came to share Rommel's pessimism about the military situation. The basis of Rommel's despair was that, although by mid-July the field army had lost 100,000 men in Normandy, only 6,000 replacements had been received. To him it was clear that, given the present imbalance between losses and reinforcements, it could only be a matter of a few months before there were no longer enough soldiers to man the battle line. His defensive strategy was still able to confine the Allies within their beachheads, but any major German offensive operation was out of the question.

Rommel, who had always been conscious of Allied superiority in the air, was attacked by fighter-bombers on 17 July. His car crashed and he was seriously injured. Three days later a bomb exploded in Hitler's headquarters but failed to kill the dictator. Under interrogation, prominent people arrested for complicity in the bomb plot mentioned Rommel by name. Whether or not, or, indeed, how deeply he was involved in the assassination attempt did not matter to the Gestapo. Rommel was visited by two senior Army officers who gave him the choice of a public trial followed by the persecution of his family, or a suicide which would be disguised as a heart attack. Rommel chose the latter, took poison and was given a State funeral. An inspiring commander and a man respected even by his enemies was no more. Shortly after his suicide, the beachheads in which his defensive operations had penned the Allies burst open. The Allied armies swept out of Normandy, and in a series of offensives brought the war to an end within eight months.

The Panzer Count

Generalmajor Hyazinth von Strachwitz

Although the Christian name Hyazinth is an unusual one for a warrior, its use in the Strachwitz family dates back to the Middle Ages, when the custom was begun of giving that name to the first-born son in each generation. The Strachwitz's were rich and noble Silesian landowners, and across the centuries they served in the army of the Hohenzollerns when that family were the Electors of Brandenburg. They continued serving that family when they were elevated to become the kings of Prussia, and on into the time when the Hohenzollerns were proclaimed Emperors of Germany.

The Hyazinth von Strachwitz dealt with here was born on 30 July 1893 in Grosstein, Silesia. After undergoing cadet training in the Guards Depot at Lichterfelde and later at a military academy, he was gazetted as a second lieutenant in the élite Gards du Korps cavalry regiment. It was with that regiment that the young Lieutenant Strachwitz rode out to war in the autumn of 1914.

As the German battle plan unfolded, there was uncertainty in Supreme Headquarters as to where the main body of the French Army was located and how that army was deployed. In the days before the internal combustion engine made reconnaissances by motor vehicle or by aeroplane possible, cavalry patrols were the chief means of obtaining combat intelligence. German Supreme Command needed accurate intelligence, and the Chief of Staff of Guards Cavalry Corps asked for officer volunteers to carry out long-range patrols behind the French lines. Not only were the patrols to gain information such as numbers of French troops observed, the routes they were using and the sites of their camping grounds, but they were to cut telegraph lines and blow up railway tracks. Through such operations the rear areas of the French Army might be flung into a state of confusion. Furthermore, if confusion also entered into French civilian life, the consequences would affect the French political administration, which would be particularly disastrous if the government was forced to leave Paris.

The patrols, six in total from the Guards Cavalry Corps, were to carry out a half-circle sweep, meeting at a prearranged point when the sweep was concluded. There they would pool their accumulated knowledge, evaluate it and then return to base. To make them more mobile and less conspicuous, the patrols would not carry lances, and nor would they wear heavy metal parade helmets. Instead they would be dressed as Pioneers and would carry explosives and detonators.

Lieutenant Strachwitz, who had already carried out a number of short patrols, was one of the first officers to volunteer, and his action was followed by all of his Troop. He chose the sixteen best men, was briefed on the mission, then explained the tasks to his men and led them out. Less than an hour after the ride began Strachwitz and his men saw a French cavalry detachment, attacked it and drove the Chasseurs from the field. The patrol then rode on in the direction of the Seine. En route it clashed with an English cavalry patrol, and Strachwitz sent back his first report that French and British forces seemed to be concentrating along the line of the Marne river.

Two other German patrols, whose advance had been blocked when they met superior enemy forces, then linked up with Strachwitz. He assumed command and led the whole group on a 120km march to Melun on the Marne, having been told to check whether the Allies were concentrating their main armies in that area. Throughout the whole time that the patrol was moving deep into France, Strachwitz sent out small troops to blow up sections of the railway line. In a fashion which he was to repeat throughout his military life, he then chose to ignore the orders he had been given and, in a wide sweep, advanced so far behind the French front that he and his patrol reached the outskirts of Paris. The appearance of German cavalry so close to the capital caused an outbreak of panic. One aspect of the High Command plan had worked; small groups of German cavalry had indeed created confusion in the French capital. The French government and Army organised special detachments and spared no effort to locate and catch Strachwitz's patrol.

For more than six weeks he and his group rode across France, carrying out reconnaissance and blowing up bridges. Food was bought from villages and farms, because Strachwitz did not want his group to be accused of looting. Late one night he halted his patrol and sent out a demolition team to blow up a railway track. Although the horse minders had been keeping a good watch, they were surprised by the sudden appearance of a French patrol, whose first action was to stampede the German mounts. In the opinion of the French officers the Germans, now without horses, would be forced to surrender, but Strachwitz had no intention of giving up, and led his men on foot.

One autumn morning, after a night spent in the open in pouring rain, he and his soldiers were drying their wet clothes when they were attacked by a large body of French colonial troops. Snatching up what pieces of uniform they could, the Germans fled. Later that day they stopped at a farmhouse, where the young lieutenant bought old clothes and boots to clothe his men. He knew and accepted the risk that in the event being captured in civilian clothes they might not be considered soldiers deserving of prisoner-of-war status, but might be summarily shot as spies or saboteurs. Indeed, capture was not far off, and when it came, as Strachwitz had feared, the drumhead court-martial sentenced them all to death. The sentence was commuted, and Strachwitz was condemned to serve a prison sentence in a French penal colony. That sentence, too, was revoked, and he was moved from one civilian prison to another, on many occasions being taken from his cell and told that he was to be executed.

In the last years of the war Strachwitz was finally treated as a soldier and sent to a prisoner-of-war camp in south-east France. In the company of a fellow officer he carried out an escape attempt. The two men intended to climb the alpine peaks between France and Switzerland and thereby reach neutral Switzerland, but the attempt failed when Strachwitz fell from a rock face and was badly hurt. Because he needed medical treatment the two were forced to give themselves up, and there followed yet another court martial and the now ritual death sentence. Instead of facing a firing squad, Strachwitz was sent to a new camp, but by this time his physical condition had deteriorated. The wounds he had suffered in the fall from the rock face had not been treated by his French captors, and blood poisoning set in. His poor physical condition so alarmed the Swiss doctors of a medical commission that they insisted he be sent to Switzerland to recover. There he was restored to good health, but then learned that he was to be sent back to the prison camp. His avoided this by pretending to be mad. He worked so hard and played the part so convincingly that he was actually admitted into an asylum, and stayed there until the war's end.

When Strachwitz returned to post-war republican Germany he was so ill that he was discharged from the Service and spent a year on convalescent leave. Although Germany was in the throes of Red revolution, Strachwitz set out, initially on his own, to work against the communists and the terror regime they had set up. Members of the soldier-soviets had taken to tearing the epaulettes from officers' uniforms as an act of degradation. Strachwitz would not allow himself to be intimidated, and to show his contempt for the Reds and their actions he walked through the streets of Berlin wearing Garde du Corps uniform and defying the Soldateska to attack him.

There was also trouble at national level. The government of the newly created Polish State, determined to exploit Germany's military weakness, invaded her eastern provinces with the aim of annexing them and thereby gaining control of their rich coal and iron resources. Despite his poor health, Strachwitz flung himself into the task of forming local paramilitary defence units to fight Polish incursions and terror raids. Those defence formations eventually became known as the Freikorps, and the greater number of men who served in them were former front-line soldiers. The units were poorly armed to begin with, but the shortage of weapons and equipment was balanced by the greater combat experience of the Freikorps, and the determination that came from knowing that they were fighting, quite literally, for their home and hearth. Strachwitz had an answer to those men who complained that they were short of weapons and ammunition. He told them to take what they lacked from the enemy.

The term 'Freikorps' was an evocative one to Germans, recalling the volunteer militias created during the national uprising against Napoleon. Years after the Freikorps was disbanded, the Nazi Party sought to strengthen its claim to represent the 'real' Germany by claiming that its party formations were directly descended from the Freikorps organisation. It was true that much of the Nazi uniform insignia, as well as many unit descriptions, were taken over *en bloc* from that body. In the first months of its life, while the Freikorps was a grouping of local defence units, the tactics and combat efficiency of such formations as Strachwitz's held back the enemy incursions. The reputation gained by the Count and his group was such that the Poles placed a price on his head.

The last major battle of that war of the eastern frontier – one almost unknown outside the east German provinces – was fought around the Annaberg, a tactically important hill, but more importantly a place of great emotional and historic significance to the German population of Silesia. The key position of the Annaberg was stormed and taken first by one side and then by the other. When one major Polish assault captured the summit, a counterattack was launched to retake it. The honour of spearheading it was given to Strachwitz's detachment. Leading his men in a classically executed attack, and beating down at close quarters the opposition of the Polish defenders, Strachwitz fought his way uphill until he stood, as the first of his men, on the crest of the Annaberg. Shortly after that victory Polish efforts to detach the eastern provinces came to an end, and when hostilities ceased Strachwitz decided to go back to repairing and restoring the family estates, which had been neglected through the years of war. But he was too active a man to find satisfaction in a farming life, and his thoughts turned more and more to the military. By this time he had recovered his lost strength, and was aching to return to the Army.

The chance came when he attended the 1934 Army manoeuvres in Breslau, and was impressed by the armoured fighting vehicles. It was the first time he had seen motorised units being used in simulated attack and defence, and, fired by this, he reapplied to join the Army, choosing the armoured force as his Arm of Service. His application was approved, and he was gazetted to 2nd Panzer Regiment, there to learn the skills of his new trade. How well he succeeded was demonstrated in the campaign in Poland, where he made a name as a daring commander and led his men with such panache that stories about the exploits of the 'Panzer Graf' were soon current in Berlin.

He added to his reputation for daring action during the fighting in France and the Low Countries during the summer of 1940, carrying out deep raids in the Allied rear areas. The most celebrated example of his actions came during the campaign in France, when he and his driver entered a French town and found themselves isolated and driving towards a military barracks. Strachwitz realised that if his vehicle turned round and fled it would draw French fire. His panzer was quite alone; he was without any sort of support or back-up. Nevertheless, he boldly walked up to the sentry at the main gate and demanded, in fluent French, to speak to the orderly officer. When the man appeared, Strachwitz ordered that all the troops in the building be directed to surrender. If they did not immediately comply, he would order his panzer regiment to open fire. There was no panzer regiment behind him, but the French officer did not know that. The Frenchman gave the order and the garrison laid down their arms and allowed themselves to be taken prisoner.

A year later, as the commander of a tank battalion in 18th Panzer Division, Strachwitz led his unit into the war against the Soviet Union and into a number of such enterprises. During one mission in the first days of the new war, Soviet infantry attacked and great masses of men swarmed round his unit's vehicles. One panzer was hit and knocked out. Strachwitz immediately leaped from his own machine and attacked the Soviet soldiers closing in on the immobile machine, firing on them at close quarters with a machine pistol and showering them with hand grenades. During the fighting he was hit by a bullet which lodged in his body. Realising that it was neither dangerous nor painful, he had it cut out on the spot and carried on fighting.

Just as he had shown himself to be competent in the offensive, he proved that he was equally proficient in defensive fighting. At Vewrba he launched counterattacks against Russian tanks which had broken through the German line and were threatening the regimental supply columns. So ferocious was his opening charge that the Soviet armoured detachment halted in confusion. The enemy tanks then spun on their tracks and tried to retreat, but Strachwitz had no intention of letting them escape. He chased the fleeing Red armour, firing on the move, and the battle of pursuit continued even after nightfall. In that furious drive he crashed through the Soviet front lines and into their rear areas, passed through the artillery belt and shot up the batteries. For that action, the most recent of a whole series of such singlehanded missions, he was awarded the Knight's Cross.

For the crossing of the Bug river, panzers of his battalion were fitted with watertight rubber skins to make them submersible, and they crossed the river, climbed its eastern bank and set up a bridgehead there. When Strachwitz's panzer drove across the river bridge he was accompanied by General Nehring, the divisional commander. The General dismounted and the Panzer Graf promptly led the battalion into an action in which he destroyed a column of more than 300 soft-skin vehicles and a number of Russian gun batteries. Later, in the fighting around Uman, he again broke through the Russian front to attack and disperse enemy formations in the rear areas.

In the summer of 1942 the German Army opened a new offensive, Unternehmen Blau, and the opening assaults tore open the Red Army's battle line on the sector held by Paulus's 6th Army. Through that gap, Strachwitz, now a lieutenant colonel, pursued the retreating Russians and chased them towards the Volga. The objective of the German Army on the Eastern Front required that Paulus's 6th Army take out the city of Stalingrad. If the Germans could stop Russian shipping using that river, the Red Army's supply system would be deprived of one of its principal routes. Hube's XIV Corps was one of the finest units of 6th Army, and von Wietersheim's 16th Panzer Division, in which Strachwitz was now serving, was one of the best units in Hube's Corps. During the night of 23 August 1942 Strachwitz received a signal from Divisional Headquarters for his battalion to attack at 0415. First, however, he was to report to headquarters for a final briefing. It had been the Corps commander's understanding that 6th Army's principal objective was to reach the Volga. On the basis of new directives it now seemed that Supreme Headquarters had altered the priorities, and that reaching the river was to be an interim phase of 6th Army's operations. More important than the capture of Stalingrad, or so it now seemed, were the preparations for an advance into the steppeland leading to Astrakhan.

The plan of attack towards the Volga, which Hube's XIV Corps was to undertake, placed 16th Panzer in the centre, with 3rd Motorised Division on the right flank and 60th Motorised Division on the left. The distance from the Corps front line to the Volga was only 60km; less than a day's march under normal circumstances, and Soviet resistance had, to date, been weak. It seemed that the enemy had pulled out of his positions to the west of the river and had concentrated his forces either on the east bank or in the north, where they would threaten the advance of 6th Army's left flank.

When the advance to the Volga opened there was still little resistance to Strachwitz's panzer thrust. Opposition grew when his unit reached the airfield of Gumrak, but Strachwitz called down the Stukas and, in a combined air and ground strike, the Reds were dispersed and the advance rolled again. Within twelve hours of the operation opening, Strachwitz and his men had reached the Volga between Rynok and Spartakova and stood at the northern end of the city. His was the first vehicle to enter Stalingrad, and German reports spoke of the panzers being greeted by the local civilians with flowers and fruit. It seemed that even that far into Russia the ordinary people saw the Germans as liberators.

In his usual confident fashion Strachwitz radioed to divisional headquarters: 'Have reached the Volga as ordered. Losses; one man. Am organising a crossing of the river so as to create a bridgehead on the eastern bank.' Upon receipt of that news both the Corps and divisional commanders drove to Strachwitz's tactical headquarters. There the Panzer Graf pointed out that the opportunity to cross the Volga had to be taken without delay, otherwise the enemy could bring forward such a mass of reinforcements that a crossing of the river would soon be impossible. A report from 3rd Motorised Division affected the Corps commander's decision. The wireless message stated that strong enemy attacks were coming in from the north against his left flank. Hube decided that, attractive though Strachwitz's proposal was, it could not be realised.

Instead, the Panzer Graf and his battalion were sent forward to support 3rd Motorised and directed to reach a point about 20km from the outskirts of the Stalingrad city area. From there, he and his unit went out on a deep-penetration patrol and surrounded a Soviet aerodrome. His battalion's vehicles were driven forward to within gun range and were so well camouflaged as to be undetectable. The panzers opened fire on Russian aircraft trying to land and destroyed 158 of them. But that and other tactical successes could not change the fact that the attitude of the Russian civilians had changed under direction of the Party officials, and the Red Army's resistance was now rock hard. Stalingrad had become a prestige objective, and Stavka poured masses of men and material into the battle.

In the weeks of bitter fighting the German military situation began to deteriorate, and as the Red Army closed in on 6th Army the supply system was affected. Not only food, but arms and ammunition began to run short. Strachwitz adopted the solution he had found during the 1920s war with Poland; take what you need from the enemy. At night he led infantry-style commando raids which took from the Red Army the material his battalion lacked. He did not spend much time in Stalingrad town, but operated in his usual fashion, creating confusion in the enemy's rear areas and 'killing' a great many Russian vehicles in a succession of panzer battles. Russian counteroffensives soon surrounded Hube's Corps, and the commander ordered all units to break out. The move was detected by the Russians, who raced forward, overran the rearguard detachments and slaughtered them.

In the middle of the battle which ensued as the Red hosts struck the main body of Corps, an order came from Hitler, cancelling the withdrawal and directing the units to retrace their footsteps and fight to regain and reoccupy their old positions. The order was carried out but the losses, particularly in Strachwitz's battalion, were high. With the few vehicles remaining to him he could not afford to fight prolonged battles. Instead, he had to mount lightning hit-and-run strikes which held down and dominated the Soviet armoured armadas. He had to undertake small hit-and-run operations because he was under orders to prevent his last panzers from being destroyed. They had become the backbone of Hube's force.

In military history there are many men who have gained a reputation for skill, bravery and outstanding ability in a short period of time. Strachwitz was such a man, and he was known throughout the German Army on the Eastern Front. He nonchalantly ascribed his battle successes not to his skill, but to a sixth sense which warned him if he was about to be attacked by the enemy. One example of this occurred when he was carrying out another of his deep sweeps. A long column of T 34s rolled over the crest of a hill and came down towards the area in which his small group lay camouflaged. He did not lead his panzer detachment out to engage the enemy, for his instinct told him that there were more Soviet machines beyond the crest. Slowly and carefully he positioned his vehicles so that they formed an ambush.

The Soviet machines advanced, unaware that a German force was lying in wait. Strachwitz gave orders that no shot was to be fired until he opened the battle. He then allocated to the crews the Russian tanks which each was to engage. Only when everything was ready did he open fire, destroying the leading T 34 with the first round. He then 'killed' the next one. One of his group took out another vehicle of the Russian detachment, and the battalion went on to smash the machines in the centre of the Russian line. Within an hour more than 150 enemy tanks lay broken or burning, and not one of Strachwitz's group had even been hit. He emerged victorious from such small unit actions again and again. A couple of days after that success Strachwitz was badly wounded and was flown to a hospital in Breslau. While he was undergoing treatment he learned that he had been awarded the Oak Leaf to the Knight's Cross. By the time he was fit enough to return to active service, 6th German Army had surrendered at Stalingrad and his old battalion had been destroyed in the fighting there.

His superiors' confidence in him was shown when Strachwitz, now holding the rank of colonel, was given command of a battalion of the new 'Tiger' tanks in the crack 'Grossdeutschland' formation. He was desperately keen to test the Tigers in action, and the chance came during the battle for Kharkov in 1943. The Red Army's winter offensive was advancing upon the city, threatening to trap the defending forces of Field Marshal Manstein. The Soviets were prepared to fight hard and long to capture the city, and anticipated a hard battle because they knew Hitler had ordered his Divisions inside Kharkov to hold it to the last.

As part of the Kharkov garrison, 'Grossdeutschland' was bound by Hitler's no-withdrawal order. To obey such a command was against all military logic, and Manstein explained to SS General Hausser the strategy he intended to follow. To Manstein it was clear that the Soviet offensive was losing momentum. The Red Army, driven on by Stavka's orders, had overreached itself and had outrun its supplies. Manstein intended, first, to evacuate Kharkov, and then, choosing the moment, to charge forward in a counterattack of such weight that it would roll back the Russian forces in utter confusion. To carry out such an operation meant disobeying the Fuehrer's order not to evacuate the city, but both Hausser and Manstein were prepared to face Hitler's wrath to save their soldiers from being needlessly sacrificed. Kharkov was evacuated and then retaken in the planned counteroffensive.

During the operation to recapture the city, intelligence reached the 'Grossdeutschland' Division that a column of T 34s and KVs was bearing down, and the order was given for the enemy tanks to be engaged immediately. It was late evening, and Strachwitz, in an outpost position in a village forward of the main battle line, saw the Russian armour pour over the crest of a ridge some 4km distant. He decided not to engage them at that time and at that range, but to gain the element of surprise by waiting all night and withholding fire until first light. By that time the enemy machines would not only be closer and clearly visible, but, because there had been no opposition to their advance, they would also be off guard. During the hours of darkness, as Strachwitz's group lay waiting, the sound of Russian AFVs was clearly heard. Another wave of enemy machines was coming forward over the crest to reinforce the first group.

Initially, the Soviets made no attempt to move forward. Clearly, the Russian commanders, not knowing the strength of the Germans facing them, were loath to advance into the unknown. They were waiting for the German panzer men to move and betray their positions. Strachwitz knew the value of concealment, and had ensured that all of his machines were completely hidden from sight. Many had been driven inside the peasant huts of the village. Late in the night, believing the village to be undefended, the Red commanders issued the order to advance, and two groups of Russian tanks drove down toward the seemingly deserted huts and houses. But there was still some hesitancy on the Russian side, and the groups halted and waited outside the semicircular collection of straw-roofed huts. Later during the night the Soviet armoured fighting vehicles moved forward again, slowly. Some tanks fired incendiary shells which set alight the straw covered huts and lit the darkness. Still there was no movement from the German side, and the Soviets, becoming more confident, at last entered the village and settled down to rest for the remainder of the night.

At first light Strachwitz saw that the Soviet command vehicle was less than 50m from his own. In whispers he passed fire orders, and the 88mm gun on Strachwitz's Tiger fired an armour-piercing round which took off the turret of the enemy vehicle. The firing of the guns of Strachwitz's other Tigers was submerged in the crashing detonation of the exploding T 34, but the effects of those shots were soon visible. Within minutes eighteen T 34s or KVs were burning. The remaining machines spun round on their tracks, making every effort to escape, but were shot to pieces before they could get out of the village. The entire group lay wrecked upon the battlefield. For that success the Panzer Graf was awarded the Swords to the Knight's Cross.

Strachwitz's active mind was always considering new tactics to gain the advantage over the enemy. One idea he put forward was to mount a loudspeaker on a panzer and broadcast an announcement inviting the Red Army soldiers to desert and bring their arms with them. His proposal was tried, and brought almost immediate results, with a stream of deserters coming in. One morning a Red Army man in an unkempt condition was brought in. He claimed to be the commander of 190th Division of the Red Army, which was in the line opposite Strachwitz's unit. In a casual fashion the Panzer Graf told the Russian officer that he would not accept his individual surrender, but that he must return to his own lines and bring his Division back with him. The Russian colonel protested that for him to return to his own lines was to invite summary execution, but his arguments were in vain, and after a great deal of discussion he realised that Strachwitz would not give way. The colonel left, and within two hours returned to the German lines followed by his men.

Shortly after that episode Strachwitz was wounded once again, but he insisted upon returning to his regiment before his wounds had healed. On 1 April 1944 he was promoted to the rank of generalmajor, and was told that he was to take over command of 1st Panzer Division, with the additional responsibility of senior panzer officer in Army Group North. Under his command there would be, in addition to 1st Panzer, two other panzer Divisions and a Tank Hunting Brigade. The one drawback to the new command structure was that not one of the formations he was supposed to command had yet arrived on his sector. The Panzer Graf complained, and Field Marshal Schoerner, the officer commanding Army Group North, ordered him to fly to Libau on the Baltic, where it was believed the panzers were to be unloaded. Strachwitz found that the port had no facilities to cope with heavy armoured fighting vehicles, and worse was to come. Despite repeated assurances from Fuehrer headquarters, the Divisions placed under his command had not even left en route to Libau. Again Strachwitz complained, and finally Guderian sent ten panzers and fifteen armoured troop transports. That was all that could be spared.

During this period of frustration Strachwitz demonstrated another example of his calculated casualness. He radioed the Red Army units opposing him, stating his intention to attack them and giving the exact time and precise place. He carried out the attack at the time and place specified, but the Soviets had pulled their units from that sector, hoping to lure him into a trap. The withdrawn enemy forces were concentrated in a small area from which they intended to launch their own destructive counterattack, aimed at destroying the Panzer Graf. Strachwitz's group cruised through the Russian line, reached the enemy's concentration area and immediately shot the Soviet force to destruction. The group then drove on into the Red Army's rear areas, engaging and destroying every target it met. Driving and firing, it maintained its advance until it reached a point some 150km behind the Russian line. Then, making an about turn, the group set course for their own lines. Despite the long march and the opposition, the detachment returned with all vehicles intact and undamaged.

A short time later the Panzer Graf undertook another operation of the type for which he had become famous. OKH needed to launch an offensive to break the Russian encirclement of Riga and recapture the town. German intelligence had learned that Stavka intended to launch an offensive aimed at the destruction of Army Group North. That Soviet assault would start from the town of Tuccum, which the Red Army had recently captured. That town was equally as important to the defence plans of OKH as it was to the Soviet attack plans, and

Army Group North ordered that it was to be recaptured. German intelligence was of the opinion that Tuccum was strongly held by the Red Army and that, therefore, any attack to capture it would have to be made in force. Such an operation could have succeeded had Strachwitz had the formations of his new Command to hand, but his three panzer Divisions had still not arrived.

He asked for authority to operate independently, and his requested was granted. He planned to advance eastwards, moving along a line to the south of Tuccum under a strong artillery barrage. Before the panzer group reached the city he would swing it northwards and the advance would bypass the town. He would then change direction again, and in a wide, southward-looping drive descend upon the town and seize it in a *coup de main*. He hoped that his frequent changes of direction would confuse the Soviets and unbalance their defence. It was a glorious morning when the Panzer Graf led his group of ten panzers and fifteen troop carriers across the start line. Driving at top speed, his small column attacked and captured a river bridge, together with a battalion of Soviet infantry. These he ordered to march back into the German lines, but he could only supply two of his men as escort. One Tiger stayed behind to hold the bridge, and his group raced on, shooting up Red Army columns on the road. More prisoners were taken, together with guns and tanks, and again these were marched into captivity under a minimal escort. The drive lasted all day, without pause or rest, for he had told his crews that they would eat in Tuccum. At daybreak the group reached the outskirts of the city, and saw drawn up before them a battalion of 48 Red tanks, arrayed as if for a parade.

The gunnery officer of the German warship *Lutzow* had travelled with Strachwitz's column to act as an artillery forward observation officer, and he directed the fire of the ship's 28cm guns on to the tanks packed nose to tail in the town's market square. Within seconds shells crashed down and destroyed the majority of the Soviet machines. Strachwitz shot up the only two tanks not destroyed by naval gunfire, then organised the collection of prisoners before reporting to Army Group North that he had captured Tuccum. From a nearby Russian petrol point he filled the fuel tanks of his group and ordered two of his panzers to stay in the city while he and the other three machines set out to break the ring around Riga. As his group raced northwards he saw dust clouds on his right flank. A Soviet tank Corps and two infantry Divisions were moving forward to reinforce the encirclement. Seeing the German AFVs in his own army's rear area, the commander of the Soviet group drew the wrong conclusion. Thinking that he and his unit were surrounded, he promptly surrendered his whole force to Strachwitz, who delegated five of his transport lorries to guard it.

On the outskirts of Riga his few vehicles shot and destroyed a number of Red Army tanks and captured a field hospital, which he left to be guarded by two panzers. He then took the remaining troop transports and broke through the Soviet lines. The Grenadiers debussed from the transports to fight down the

Soviet units which were now counterattacking his very small group, while he drove on and entered the town. On the way into the centre of Riga his Tiger was halted by a group of German generals who greeted him with cries of 'Well done, lieutenant'. Strachwitz wore no rank badges, so the mistake was understandable, but as he climbed down from the turret he told the group members that they were mistaken; he was a general. When they asked the whereabouts of the other vehicles of his Command, he replied that they were guarding prisoners. Days later a strong panzer group reached Riga. The ring around the town was broken, and the transport of wounded and civilians began. The Panzer Graf's achievements had led to the capture of 18,000 prisoners, 28 batteries of artillery, and a mass of tanks, anti-tank guns and other weapons.

That victory brought the award of the Diamonds to the Oak Leaf of the Knight's Cross. Shortly after receiving that distinction the Panzer Graf was involved in a car crash so severe that it was considered unlikely he would survive. He had severe injuries to his head, ribs, legs, arms and hands. A strong constitution and personal determination pulled him through, and although he could barely hobble he reported himself fit for duty and set out to raise tank destroyer Brigades, Within weeks he had a unit of battle-hardened veterans, equipped with modern weapons. The war was now in its closing stages, and Strachwitz had no chance to lead his new unit into a major action. Nevertheless, he sent out small detachments and employed these in minor and tactical operations. At the war's end he fought his way through Czech partisan infested country to reach Bavaria, where he surrendered to the American forces.

When he was released from prisoner-of-war camp he had nothing but the clothes he wore. His estates had been confiscated by the Soviets, his wife and younger son were dead and his family dispersed. Strachwitz accepted an invitation from the Syrians to reorganise their agriculture and their army, but had barely completed the long and arduous task when a coup overthrew the government. The revolutionaries ordered his arrest. He and his new, young wife escaped across the border. Once more the Panzer Graf found himself penniless. He returned to Germany in 1951 and died there shortly afterwards.

The Airborne Innovator

Generaloberst Kurt Student

K urt Student was born in Neumark, Brandenburg, in 1890, the third son of a family of minor landed gentry. Despite its social position his family was not wealthy enough to give financial support to all four sons in the choice of their career. Kurt elected for the Army, joining the Military Junior Cadet school at Potsdam, from which he passed out at the age of 15 into the senior academy in Lichterfelde, Berlin. On 3 March 1910 he graduated and was accepted as an Ensign in the 1st Battalion of the Graf Yorck von Wartenburg Regiment. A year later, his probationary period ended, he was promoted to the rank of Leutnant.

Upon the outbreak of the First World War Kurt was sent on a pilot's training course, and was eventually transferred to the Air Force, serving for the whole of the war as an airman. In October 1916 he was given command of Jagdgeschwader 9, and during 1917 was wounded in aerial combat. At the war's end Student returned home and became another ex-serviceman bitter at the Allies and their harsh treatment of Germany, but he was not long out of uniform. Although a German air force with military aircraft was forbidden under the terms of the Treaty of Versailles, gliding had not been banned. It was to the Fliegerzentrale, the camouflaged name for the Air Ministry, that Student was posted, and there he joined other officers who, like him, were employed to pass on the knowledge they had gained on active service to the cadets of the forbidden air force.

In 1922 the German and Soviet governments signed the Rapallo Treaty, the undisclosed conditions of which included the offer of facilities for Germany to train her armed forces on Soviet territory. Thus the German Army and Air Force, denied the opportunities to test out new military theories in their own country, simply moved eastwards into Soviet Russia where those facilities were available. The principles of armour used in mass and closely supported by aircraft acting as flying artillery, the concept of fast warfare or blitzkrieg, had already been formulated. Now the theories needed to be tested in practice, and the vast steppeland gave the theorists the chance to prove and/or adapt their ideas. The panzer men were already training around Kazan when the candidates from the Fliegerzentrale arrived to carry out in powered aircraft those manoeuvres and tactics which glider training had not been able to duplicate. Although Student was once again able to pilot an aeroplane, he retained an interest in gliding and, as we shall see, was able to use that knowledge and expertise later in his career.

His time in Russia was brief, for he was ordered back to Germany to take up a regimental command in order to qualify for promotion. He returned to his parent regiment and spent five years in the post of battalion commander. During this period of regimental duty there was a political change in Germany. Adolf Hitler, leader of the Nazi Party (NSDAP), was named as Chancellor and lost no time in preparing to expand the armed forces of the Reich. This proved to be an easier task than he might have expected, for the western powers saw in Germany a bulwark against Soviet Russia, and were therefore complaisant in Germany's flagrant abuse of the restrictions of the Treaty of Versailles. The German Army, which the treaty had restricted to a strength of 100,000 men, had become, in reality, an Army of 100,000 NCOs and potential officers who would lead the Service when it expanded, as it was sure to do. A cadre of panzer men had been established out of those who had trained on the Russian steppes, and the officers of that armoured force were the men who would lead the panzer Divisions and Corps. An embryo Luftwaffe, still as yet without powered aircraft, had been created. The German armed forces were indeed expanded under the chancellorship of Adolf Hitler, and within two years the bayonet strength of the Army had been tripled, and the tanks and heavy artillery which had previously been forbidden were once again in its arsenal.

While these moves were taking place at Supreme Command level, Student, still serving as a battalion commander, was chosen to be Director of the Luftwaffe Technical Training School, and was transferred from the Army to the Air Force. Evidence of the growing power of Hermann Goering, Hitler's Party comrade and commander of the Luftwaffe, was seen in his insistence that the Training School of which Student was Director be detached from War Ministry control and placed under the Air Ministry. Goering was determined to make the Luftwaffe a separate branch of the armed forces, as completely independent of Army control as the Royal Air Force was in Britain.

Student was given the task of creating, almost from nothing, a new arm of Service comparable in power and influence with the long-established Army. He had to raise squadrons, organise the laying out of operational airfields, and set up barracks for the air and ground crew personnel, as well as organising the work schedules of the air staff whom he had to train. He was also given the responsibility of organising aircraft production. In common with most of his contemporaries, Student worked hard and long at these and all the associated tasks, driven on by the work ethic in which they had all been raised, and animated by the thought that they were rebuilding national pride in setting up highly efficient fighting forces.

In August 1935 Student was promoted to the rank of colonel, commanding the Flying Equipment Test and Research Centre in Rechlin. During his period of service in that establishment the aircraft types which Germany was to use in the Second World War were tested, found suitable and passed into series production. There was no mass production, as German industry had not yet reached that stage of development and aeroplanes were practically hand-built. That method of construction was to prove a disadvantage in time of war, but among the aircraft which came on stream at that time were the Messerschmitt Bf 109 and Bf 110 fighters, the Junkers Ju 87 dive bomber and the Heinkel He 111 bomber.

At the end of three years' hard work Student was posted from Rechlin to take up a field command. On 1 July 1938 the High Command of the Luftwaffe (OKL) decided to create an Airborne Division, and selected Student as the man to raise and lead it. From the start it had been accepted that the units of the new formation, 7te Flieger Division, would be transported by air to the combat zone and dropped by parachute over their objective. In the setting-up of his Division Student displayed his talent for organisation as well as a grasp of the role for which the paratroops would be trained. He had an interest in unusual weapons and tactics, and an almost intuitive feel for adapting these to his new command. Although that grasp was to lead him to consider new techniques for his paratroop force, he saw as his first priority the need to inspire the men under his command with the conviction that they were an unconquerable élite. He instilled this 'Springer Geist' (Paratroop spirit) thoroughly and at every level of command.

At the General's disposal in the formation of his Division was the paratroop training school in Stendal, which opened in 1937, and a fleet of Junkers Ju 52s which could be used not only to train the recruits but also to transport men or supplies. Student also had a small nucleus of trained paratroops around which he could form his division, for Hermann Goering, the Luftwaffe Commander in Chief, had established a paratroop unit from the Berlin police force. In addition, a paratroop battalion had been raised by the Army.

Because there were two types of paratroop formation; one controlled by the Army and one administered by the Luftwaffe, there were two points of view on how those units should be employed in war. The Army envisaged their employment in a strategic mode, while the Luftwaffe saw the airborne operations as being more tactical in nature. Both Services appreciated that, as in all operations, it would be necessary in an airborne mission to create a point of maximum effort (a Schwerpunkt), but they differed as to how this could be achieved. The Army favoured either mass paratroop drops or troops being airlanded behind the enemy front, on such a scale that they would overwhelm the opposing forces on the ground. The Luftwaffe solution was the 'drops of oil' technique, in which small groups of paratroops were dropped simultaneously and, upon landing, combined to form perimeters which would threaten the enemy line at a number of places. Any Luftwaffe perimeter which showed the potential to be successfully exploited would be reinforced and expanded to become the Schwerpunkt.

A compromise at OKW level laid down that in any operation carried out in conjunction with the Army, but in which the paratroops had a role, the Luftwaffe was to be responsible for the preparation and execution of its part of the battle plan, as well as for supply missions. Once the airborne drop had been completed and the formations had made contact with the main ground forces, the Luftwaffe units would come under Army control. Operations which would be wholly a Luftwaffe responsibility were those in which tactical targets which had not been destroyed by aerial bombing were to be attacked and captured by para-dropped or glider-borne troops. Despite that compromise, the Army authorities insisted that a mass of men would be needed to form a Schwerpunkt, and that the German forces had not, at that time, any such mass on establishment.

To overcome the Army's objection, OKW selected a standard infantry Division, the 22nd, and converted it to the role of an air-landing formation. That air-landed component would be carried in transport aircraft which would land on the aerodromes which other airborne forces, either dropped by parachute or glider landed, had captured. Student was involved at the highest level in the conferences and committees dealing with the tactics, weapons and equipment which the paratroops would use. Drawing upon his own experience, he pressed for the use of gliders, which could bring a group of men to within a metre or two of a given objective, thereby fulfilling the airborne need for landing a complete group of men directly on to the target.

When Student took over command, the 7th Airborne Division consisted of only two rifle battalions, an air-landing battalion, several companies of Service troops, a glider detachment and a training school. The General ordered a speeding up of recruitment and a tightening up of the divisional structure. He succeeded so well that, at the outbreak of war in September 1939, the 1st Regiment and two battalions of the 2nd were on establishment, with the third battalion of 2nd Regiment almost completely raised. An infantry regiment was also on strength, as was an artillery component fielding both field and anti-tank artillery and, in addition, the usual Service units. When war came, neither of the embryo airborne Divisions was employed operationally and both were held in reserve.

Standard German Army organisation specified that a force of two Divisions constituted a Corps. In the case of the airborne forces, that administrative move was not carried out, probably because the Army High Command was unwilling to relinquish one of its Divisions to the Luftwaffe. Student did not, therefore, become a Corps commander at that time, although he was GOC of 7th Division and had been appointed Inspector of Airborne Forces.

At the end of the Polish campaign, plans were laid for a War in the West to be carried out against the French and British armies positioned along the Belgian frontier. The German battle plan depended for its success on the bulk of the Army overcoming the defences of the Maginot line, but because of its great strength that line could not be taken by a conventional, direct assault. Alternative forms of attack would have to be employed if the German Army was to drive rapidly westwards, violating the neutrality of Holland and Belgium, before swinging southwards into France. To bring about that rapid westward advance the assault Armies needed to move without hindrance across a great number of strategically important rivers, so it was vital that the bridges spanning those rivers be captured intact. In addition, certain aerodromes needed to be taken so that the aircraft carrying the 22nd Division could land.

Student convinced Hitler that airborne operations would help win the forthcoming campaign, and he was given a number of feasibility studies. Having examined these thoroughly, he decided that certain major objectives were vital to the success of the invasion plan, Unternehmen Gelb. One of the major obstacles in the path of 6th German Army, which would be thrusting towards Liége, was the fortress of Eben Emael. Its heavy-calibre guns dominated the crossings and bridges across the Albert Canal. In addition to the fortress, there were also three bridges across the Albert Canal whose capture, intact, was essential for the passage of 6th Army.

Further to the north, in Holland, there were waterways which needed to be taken, and a force would also have to be dropped or air-landed behind the main Dutch defensive area, the Peel position. This was a water barrier which the Dutch could create by flooding the land to make it impassable to German armoured fighting vehicles striking for the heart of western Holland. The use of airborne forces in the Dutch operation had not been part of Student's initial brief, but the Army Group commander demanded airborne operations, and Student was keen for his airborne force to play a more active part in Operation Gelb. Hitler approved the use in Holland of the 22nd Airlanding Division and elements of 7th Airborne.

The plan for the Dutch operation featured both a parachute drop and an airlanded assault. The paratroops were to capture the all-important bridges, and the airlanded 22nd was to supply the necessary back-up to create the strategic Schwerpunkt. Of the two operations on which Student and his staff worked, the Belgian one seemed likely to be the more difficult to resolve, because Eben Emael seemed impregnable. Then the proposal was made to land gliders on its roof; it is unclear who suggested this. Some authorities state that Hitler proposed it, while others say that Student, drawing on his glider expertise, conceived the plan of a silent descent upon the individual cupolas of the Belgian fortress. He realised that a glider-borne operation offered several advantages. The Belgians would not expect an assault from the sky, so the units defending the fort would be few in number and, in addition, the main enemy infantry force would be east of the Maas river along the Belgian/German frontier.

Student was a careful and methodical planner who worked in a calm and direct way towards finding a solution which not only produced the immediate result required, but also took into account long-term consequences. He would deliberate long and deeply, then write in longhand very precise details for a mission. It has been said that when he wrote the orders for the attack upon Holland, they specified the landing zones and objectives down to individual Company level. This would have been typical of his work style. In considering the problems of taking out Eben Emael and the Albert canal bridges, Student realised that a paratroop drop would disperse the troops over a wide area, and that the time spent concentrating the group would lose the vital element of surprise. The solution was to bring small groups of men to the target in single 'containers', such as aircraft fuselages, ie., gliders.

Also because of the nature of the terrain on the roof of the fort and its restricted area, a landing by powered aircraft was out of the question. He decided to use gliders. The assault would have to be made late at night so that the machines landed on the fortress area at first light. Approaching silently, the gliders would come in under the cover of darkness and catch the enemy garrison totally by surprise. Student then created an élite unit to carry out the several tasks. By November 1939 a detachment had been formed. Eventually named Assault Battalion Koch, it was made up of an airborne infantry detachment, a pioneer platoon and a glider section. Over the ensuing months Koch's battalion trained for the mission, carrying out mock ground attacks against the fortifications in Czechoslovakia, while the glider pilots practised landing on an area no larger than a tennis court. The OKW plan for the campaign in the west is covered more fully in the chapter dealing with Manstein, while the Eben Emael mission is dealt with in the chapter on Rudolf Witzig. It is enough to say that Student's careful planning and attention to detail resulted in 'an operation of exemplary daring and decisive significance'.

The original plan for the invasion of Holland and Belgium was compromised when the aircraft carrying an officer with the plans forced landed in the Low Countries. OKW was compelled to produce a new plan, and that meant laying out fresh targets for Student's airborne force. Before the War in the West opened in May 1940, Student was ordered by OKW to mount a series of minor airborne attacks to open the war against Denmark and Norway. The first of these was launched on 9 April, and captured intact the important bridge linking the Falster and Seeland islands. Concurrently, air-landing operations seized a number of important airfields. Later in April there was a drop over Dombas to cut the road and thereby delay the advance of the BEF in Norway.

As the time approached for the campaign in the west to open, Student was given a list of missions for the 7th Airborne and 22nd Airlanding Divisions to carry out. In addition to the Eben Emael and Albert Canal missions in Belgium, his men were to capture the bridges over the Maas at Moerdijk, Dordrecht and Rotterdam, and hold these open until 18th Army relieved them. The airfields around the Hague were also to be captured and held. Student disposed his forces in three battlegroups. Koch's battalion was to attack the Albert Canal and Eben Emael objectives, Paratroop Regiment No. 1 had as its tasks the capture of the Moerdijk and the Dordrecht bridges and the Maas bridge at Rotterdam and Waalhaven, and a reinforcement wave made up of 1st Battalion 2nd Paratroop Regiment was to capture the Hague airfields at Yperburg and Valkemburg. Student's operations did not always go according to plan, chiefly because the Dutch reacted more quickly than expected and their resistance involved the paratroops in heavy fighting. Another problem arose when the pilots of the Ju 52s were unable to locate the correct targets and dropped the paratroop 'sticks' over the wrong areas.

His determination to be with his men led to Student flying into the Hague with the 22nd Division. On the fourth day of the campaign Rotterdam capitulated, and during that last day of fighting Student was wounded in the head. Hearing sounds of gunfire, he walked across to a window in the house he was using as a temporary headquarters and was struck by a bullet. It was long believed that the wound was inflicted by a shot fired by a sniper in an SS unit. The wound took him out of command for several months and left him with a permanent impairment to his speech. During his period of enforced absence the 7th and 22nd were amalgamated to form XI Flieger Korps, and Student was promoted to the rank of lieutenant general and given command of the Corps. During his absence a few minor paratroop drops were made around Narvik in Norway; missions which he had not helped to plan.

A year was to pass before his Corps went into action again, and despite Student's active lobbying no further airborne Divisions were raised at that time. During his convalescence, Student's active mind ranged over a series of matters concerning his airborne force. His immediate concern was that the Jaeger were too lightly armed and needed artillery back-up. He realised that those artillery weapons on issue would either have to be restructured using lighter carriages, or else a completely new design of gun would have to be brought in. The newly designed recoilless gun was the answer, and it was introduced into service in time for some pieces to be airlanded and used in the Crete operation.

The strategic situation had changed during Student's absence. A German force was operating in Africa, and in Student's opinion a secure supply line needed to be set up between the mainland of Europe and Rommel's Afrika Korps. That lifeline needed to be based upon one or more of the islands in the eastern Mediterranean, so one of these would have to be captured. There was general agreement at OKW level of the need to operate in the Mediterranean and to break the British lifeline to the Far East. Goering and Student discussed likely objectives, and both decided on Crete. On 20 April 1941 Student met Hitler, and it became clear that the Fuehrer, too, had made the same choice. Meanwhile, the BEF in Greece was evacuating that country, and an unsuccessful paradrop was made over Corinth to trap the escaping British forces.

Student was now given orders to launch an air invasion of Crete, and his staff began to plan. Landings would be made on the northern side of the island.

Along a west-east line running the length of Crete there were two major objectives; the airfield at Maleme in the west, and Canea, with its harbour facilities in Suda Bay, in the centre. A number of logistical questions concerned Student. Although he could call upon every Ju 52 transport aircraft on the Luftwaffe establishment, there were still too few aircraft to carry the whole Division in one 'lift'. At least two separate waves were needed. Once the initial drops had been made, the paratroops of the second wave would seize and hold the airfields at Rethymnon and Heraklion. The course of operations after that would depend upon how quickly the principal objectives of Maleme and Canea were taken, for, until they were, the airlanding component, Ringl's 5th Gebirgs Division substituting for the 22nd (Airlanding) Division, could not be brought in. The Fallschirmjaeger on the ground lacked heavy support weapons and would be without these until a convoy of caiques brought the equipment from mainland Greece to Canea harbour.

In an operation which depended for its success upon so many incalculable factors, the failure of any one of them might have a knock-on effect which would endanger the whole. Were the worst to happen and neither heavy weapons nor reinforcements reach them, the 'Springer Geist' of the lightly-armed Fallschirmjaeger would have to bring victory out of possible defeat. Student, operating from Corps Headquarters in the Grande Bretagne hotel in Athens, organised and planned every detail of Operation Mercury. It would go in against three targets in the west and centre of the island. The assault regiment, the most experienced of his formations, would para-drop and land in gliders around Maleme. The Junkers transports, having dropped their 'sticks' of men, would fly back to the airfields in Greece, refuel, load up with new 'sticks' and take off for the second-wave drop over the two objectives in the centre of the island.

The landings at Maleme failed to capture the given objectives. The airfield was not taken, and in any case it was overlooked by a hill from which New Zealand artillery fire was directed, preventing the Ju 52s from landing. Nothing could be done until the hill was taken and the airfield captured. Only then could aircraft touch down with the airlanding component of 5th Alpine Division. How the objectives were taken is covered in the chapter dealing with Bernhard Ramcke.

Drops made over the centre of the island went badly wrong when faulty navigation by some pilots led to whole units being dropped over the wrong areas. Other 'sticks' were widely scattered and found difficulty in grouping. The set objectives for the morning drop (the first-wave mission) were not taken, and the second wave, which came in during the afternoon, met determined opposition from the British and Imperial forces and suffered heavy loss. At the end of that first day, Student's 7th Division was in a serious situation, and if the British/Imperial ground commander had been more aggressive the unsupported paratroop formations might have suffered total defeat. Instead he withdrew the New Zealand units from Maleme airfield and the tactically important hill, allowing the German ground operations to develop. The airlanding of Ringl's Mountain Division made the capture of Crete only a matter of time. Eventually the end came, and on 19 July Hitler bestowed upon Student the Knight's Cross of the Iron Cross.

The invasion and seizure of Crete had shown the strategic potential of airborne operations, but it was to be on largely tactical operations that future missions were flown. The combat efficiency and élan of the Fallschirmjaeger were, paradoxically, the reasons why so few airborne operations were undertaken in the remaining years of the war. The Jaeger had shown themselves to be élite infantrymen, and it was in that role that they were eventually to serve on every front. Student was condemned to watch in despair as his paratroop regiments were taken and used piecemeal in ground operations in Russia, Africa, Italy and north-west Europe. Some paratroop and glider operations were planned and then aborted; an air-drop over Gibraltar, and then a mission to capture Malta, to be carried out in conjunction with the Italians. Some operational missions were flown, the first occurring in 1943, but at the end of 1941 Student's 7th Division fought exclusively on the Eastern Front.

At that time, on the northern flank of the German Army in Russia, Hitler had halted the panzer drive upon Leningrad. Stavka, the Red Army's High Command, exploiting the blunder, struck at the German encircling ring and came close to breaking it. On 24 September the 7th Airborne was ordered to fly in by battalions to fight in a ground role, but before it could concentrate as a Division some of its battalions and even Companies were taken away and used to plug gaps in the German battle line. By the middle of October, although only one regiment remained in position on the divisional sector, the 7th had taken over the whole area of the river Neva. Only two regiments of the Division were actually employed in the Leningrad area. The 2nd Regiment was first held in reserve and then posted to Army Group South, to a sector along the river Mius around the town of Charzysk. Battle casualties so reduced the regiment that during February 1942 a battlegroup had to be formed out of the last uncommitted units of the Division and rushed to the Mius river sector.

The German summer offensive of 1942 included within its framework the plan of an airborne mission around Tuapse on the southern side of the Caucasus mountain range, to be followed by an advance to the main oilfields. Student and his staff worked hard, but the planned operation was aborted at the last moment. The 7th returned to active service in an infantry role, but within months Student had received orders to send a paratroop ground force to Libya. He chose units from his Command which would produce an all-arms, Brigade-sized battlegroup, and entrusted its leadership to Bernhard Ramcke. The chapter dealing with Ramcke includes an account of his battlegroup in action in the desert. Later came another call to send more paratroop units to Africa. The Anglo-American invasion of French North Africa was countered by paratroop units which were flown across to Tunisia. Although Student's whole Corps was being fragmented, he continued to press for other airborne formations to be raised.

In January 1943 OKW issued orders for a second airborne Division to be created, and when that came about the former 7th Division was renumbered and became 1st Paratroop Division. Late in 1943 3rd Paratroop Division was raised, and during the final two months of that year the 4th was formed. Those formations were to be followed by a 5th and 6th, both in April 1944, a 7th and Eighth in September 1944, a 9th in January 1945, a 10th only a month later and an 11th during March 1945. That expansion can only be seen as absurd, as there would be no opportunities to mount major airborne operations and, indeed, few Jaeger were able to receive their full 'jump' training. The expansion can only be seen as 'empire building' on the part of Reichsmarschall Goering, who was determined to have a ground force under his control. Student was drawn into this raising of airborne formations which would seldom if ever be used in that role.

However, there were exceptions. During the summer of 1943 the Allies invaded Sicily in an operation which would lead to the fall of Fascist Italy. They then landed at Salerno and in Calabria on the Italian mainland, and two Divisions of Student's Fallschirmjaeger fought throughout the duration of that campaign. There had been paratroop drops over Catania in Sicily, as well as around Rome, to take out the command structure of the Italian Army. In that connection Student also organised the rescue of Mussolini from his mountain-top prison. Another paratroop drop was made over Leros in November 1943 to recapture the island from the British.

Late in 1943, with four airborne Divisions raised, a reorganisation of that Service arm was begun. The Luftwaffe High Command decided to create an Airborne Army, and gave command of the new force to Student. The composition of that new force was I Corps (the former XI Corps) and II Corps.

Although airborne formations were heavily committed on the Eastern Front, they were also active in Italy as the defenders of Cassino, as well as in north-west Europe, where they were put in as part of the forces to counter the Allied invasion of June 1944. When the German front collapsed in Normandy, the remnants of 7th Army and Panzer Group West retreated so quickly and in such disorder that no firm line existed. Into the gap that had opened across much of Belgium, von Rundstedt, Supreme Commander West, put Student's airborne army, even though it had not been completely raised. Of that time, Student said:

> We had no disposable reserves worth mentioning, either on the Western Front or within Germany. On 4 September I took over command of the sector of the Western Front along the Albert Canal. At that time I had only recruit and convalescent units and a single coast-defence formation from Holland. These were supported by a panzer detachment – 25 panzers and SP guns.

With that collection of fragments Student knitted together the Western Front, but the fighting was so hard that the 1st Battalion of 2nd Regiment was reduced to less than Company strength. The 1st Airborne Army, numbering nearly 160,000 men, fought across the ground leading up to the Rhine and then on that river's eastern bank.

When the Allied airborne operation was launched at Arnhem, Student, promoted to colonel general during September 1944, watched with envy when the British Airborne Division flew in. 'If only I had had such resources at my disposal,' he commented to one of his Staff officers. One of his regiments, commanded by von der Heydte, carried out the last German paratroop drop in the west, during the Battle of the Bulge in December 1944. For that operation Student was given command of Army Group H, but he was soon replaced by Blaskowitz, whom he served as deputy.

In April 1945 Student was posted to Mecklenburg and given the task of reorganising the defence of that area. While on an inspection trip to Schleswig-Holstein he was taken prisoner by the British, and at the end of the war he was charged with committing war crimes in Crete but found not guilty. Released from prison, he lived modestly in retirement in Lemgo, where he died on 1 July 1978.

The Finest Battlegroup Commander

Otto Weidinger, Sturmbannfuehrer der Waffen SS

Otto Weidinger was born on 27 May 1914 in Würzburg, the son of a postal worker. He followed the standard educational route of a German boy, and in 1934 was preparing to enter upon higher education when he received a response to an application he had made a year earlier. That application, made in July 1933, was to change his whole life and bring him recognition as one of Germany's finest field commanders at regimental level. He had applied to join the Allgemeine branch of the SS, and it had been approved.

Weidinger carried out the probationary period of his service in his native city, and showed such promise during his recruit training that, on 16 April 1934, he was sent on a posting to the SS Training Depot in Dachau. On 20 March 1935, when his probationary period finally ended, he passed out with the rank of Sturmmann (trained soldier). His superiors had already recognised his potential as an officer, and he was posted, with the title of Junker (a type of cadet officer grade), to the officer training school in Braunschweig. He started the Junkerschule's course of studies on 1 May 1935, and within six months had risen to Standartenjunker and from that post to the highest cadet rank, Standartenoberjunker. Weidinger passed from the theoretical stage of instruction at Braunschweig to the practical stage when he was sent on a course for potential platoon commanders at the Dachau training establishment. During this practical training he was given command of recruits from 2nd Battalion of the 'Deutschland' Standarte. On 1 April 1936, at the end of the Platoon commander's course, Weidinger was commissioned and posted as a second lieutenant to lead a platoon in No. 9 Company of the 'Deutschland' formation. The official notice of his gazetting as an officer was dated 20 April.

During the summer of 1936 a reorganisation of the SS was carried out, to bring that force more into line with Army nomenclature. As a result the unit designation was changed from Standarte to Regiment, but its organisation as a four-battalion unit was retained. SS headquarters then decided to raise a new 3rd battalion, and the original one was renumbered and became 4th battalion. The Company to which Weidinger belonged, No. 9 Company, was also renumbered, becoming No. 16. In the spring of the following year, 1937, he handed over his Platoon in order to attend a month's course in the SS Engineer College in Dresden, returning at its end to 'Deutschland' regiment.

In 1938 there were a series of political crises in central Europe. The first of these ended on 13 March when the German armed forces invaded Austria, an operation in which Weidinger's regiment played a prominent part. Another leaders' training course, during the summer of 1938, was held to give junior commanders experience of active service conditions on the battlefield. Weidinger served as a platoon commander on this course, and led his group so well that he was promoted to the rank of full lieutenant on 11 September.

Although the SS had several academies and establishments capable of training entrants to junior leadership positions, there were none in which promising students could be taught the disciplines of the Staff and of the High Command. Only the Regular Army colleges of higher education could provide such courses, and it was only by reverting and taking up Army service, carrying out duties as an officer with an Army unit, that SS entrants could gain a place in the War Academy. Weidinger took the first step towards senior command status when he reverted and was posted from his SS Company on a four-month secondment with the Army's 14th Jaeger Regiment.

Upon his return to 'Deutschland' he found that there had been a fresh reorganisation within that regiment. The 4th Battalion had been converted to motorcycle status, and had been taken on charge as 2nd battalion of the newly created SS regiment 'Ellwangen'. Weidinger was appointed Adjutant of that unit. 'Ellwangen' had only a brief life, for it was broken up during the summer of 1939, in common with a number of other SS detachments which were being amalgamated. Himmler had decided to create an armed SS Division which would be known as the Verfuegungs Truppen (VT; troops available for special use). When 'Ellwangen' was broken up, the 2nd battalion to which Weidinger belonged was converted to become the reconnaissance battalion of the proposed new Division. Weidinger served as the adjutant of that battalion, and held the post throughout the war against Poland. For his work in that campaign he was awarded the Iron Cross Second Class on 15 November 1939.

The VT Division did not serve as a Division during the war with Poland, but was split up and its components posted to other major formations. Nevertheless, experiences in that campaign highlighted deficiencies in the organisation and training of SS units. There was a need to tighten standards in the embryo Division, and these changes were put in hand. As the result of one change Weidinger was posted to and took command of the armoured car platoon of the reconnaissance battalion. Late in 1939 he was sent on a Company Commander's course, and acquitted himself so well that when the platoon he commanded was expanded to a Company during the spring of 1940 he was the obvious choice to be its commander.

Like the campaign in Poland, the war in the west was also brief, and at its end Weidinger was not only promoted to the rank of Captain in the SS but he had also been awarded the Iron Cross First Class. He was confirmed in his appointment as Company Commander during September 1940, and held it, alternating with several junior Staff appointments, throughout the campaign in Yugoslavia.

For the opening offensives of the war against Russia, in 1941, he served in the post of IIa, but during July 1941 he was transferred back to a field command and took over No. 5 Company, the heavy weapons unit of the motorcycle battalion. The fierce fighting of the first month on the Eastern Front inflicted a great many casualties on the SS 'Reich' Division in general and on the regiment in particular. When the commander of No. 3 Company was wounded, Weidinger was ordered to take over and lead it. The Rifle Company he now led was heavily committed to close-quarter combat on a 14km-wide sector of the front against an enemy superior in number and firepower.

When he reached No. 3 Company's area, Weidinger's first action was to form a battlegroup and lead it in a counterattack against Soviet troops flooding through the Company's broken front. That vigorous counterattack was fought without halt for more than a day, but when the battle died down the breach had been sealed and the German positions were once again firmly in the hands of No. 3 Company. As evidence of how hard the fighting had been, more than 480 Soviet soldiers lay dead on Weidinger's sector of the battlefield, and hundreds more Red Army men were wounded. It was Weidinger's 'blooding' as a commander leading men in action, and he had acquitted himself well. It was not just on that single occasion that he showed his skill. He repeated it throughout the weeks he spent in command of No. 3 Company. His reputation as a calm, confident and, above all, courageous commander grew with every action, and he frequently demonstrated his ability during the fighting which marked the autumn of 1941.

The battle for Yelnya was fought around a small town on the banks of the Desna river, about 75km east of Smolensk and approximately 300km from Moscow. Army Group Centre, with which SS Division 'Reich' was serving, had as its first strategic objective the ridges of high ground around Yelnya. These dominating features were a springboard for any army advancing from the west, as well as a shield defending the capital, and were therefore important to both sides. To improve the already strong defences along the Desna river, the Soviet commander-in-chief on that sector, Marshal Timoshenko, conscripted the entire civilian population to dig trenches and anti-tank ditches and lay minefields

On 22 July 'Deutschland' regiment of 'Reich' Division was ordered to attack the high ground to the east of Yelnya. The regiment had its 1st and 2nd Battalions 'up', with 3rd in reserve, and the 10th Infantry Division was on its left flank. Very soon the German forces on that sector were engaged in a bitter struggle against an enemy in well-prepared positions who held the additional advantages of occupying the upper ground and of being strongly supported by artillery. But the men of 'Deutschland' would not be gainsaid, and the battle, which began at 0900, had been won by late evening. The Yelnya heights were in their hands.

On another occasion Weidinger halted the panic flight of soldiers from 10th Division, regrouped them, and led them, together with his own SS unit, into an assault. The charge recaptured ground which had been lost, including Avdeyevka, a tactically important village. As a result of one counterattack, Weidinger's men not only took more than 400 prisoners but also captured 30 machine-guns and four anti-tank rifles. On that day Weidinger led another bayonet charge. With shouts of 'hurrah', he and his No. 3 Company rushed into the attack, and by furious assault captured an objective on the Dedy sector which it had been thought could only be gained by an assault by the whole battalion. He and his men then pursued the fleeing enemy, inflicting more casualties. During the bayonet charge Weidinger was wounded, but refused to leave his men until the objective had been gained. Upon his return from hospital he took over command of the motorcycle battalion's 1st Company and led it during the fighting near Yosevo, to the south of the Moscow highway. The fighting was sometimes hand-to-hand, and the Russian counterattacks were hard, made in overwhelming strength and very frequent. During one enemy attack, once again fought at close quarters, Weidinger went out to destroy a Russian tank and was wounded for a second time.

On 21 October 1941 came the award of the Infantry Assault Badge, and on the following day he was posted back to the SS Junker Schule Braunschweig. There he took up a post as an instructor so that he could pass on to the students the knowledge he had gained in active service. His period as an instructor lasted until 8 May 1943, when returned to his unit. During his absence from 'Deutschland' regiment Weidinger had been awarded the War Service Cross Second Class, had passed a battalion commander's course in Paris, and had been promoted to the rank of SS Sturmbannfuehrer (major). In that rank he assumed command of 1st Battalion of 'Deutschland' regiment on 1 June 1943.

On the Eastern Front in the summer of 1943 the German Army was preparing to undertake a major operation codenamed Zitadelle. The imperative for that operation was that, before the 1942/43 Russian winter offensive was finally halted, the Red Army advance had left a large, blunt-headed salient projecting into the fronts of German Army Groups Centre and South, to the north and south of the town of Kursk. Unternehmen Zitadelle had a two-fold purpose. Firstly, by cutting off the salient the German battle line would be shortened and would require fewer units to man it. The formations thus released could then be concentrated to form a reserve. Secondly, the mass of Red Army soldiers whom Hitler confidently expected to be taken prisoner during the offensive would be employed on the farms and in the factories of the Reich. Both the Germans and the Russians had carried out intensive preparations for the coming battle, for both sides knew that it would be a climacteric. To anticipate the outcome of Zitadelle, it was Germany which was forced to break off the battle. Thereafter, she was never able to recover the military initiative nor to launch a successful major offensive on the Eastern Front.

For Unternehmen Zitadelle SS Division 'Reich', forming part of II SS Panzer Corps in 4th Panzer Army, was located on the southern side of the Kursk salient. The battle plan was that 4th Panzer Army was to advance northwards and join hands with Model's 9th Army, which was striking down from the north. On 5 July 1943 the Panzer Army opened its offensive, thrusting out of the Bjelgorod area towards the intermediate objective of Orel, with the intention of driving from that place to Kursk, the final objective. 'Das Reich' Division was positioned on the right flank of the SS Panzer Corps with SS 'Totenkopf' Division in the centre of the Corps line and the 'Leibstandarte' Division on the left flank. On its sector of the front 'Deutschland' regiment faced a succession of strongly-built trench lines, each of which was protected by minefields, flamethrowers and barbed wire entanglements.

The orders issued by 4th Panzer Army for Zitadelle placed upon the II SS Panzer Corps the burden of that Army's main assault. The orders directed Corps to '... break the enemy's defensive zone and, [go on] to attack the second enemy position .... to hold itself ready to cross the Psel sector and to advance in a north-easterly direction with its right wing on Prokharovka ...' Weidinger's battalion opened 'Deutschland' regiment's operations by moving out during the hours of darkness to capture the Russian outpost line protecting the anti-tank ditch at Jakantov. Covered by the flamethrowers of No. 16 Company, Weidinger's Grenadiers went in and quickly gained their objectives. Their successes opened the way for the remainder of the Regiment to advance northwards. Despite its early successes, the German offensive at Kursk was called off on 16 July, and 'Reich' Division was rushed to the sector of the Mius river, where a Soviet offensive was gaining ground. When the Division had restored the situation it was then put into a counterattack to the north-west of Kharkov.

Shortly after the offensive at Kursk failed, Weidinger was ordered to take command of the divisional reconnaissance battalion. Almost immediately he was confronted by a crisis when Soviet troops broke through at Lyubotin, to the south-east of Kharkov. The battalion commander concentrated all the forces he had been able to muster, and by personal example inspired his men to hold out against the Soviet assault for more than six days. When the German line was broken again, Weidinger created a new battlegroup and once again restored the situation. On 19 August he was awarded the Wound Badge in Silver in recognition of his third wound. The fighting east of Kolomak, in which the reconnaissance battalion was heavily involved, was the hardest in his military career, according to Mark Yerger's excellent biography of Weidinger. During that action more than

100 enemy tanks were active on his sector, but Weidinger had trained his men well and they knew how to deal with the situation. They allowed the enemy armour to over-roll their slit trenches, then rose up out of them to open fire upon the accompanying Red infantry, knowing that the divisional panzers would take on and defeat the Russian machines. At the end of the fighting 22 of the 60 enemy tanks which had attacked the reconnaissance battalion's positions lay destroyed in front of Weidinger's TAC headquarters.

The fighting in the bend of the Dnieper river was nearly as bitter and, when an Army unit retreated in panic flight, Weidinger, realising the danger to his exposed flank, scraped together a small counterattack unit of seventeen men and led them into a charge. That prompt action restored the situation. When, later in the day, some panzers came into the area, Weidinger used them to seal the break in the German front. The divisional commander's recommendation that Weidinger be awarded the German Cross in Gold was approved, and the decoration was bestowed on 26 November.

'Das Reich' had been in almost continuous battle from the Kharkov offensive in the spring, throughout Zitadelle in the summer and on into the defensive fighting of autumn and early winter. It was accepted at OKH that the Division was no longer able to carry out the tasks of a fighting Division. It was too weak in numbers. Those divisional units which were still battleworthy were then formed into Panzer Kampfgruppe 'Das Reich'. Weidinger led one of the formations of that battlegroup until 8 March 1944, when he took command of the whole unit. The Kampfgruppe then bore his name. On 20 April the unit, some 800 men in number, left the Eastern Front, entrained for Germany and arrived a week later in the Toulouse area, where 'Das Reich' Division was being re-formed. The battlegroup was greeted by the regimental band as well as by Wisliceny, Deutschland's commander. After his speech of welcome he announced the award to Weidinger of the Knight's Cross of the Iron Cross for his actions during the fighting by the reconnaissance battalion at Negrebovka. The Cross was officially presented that afternoon by the divisional commander. After a formal parade on the following day the battlegroup was broken up and its constituent units returned to their parent formations.

At a civil level, Weidinger's home city, Aalen, presented him with an oil painting after a ceremony in which he was honoured by the Mayor and had his name entered in the city's Golden Book. Then, on 30 April, he received the Close Combat clasp in bronze and, at the end of a short period of leave, was told that his new appointment was a posting to 'Der Fuehrer' regiment as Officer in Charge of Training. He did not serve long in that post. The Allies invaded France on 6 June 1944.

'Das Reich' had been held at Toulouse as part of the reserve of the Supreme Commander West, to defend southern France against an Allied landing. When the invasion of north-west Europe came in over the beaches of Normandy, the formation was ordered to move to the battle zone. After delays it reached Normandy, where it was again placed in Army reserve. It was not until 14 June 1944 that the first elements of 'Das Reich' Division reached the concentration area south of Domfront. During the march to battle Weidinger was informed that he had been given command of 'Der Fuehrer' regiment in succession to Standartenfuehrer Stadler.

During the evening of 26 June German 7th Army sent a signal placing Weidinger's Grenadier regiment under the command of the Army's 2nd Panzer Division for the duration of a planned offensive. The 7th Army intended to mount an attack along the highway from Villers Bocage to Caen to clear up the penetrations made by the British 2nd Army. On that particular sector fighting had been so hard that the German divisions had been badly mauled and were in no condition to undertake a new and major offensive. For those reasons the opinion of the commander of Panzer Lehr Division was that 7th Army's operation must fail. He thought it would be far better for Weidinger's regiment to take up a position to the east and north of Noyers, between his own Division, Panzer Lehr, on the left and 12th SS Panzer Division 'Hitler Youth' on the right, thereby closing the gap in the German line. Only after the breach in the line had been sealed could a general offensive in the Villers Bocage area be considered. His proposal was adopted, and Weidinger's regiment moved off to its new position, taking casualties as the Grenadier Companies passed through a heavy artillery bombardment. British preemptive strikes, intended to throw the SS Panzer Corps off balance, came in almost as soon as Weidinger's Grenadiers entered the area, and were so strongly mounted that they separated his 1st and 2nd Battalions from each other.

For the German offensive which was to open at 1430 on 29 June, 'Der Fuehrer' regiment passed from the control of 2nd Panzer Division and came under the aegis of SS Division 'Hohenstaufen'. The Corps attack began to roll but then met, head-on and quite unexpectedly, an assault by British VIII Corps aimed at gaining ground to the south of Caen and thereby isolating that city. Although Weidinger's men made some progress in the first hours of their attack, the advance was slowed and then halted. But fighting continued and lasted throughout the short, rainy night, the SS and the British infantry often battling hand-to-hand. According to British official sources, the tactics employed by Weidinger's Grenadiers were most effective. The SS allowed the British troops to pass by their well camouflaged positions, only emerging when 'suitable targets presented themselves. It is worthy of note that in every case groups of the enemy fought until they were all killed or until [our troops] had taken the position.' Such tactics were typical of those used by the SS on the Eastern Front, and which Weidinger had taught his men. They were techniques which the British infantry had not been taught, and with which they were unfamiliar.

A terrain factor which might have favoured the Germans more than the Allies was the closeness of the bocage, a system of small fields enclosed by hedges so high and thick that they reduced the field of fire. Weidinger, appreciating the problem besetting his Grenadiers, issued the directive that 'a good field of fire takes precedence over cover'. Although such terrain might have been expected to give the defender certain advantages, Weidinger was to write that the bocage conditions reduced observation so badly that there could be no direct control exercised over his formation except at platoon level. Because of the failure of the German daylight attacks, operations at night were tried, but the first attempts to mount such assaults were unsuccessful.

The men of Weidinger's regiment faced an enemy who could call upon the support of overwhelming firepower; a superiority found not only on the ground but, more especially, in the air. Control of the air on such a scale as the Western Allies held in Normandy had not been met on the Eastern Front, and it took its toll not only of vehicles and men but, more importantly, on the nerves of the Grenadiers. The exhaustion of Weidinger's units soon brought the operation to a close, allowing British VIII Corps to sweep forward in a counterattack so furious in its pace that some Shermans from a British armoured unit penetrated almost as far as TAC headquarters before AA guns and flamethrowers destroyed them. But such German successes were minor. More seriously, the scale of battle casualties, which to begin with had been as high as 40 per cent in 1st Battalion of 'Der Fuehrer' regiment, had risen to 60 per cent by the time the offensive was brought to an end.

Weidinger's decimated regiment had lost 846 men in the offensive, but despite those losses he was ordered to make a night attack on 1 July, to wipe out the salient which VIII Corps had punched into the German line. Although the warning order was received in time, no further details of the attack came until shortly before H-Hour. Weidinger therefore had no time to line up his regiment. In addition, the radio silence imposed on all units meant that he could not liaise with the panzers of the 'Hohenstaufen' Division which were to support him. As a consequence of SS Corps not issuing its orders in good time, and the 'knock-on' effect of that delay from Corps to Division and then to Regiment, it was full daylight before preparations for the attack had been completed. Shortly before the Grenadiers set off, Weidinger was told that the ground was unsuitable for the panzers and that the armour could not give the promised support.

Then a worse situation developed. His battalions had crossed the start line and were making good progress when, without warning, 'Hohenstaufen' cancelled the entire attack and ordered the Grenadiers to return to their former positions. Those men who had advanced through a British barrage now had to retreat under shellfire. For infantrymen this is a bitter experience. The operation had been aborted, and the burden of the fighting over those past days had been carried by Weidinger's regiment. The sacrifice made by the regiment had not been in vain. The Grenadiers had played a significant part in preventing British 2nd Army from capturing the high ground south of Caen.

The regiment was taken out of the line and formed into a battlegroup made up of 3rd battalion 'Der Fuehrer' regiment as well as the Panzer Reconnaissance Battalion, the SP Battalion and the 2nd Artillery Battalion, all from 'Das Reich' Division. The task given to Weidinger's battlegroup was to support 353rd Infantry Division in its defence of La Haye des Puits, which was under attack by the 3rd, 9th, and 30th US Divisions. Because of the command of the air exercised by the Allies, Weidinger issued orders during the afternoon of 5 July that 'patrols are to mark out Company routes ... Officers are to regulate the flow of vehicle groups by holding those groups until Allied fighter bombers have left the area and [those officers] are to bring groups forward by bounds from one piece of cover to another until the target area is reached...'

Just as on the British sector, so in the Canadian and American areas the pattern of a German counterattack succeeding an Allied attack continued. The fighting was again hard, the battlegroup eventually having to retire because it was so frequently in danger of being surrounded and cut off. One such withdrawal brought the group to Percy, where it was intended that a stand might be made, but US Army pressure on 7th Army's left flank had opened a gap through which American armoured divisions swept forward to reach Avranches. Not only had the German left wing been torn away from the sea, but through the breach which now existed the way was clear for an American advance into Brittany.

Hitler responded to the threat by ordering an offensive with unrealiseable objectives. On 5 August 7th Army opened that operation. Hitler intended to reseal the battle line near Mortain at the base of the Cotentin peninsula and then sweep the Americans back to the original invasion bridgehead and into the sea. The 2nd SS Panzer Division, 'Das Reich', had by this time been moved to the US sector, and Weidinger's 'Der Fuehrer' regiment came back under its command. His was one of the three battlegroups fielded by Division for the Mortain mission. Lack of detailed planning by XLVIII Corps resulted in confusion, delay and then in a situation where 'Der Fuehrer' was caught in the open by RAF fighter-bombers and savagely mauled.

Hitler would not at first call off the offensive on which he had pinned his hopes but which had never had a chance of success. When he did abort it, the situation in Normandy had deteriorated and most of the German forces there, the 5th Panzer Army and the 7th Army, were being enclosed in a pocket based loosely around the town of Falaise. A report issued by 'Das Reich' Division during the afternoon of 20 August stated: 'The enemy has surrounded the main body of 7th Army in the Trun–Chambois–Falaise and Argentan areas. Das Reich Division, which has already passed out of the enemy encirclement, will carry out an attack on 21 August in the area of Le Moulins–Mardilly, with the aim of breaking the enemy ring.'

Weidinger's regiment was ordered to undertake that attack with the support of the remnant of 'Das Reich' Panzer Regiment. The march route was via

Champosoult–Mount Ormel and Chambois. The regiment attacked with 3rd Battalion 'up' and carried in armoured personnel carriers, advancing behind the AFVs of the Panzer Regiment. Weidinger's 2nd Battalion was in support. Opposition, light to begin with, grew in intensity, particularly from tank units of 1st Polish Armoured Division. A single Panzer surprised and 'killed' twelve of the Polish machines, and by that action played an important part in breaking the enemy ring around Champosoult. In every attack there comes a time when it begins to flag and to slow down under enemy fire. When his regiment's assault lost its impetus, Weidinger led his men, and through his example overcame the hiatus in the advance.

Allied pressure against the open flank of 'Der Fuehrer' regiment grew in intensity as the Poles sought to reseal the pocket which had been forced open. To master this new crisis, Weidinger regrouped his men and once again led them in mounting an attack to capture Mount St Leger, a tactically important hill to the south-west of Champosoult. During that assault seven tanks of the Polish Division were destroyed and the Allied infantry was forced back. Mount St Leger dominated the road along which the German troops caught in the encirclement could escape. It was therefore imperative that 'Der Fuehrer' reach the dominant height and hold the line against the Allied assault. The regiment was ordered into the attack. During the afternoon of 21 August units of 3rd Battalion renewed the advance, covered by an artillery barrage and supported by the panzers. The attack reached the crest of the 200m-high Mount St Leger to the south-west of Champosoult. To reach the top of the steep-sided hill the Grenadiers had to pull themselves up using bushes or tufts of grass, but once they were on the summit their fire dominated the area and, by pinning down the Allied troops, broke open the encircling ring.

At 1815 Weidinger sent a signal to divisional headquarters, announcing that the attack had been successful, that contact had been made with units inside the pocket and that a stream of German soldiers was escaping from the pocket and passing through his lines. Although Weidinger had carried out the orders, Division directed him to continue the advance until Chambois was taken. His response to that order was to point out that it was now superfluous. The jaws of the area he had breached had been held open until the last units had escaped from the pocket. At about that time a report came in that the General Commanding 7th Army, SS General Hausser, had been seen wounded near Champosoult. The 3rd Battalion was ordered to send out a fighting patrol to find him and bring him in. That proved to be unnecessary, as he had already left the pocket.

Later that afternoon Weidinger drove to 3rd Battalion's reported positions to gain a personal impression of the situation. He walked past two Panzer IVs guarding the road, but could see no sign of his Grenadiers. As he made his way back towards the AFVs he was fired on and forced to take cover. Not until night fell could he escape and make his way back to TAC headquarters. The battle of Falaise then came to an end, and the units of the German army in Normandy threaded their way northwards into Belgium or eastwards towards Germany.

Towards the end of August OKW decided that the retreat of the armies on the Western Front was to halt. 'Das Reich' Division took over an area of Germany called the Schnee Eifel, by coincidence the same area out of which the last German offensive in the west, the Battle of the Bulge, was to erupt only a few months later. 'Der Fuehrer' regiment held the left flank of the Division with its 3rd and 2nd Battalions in the line. During the long retreat march through Belgium, Weidinger was not only raised in rank to Obersturmbannfuehrer on 9 November, but was recommended for the Oak Leaf to the Knight's Cross. The recommendation was approved on 27 December, in recognition of his actions at Falaise.

The Schnee Eifel area of Germany which his regiment held was part of the Siegfried Line defences. By this stage of the war those positions were obsolescent, but Supreme Command ordered them to be held to the last man. Weidinger wrote a deeply moving account of how well some of the men of his 3rd Battalion obeyed that senseless order. Equipped with only infantry weapons, they came under attack from flamethrowing Sherman tanks accompanied by bulldozers which blocked the pill boxes' weapons slits. US infantry then attacked the blind pill boxes and placed high-explosive charges on the outside walls, shooting any SS soldiers who tried to escape.

During the second week of October Weidinger's regiment was taken out of the line to prepare for the forthcoming major offensive in Luxemburg. 'Das Reich' was not immediately employed in the Battle of the Bulge, but during Christmas 'Der Fuehrer' regiment made a number of attacks supported by its sister regiment, 'Deutschland', on its left flank. It was recognised by both the Army and the SS commanders that the offensive could not succeed, and when Hitler finally called it off the 2nd SS Panzer Division 'Das Reich' had been severely reduced by wounds and sickness.

Thwarted on the Western Front, Hitler turned east again and ordered an operation in Hungary to protect the last remaining oil wells of the Reich. An offensive carried out by heavy armour over swampy ground cannot succeed, and a Red Army counterattack forced 6th SS Panzer Army out of Hungary and into Austria. 'Das Reich' Division then took part in the defence of the Austrian capital, but by 14 April the last German troops had crossed the Florisdorfer bridge and passed out of Vienna on to the north bank of the Danube. A recommendation for Weidinger to be awarded the Swords to the Oak Leaf was approved, although the regimental commander did not learn of it until he returned home after his years in captivity.

Towards the end of the war Weidinger's parent formation, 'Das Reich' Division, was fighting on the Eastern Front, but not as a single formation. It had been broken up and re-formed into several individual battlegroups. His own unit, 'Der

Fuehrer' Regiment, was in the Budweis area of southern Czechoslovakia, awaiting orders to drive to Bruenn, where it would join the divisional headquarters
group. But no such instruction came. Instead, on 30 April 1945, Weidinger was
directed to drive to Prague, where he was to report to Obergruppenfuehrer
Pueckler, the SS Supreme Commander in the area. At their first meeting Pueckler told Weidinger that, although conditions in the city were still calm, plans had
been laid to evacuate the German civilian population. Weidinger drove back to
the 'Der Fuehrer' concentration area, and it seemed as though Pueckler's assessment had been correct. The whole area was quiet. Weidinger held an officers' O
Group and followed this with a parade of the whole regiment, at which he
announced the news that Hitler was dead. The regimental commander reminded
his men that the Fuehrer's death did not release them from their oath of allegiance, that their first loyalty was to Germany and that the regiment would fight
on until the war's end. A wireless message from Field Marshal Schoerner, the
Army Group commander, then directed Weidinger to take his regiment without
delay to Prague, where he was to put down the insurrection which had broken
out not only inside the city but across the whole Protectorate.

On 6 May Weidinger led his unit out of Budweis, heading towards the
Czech capital, and almost immediately there was opposition to the battlegroup's
advance. Initially this was slight, but it grew stronger and more intense as the
group neared Prague. Among the most disturbing features encountered during
the drive was the number of German soldiers who had been disarmed, so they
claimed, by Czech partisans. As the battlegroup neared the city it met barriers
intended to slow the SS advance. The war's end was only a few days away, and
if the partisans could stop Weidinger fulfilling his mission before the final surrender came into force, not only his well-armed battlegroup but all of the SS units
inside the capital and the German civilian population would be their prisoners.

In the outer suburbs of Prague a huge road block made of cobblestones
had been erected, and this could be neither blown up nor bypassed. It would
have to be dismantled by hand, and Weidinger put his men to the task. Soon his
Grenadiers were hard at work, and at nightfall the blackout shields were removed
from the vehicle headlamps so that the work could continue. Late at night a gap
had been made in the cobblestone wall sufficiently wide for vehicles to pass
through, and with headlamps blazing Battlegroup Weidinger raced towards the
city. At the Troya bridge the column was struck by a hail of small-arms fire. The
young commander now faced a terrible decision. He knew that the end of the war
meant the capitulation of the German Army. Any act which led to bloodshed
among the Czech civilian population or the Czech partisan forces would be considered a war crime by the victorious Allies, and particularly by the vengeful Slavs.
Yet he had his orders to carry out, and he also had the lives of his men to consider. Weidinger had to decide whether to storm the bridge in a night assault or
make no move until first light. He chose the latter option.

Just after dawn on 7 May the artillery battalion of the battlegroup opened fire, and under the barrage the Grenadiers charged forward. The assault frightened the Czechs, and Weidinger accepted the offer of a mutual ceasefire, although he rejected a demand that his battlegroup should pull back to Leitmeritz. It soon became clear to the Obersturmbannfuehrer that the Czechs were playing for time and not complying with the ceasefire agreement. He reopened his delayed attack, and Grenadiers first captured the bridge and then set up a small perimeter on its far side. The SS groups concentrated, ready to begin the advance into the heart of the city, but at this juncture a Czech officer offered to negotiate between the partisans, the battlegroup and the German military commander. Weidinger was prepared to listen to the offer, but informed the Czech of the orders he had to carry out and said he was determined to complete his mission and that his men were prepared to fight. A German officer went off with the Czech, but before they left Weidinger said that if the German officer had not returned by 1500 he would feel free to open fire in order to force a way through. The deadline came, but the officers did not. Determined to prevent unnecessary bloodshed, Weidinger extended it by a further hour, during which time the Czech and German officers returned, bringing news that the German authorities in Prague and their Czech opposite numbers had come to an arrangement.

During the officers' absence Weidinger had sent out patrols to bring in arms, ammunition and supplies. A fuel dump, found close to the bridge perimeter, enabled all the vehicles to be fully tanked for the return journey, and the presence of a strong, heavily armed and determined group of SS men in Prague attracted isolated German soldiers who were fearful of being left in this Slav land at the mercy of the Czech partisan forces.

A head count soon established that there were not enough lorries to carry all the German civilians who hoped to leave Prague, as well as the battlegroup. If they were all to be carried, the vehicles would be dangerously overloaded. The agreement between the Czech and German senior officers laid down that the convoy's destination was to be Pilsen, where it was known that US units were located. There, the German civilians were to be debussed, after which 'Der Fuehrer' would surrender. To enable this move to be made without incident, the Czechs promised to remove all road blocks and were prepared to signpost the roads and provide guides between Prague and Pilsen. Then two crises arose. In the city's railway sidings ambulance trains filled with German wounded were found. These soldiers could not be left behind. Instead, they would be brought to the vehicle concentration area and loaded into the trucks. Then a large group of female SS signalling staff reported in, and they too had to be found places in the lorry convoy.

Late in the evening of 8 May the vehicle column, now numbering 1,000 lorries, set out, but in the early hours of 9 May, the day on which the Soviets had announced the war was to end, a German General and a Czech colonel halted the trucks and demanded that all weapons be handed over. Weidinger had to comply, but issued his own order that all weapons were to be rendered useless before they were given up. There were only a few details remaining. The civilians and the wounded, having been brought to safety in Pilsen, could now be debussed. The soldiers of the battlegroup held a final pay parade, there was a distribution of canteen goods and then the Grenadiers mounted in trucks drove towards Rokiczany, where the US 2nd Infantry Division was waiting to receive the surrender of Battlegroup Weidinger.

As a senior SS officer Weidinger was imprisoned for 6½ years, and was also tried by a French military court on a charge of having committed a war crime. He was found innocent of that charge. Upon his release he became a pharmacist and also wrote a number of books, including a history of 'Der Fuehrer' regiment and a multi-volume definitive history of 'Das Reich' Division. Otto Weidinger remained active in German ex-Service organisations, particularly those of 'Das Reich' Division and of his old Regiment. He died in 1992.

The Tiger Panzer Ace

Michael Wittmann, Hauptsturmfuehrer der Waffen SS

Some soldiers establish so great a reputation during their lifetime that they remain military legends even decades after their death. In former days it was a knight on horseback, not the simple bowman, who gained the honour and was remembered. Similarly, in the 20th century, in purely military terms, it is usually the panzer commander and not a humble Grenadier who is remembered. The armoured fighting vehicle is the instrument of glory, and it is a tankman, killed in battle at the early age of 30, who is the subject of this account. It is claimed that Hauptsturmfuehrer Michael Wittmann of the Waffen SS was the most successful tank commander in the history of armoured warfare. Certainly his impressive number of 'kills', 117 on the Eastern Front alone, seems to confirm that claim.

Michael Wittmann was born on 22 April 1914 in Vogelthal in the Oberpfalz region of Germany, the son of a farmer. On 1 February 1934, shortly before his 20th birthday, he joined the Reichsarbeitsdienst (the German Labour Corps) and served for six months. On 30 October of that year he passed from that organisation and enlisted in the German Army's 19th Infantry Regiment. He was soon promoted, and left the Service in September 1936 as a junior NCO. Almost immediately he re-entered Service life, not in the Army but in the SS, where he served with No. 1 Sturm of the 92nd Standarte. He must have been an exceptional volunteer, for not only was he accepted into the SS, but into the élite Leibstandarte SS Adolf Hitler (LSSAH), the personal guard troops of the German Chancellor and Fuehrer. In 1937 he trained as a driver on a SDKFZ 222, showing remarkable aptitude for mechanical vehicles. By the outbreak of war he was a non-commissioned officer, and during the campaign in Poland in 1939 he commanded an armoured car. It was in that post that he served in the War in the West; first in Holland and then in France.

With the expansion of the LSSAH, a self-propelled (SP) artillery detachment came on to that formation's establishment. Wittmann was given command of one of its vehicles, and served with this piece of artillery in the Greek campaign of 1941. Several months after the end of the Balkan campaign he was awarded the Iron Cross Second Class. In June 1941 Germany invaded Russia, and the

LSSAH served in the first stages of that war as part of Army Group South. Wittmann seems to have had a natural aptitude for panzer operations at a tactical level, and as an SP commander he swiftly showed his mastery of those skills. During the early stages of the war against the Soviet Union, Unternehmen Barbarossa, his SP came under attack by eight Soviet tanks, but by swift and frequent changes of position, together with clever use of ground, he 'killed' six of his attackers. The remaining two pulled back. That and similar acts brought the young NCO to the attention of his superiors, for those deeds showed that he had the military virtues of bravery and leadership which qualified him for commissioned rank. Between the time of his destruction of the six Russian tanks and his posting to the officers' training school at Bad Toelz, Wittmann had been twice wounded and in September 1941 had been awarded the Iron Cross First Class.

He passed out of the Bad Toelz Junkerschule in December 1942 with the rank of Untersturmfuehrer (second lieutenant). Two months earlier the LSSAH had been brought back from the Eastern Front to be rested and reinforced in France. In the west the Division was upgraded to Panzergrenadier status, which gave it a regiment of two panzer battalions. Concurrent with the formation of the panzer regiment, which was equipped with conventional panzers, was the creation of a Heavy Panzer Company with the Tiger, the formidable Panzer VI with its 88mm main armament. Within a short time of his return from Bad Toelz Wittmann was given command of a Tiger in No. 13 Company, and underwent instruction on the new vehicle at the training ground at Ploernel. His superiors were confident that he would bring to his new command the skills and courage he had already exhibited as an SP commander; coolness under fire and tactical ability.

The LSSAH returned to the Eastern Front, and towards the end of January 1943 was back in action in the Kharkov sector. In one of the first actions using the new heavy Tiger tanks, the Heavy Panzer Company was ordered to protect the ground leading up to the Donets river while the reconnaissance battalion carried out a sweep of the area. Wittmann, who now commanded a panzer platoon, moved forward with the five Tigers of his small command towards a village and, having destroyed two anti-tank guns at its approaches, drove through it. In the middle distance he opened fire on a long column of Russian armoured and softskinned vehicles which sought to escape the German panzer bombardment. The young commander allocated targets to his crews and within minutes the shells of his platoon's Tigers had smashed the cohesion of the Soviet column.

Later in the winter of 1942/43, when the crisis came in the battle for Kharkov, the Tigers were grouped as a mobile reserve in the village of Alexayovka. During the night of 14 February 1943, attacks by Russian storm troops broke through the German defensive cordon, and Wittmann was ordered into action. He drove the Soviets out of the village and restored the situation. His had been a successful tactical action, but at strategic level it was necessary that Kharkov be evacuated. The Tigers of No. 13 Company covered the withdrawal of the SS

Corps by firing long-range salvoes to keep the Soviet armour at a distance. The plan of campaign produced by Field Marshal von Manstein foresaw a counteroffensive to retake Kharkov. The task of capturing the city fell to the SS Divisions, and for that operation, which opened in the first week of March, the Tigers were grouped to form a battering ram which smashed Russian opposition and captured the town.

With Kharkov once again in German hands and a firm line established, the German Central and Southern Army Groups planned a new, major offensive at Kursk; Unternehmen Zitadelle. Hitler is said to have remarked that the thought of Zitadelle made his stomach turn over. The battle for Kursk opened, and the Tigers immediately came under massed anti-tank-gun fire. Wittmann destroyed one pak within minutes of crossing the start line, and then went on to attack the first Russian trench system. As the Tigers smashed their way across the field fortifications, squadrons of Russian armoured vehicles swept down to carry out a counterattack. The Red Army tank assault was smashed, but as the Tigers drove past the burning hulks they were struck by the shells of a box formation of anti-tank guns, known as a pakfront. The panzers passed through the shellfire without damage and went on to engage and smash the pakfront.

Early in the afternoon Wittmann heard over the radio that the Tigers of another platoon were being attacked by T 34s. Immediately he swung his vehicle round, entered a small wood, passed through it and found himself behind the enemy anti-tank-gun line. He then realised that he was in the rear of the Soviet tanks which were in action with the Tigers. One panzer of that group was already alight and out of action. While two machines of his platoon engaged the anti-tank guns, Wittmann went into action against the T 34s and destroyed three within minutes. Soon after that his vehicle was hit and shed a track. The Division's efficient workshops organisation soon had it running again, and by the end of the day Wittmann had destroyed eight enemy tanks and seven anti-tank guns. It has been claimed that his individual efforts had helped II SS Corps drive a salient 20km deep into the positions held by 52nd Guards Infantry Division.

At first light on the second day of the Kursk offensive the Tigers headed for the bend in the Psyol river. During the advance one of the machines in Wittmann's platoon was hit and damaged. Following standard SS practice, the other Tigers closed round the disabled vehicle, protecting it until it was repaired. While the Tigers of Wittmann's platoon were guarding the immobile machine, the second platoon of the Heavy Weapons Company had not been inactive, but had gone into action and knocked out a number of guns. Then the whole Company drove through Lutschky and opened a destructive fire upon retreating soft-skin columns. Wittmann's platoon roared on and advanced at speed.

At the eastern edge of another village the vehicles once again came under fire. The Soviets had erected a barricade, and from close by that obstruction a pair of KV I tanks, dug in and serving as pill boxes, had engaged the Tigers at a range of some 600m. Their shells struck and set fire to the leading German vehicles, but both KVs were then attacked and destroyed. Orders came for the thrust line of Wittmann's platoon to be changed from north to north-west, and the objective now to be gained was the high ground, Point 260, lying between Gresnoya and Verchnopenye. Another wireless message then changed the day's objective once again. Now the target was Oboyan, and, covered by a rolling barrage of bombs dropped from Stuka dive bombers, the panzers raced into the attack. During the subsequent fighting Wittmann claimed seven more tanks and a number of pak.

Slowly the LSSAH advance reached the bend of the Psyol, and by 11 July it was at a point immediately to the south-west of Bogorodiskoya. On the sector confronting the SS Division lay Prokharovka, the most strongly fortified section of the whole Kursk salient, defended by élite Red Army formations including the 1Eighth and 20th Armoured Corps. A fierce tank battle raged; Wittmann's Tiger was hit twice during the fighting, and four vehicles of his platoon were knocked out. Prokharovka was finally taken, but there was no rest for the LSSAH. Fresh waves of Soviet armour emerged from the dust and smoke obscuring the battle-field and charged forward, determined to engage and destroy the dangerously weakened German panzer force. The Tigers opened fire and the mass of attacking Soviet tanks was eventually halted.

This was one of many such tactical successes, but against fanatical Russian resistance the assault by II SS Panzer Corps could make no further headway. Despite the losses they had suffered, the SS Divisions of II Corps were still determined to continue with the battle, and during the morning of 13 July moved out once again into the attack. Before they met the enemy the SS advance was halted. Hitler had decided that the offensive would be broken off, and on 17 July OKH took the SS Corps out of the line.

Later in the year, on 3 November 1943, Vatutin's 1st Ukrainian Front opened an offensive designed to recapture Kiev from the Germans. The weight of that massive operation flung aside the handful of Divisions defending the town and had captured it by 6 November. To restore the situation Hitler rushed several formations into the Kiev area, one of which was the LSSAH, which was returning to the Eastern Front after a brief period of rest and recuperation. The strategic situation on 13 November 1943 was that the Russian offensive had shattered the front of 4th Panzer Army, one of the constituent formations of Army Group South, and Soviet armour was advancing on either side of Zhitomir. The LSSAH first took position on the right flank of XXXXVIII Panzer Corps, then struck out of the area of Rogosana with the intention of gaining and cutting the Kiev-Zhitomir highway. The initially weak resistance encountered by the Leib-standarte demonstrated that an attack from the direction of Rogosana was totally unexpected by the Soviets, and had unbalanced their defence.

The Division's Heavy Panzer Company was put in to support the attack, and entered the line on 13 November, crossing the Kamenka river to the east of

Potshniki. Russian opposition to the division's advance was still weak. Then reports came in of a strong concentration of armour in and around Brusilov. It was clear that the Red Army High Command had decided to give battle there and that, therefore, a major conflict was imminent. The enemy units holding Brusilov, identified as 1st, 5th, and Eighth Guards Tanks Corps, were élite forces, and Army Group High Command decided that its forces would carry out a pre-emptive blow by striking at the Soviet armour and dispersing it before going on to capture the town. Unit orders were issued, and the Tiger Company set out in the growing darkness, leading the LSSAH column towards the objective; Brusilov.

From his perusal of a captured map Wittmann had already worked out a plan of action. He had noted that the whole area to the south-west of Brusilov was not only covered with woods and thickets, but was also cut by a number of small streams. He decided to use the cover of the trees and the river valleys to work his way forward towards the objective. Dawn was breaking when the Tiger Company advanced, and fire was opened upon it almost immediately by tanks and pak concealed in a small piece of woodland. Wittmann ordered his platoon to increase speed to pass quickly through the barrage, and as they raced forward he issued fire orders to the other Tigers and allotted targets to their commanders. The five vehicles halted and fired a salvo. Flames were seen and detonations heard. The group of Soviet tanks had been hit, had caught fire and exploded.

Wittmann recalled from his study of the map that a minor tributary of the Sdvish river ran near the woodland, and his Tigers drove down the low embankment and along the river bed, heading north-westwards while the other platoon of the Company covered the advance with a barrage of shells. Wittmann's platoon drove along the river bed towards a small wood from which enemy tanks were firing. At a point from which he could take the Red armour in flank, Wittmann brought his Tigers out of the river bed, halted them and gave the order to open fire. Then the machines advanced in line abreast, burst through another piece of woodland and charged into the laager of a battalion of some 30 enemy vehicles. The surprised Russians had little time to react, but soon rallied. In the close-quarters battle which followed one Tiger was knocked out.

Wittmann moved from one position to another, finding locations from which he could fire at the Russian machines. During one such move he heard a call for help. Instinctively he responded, and in his drive found himself at the back of a group of T 34s which were attacking a smaller number of Tigers. He opened fire, and within seconds two of the enemy machines had been destroyed. A third T 34 tried to ram Wittmann's tank, and when that failed the Russian crew left their vehicle and climbed on to the outside of the Tiger, intending to destroy it with hand grenades. Wittmann shot them off using a machine pistol. The other AFVs of the Heavy Panzer Company then rolled into the clearing to finish off the T 34s Wittmann had surprised. In a desperate effort to halt the Tigers the Soviets brought down mortar bomb and rocket fire from Katyusha projectors which, although they could not 'kill' a Tiger, did cause heavy casualties to the Panzergrenadiers taking part in the attack.

When that small battle ended at midday, Wittmann had already destroyed ten enemy tanks and five anti-tank guns. During the afternoon he went back into action again, and once in position opened fire upon a group of eleven T 34s and pak. Four enemy machines were knocked out in a couple of salvoes. The remaining seven concentrated their fire on Wittmann's smaller group, perhaps thinking that these represented no great challenge. Then the second Tiger platoon reached the clearing, and within minutes all the Soviet machines had been knocked out. At the day's end Wittmann and his crew had 'killed' another ten panzers as well as seven pak.

By the end of November 1943 XXXXVIII Corps had cleared up the situation and, in the words of the Wehrmacht communique, 'In the offensive and defensive battles on the Kiev and Zhitomir sectors the enemy armies were intercepted and flung back. Six hundred and three enemy tanks were destroyed.' Within days 4th Panzer Army, now regrouped after those winter battles, despatched XXXXVIII Corps to a new area, west of the Zhitomir–Korosten railway. Corps was given the task of carrying out a surprise attack against the right flank of the 60th Red Army in the Zhitomir–Radomyshl area. The Heavy Panzer Company had two primary objectives, Malin and Radomyshl, but to reach those towns it had first to break the pakfront between the villages of Kortuky and Styrty.

The standard tactic used to engage such a massed concentration of anti-tank guns was to charge the gun lines with the Tigers advancing and firing high-explosive shells rather than solid shot. High-explosive shells were capable of killing or wounding a greater number of enemy gunners than armour-piercing shells. As the Company neared Kortuky the Russian artillery opened up. Wittmann ordered two Tigers of his platoon to halt and engage targets while he and the other two machines continued the charge at top speed. With all five Tigers firing salvoes of high-explosive shells, a gap was quickly created in the enemy gun line. The Panther Company which was accompanying Wittmann's platoon then raced through the breach and charged towards Styrty. The attack was supported by panzergrenadiers riding in armoured personnel carriers, who fought down enemy infantry opposition and went on to consolidate the gains that had been made.

There was a brief halt for regrouping, and the ten Tigers formed a front, ready to resume the advance. Then, out of the mist of the cold, December morning rolled a giant Russian SP machine whose main armament was nearly 8m long. Wittmann's Tiger fired the first shot at the huge machine, and although the armour-piercing shell struck full on, it failed to penetrate the SP's thick frontal armour. A second shell also failed to pierce the armour, and Wittmann ordered his driver to move the vehicle to a point from where the gunner could fire into the SP's flank. The Tiger's gun was aimed at the side of the enemy vehicle and, at a range of about 100m, a shot was fired. Almost immediately the enemy machine blew up with an enormous detonation. Wittmann's Tiger then turned to rejoin the others as they prepared to charge another pakfront.

The opposition was hard, and as Wittmann took his place in the line a Tiger caught fire and a second was hit and lost a track. The remaining panzers fought their way through to the road on the southern side of the village. This was the main Russian defensive position, and a wall of fire from yet another pakfront backed by T 34s struck the German machines. Wittmann decided that a flank attack would have a better chance of success, and his vehicles turned away, driving for the eastern end of the village. Soon he had reached a point behind the Russian defensive positions, and he saw a soft-skin vehicle column preparing to drive away and escape. Driving slowly along the column of lorries, he shot it to pieces. The next objective was Golovin, and once again Wittmann's group made a flank attack. They reached a point south of the village near the railway line and there successfully engaged the enemy armour. In this engagement his platoon lost a vehicle and its crew.

The fire fight continued; Red tank against German panzer and panzer-grenadiers against Red Army infantry. During a short pause in the battle Wittmann was ordered to report to the regimental commander, who congratulated him on his 60th 'kill'. The fighting died away at last light and the exhausted Tiger crews slept in the village of Tortchin. Day after day the struggle went on, and more and more Russian tanks were destroyed. On 13 January 1944 the radio announcer, reading the Wehrmacht communique, announced the award of the Knight's Cross to Wittmann, and added:

> From July 1943 to the beginning of January 1944 he has destroyed
> 56 enemy AFVs, including T 34s and super heavy SPs. On 8 and 9
> January he and his platoon halted and destroyed the breakthrough
> attempts of a Soviet tank Brigade, and in that battle he destroyed
> a further ten vehicles. On 13 January, nineteen T 34s and three
> super-heavy SP guns. His total then stood at 88 tanks and SPs.

The background to the long battle which followed those victories was that, at the beginning of November 1943, the Red Army had opened a major offensive to recapture Kiev. On the 5th of that month, two days after the opening of the Red Army's operation, the LSSAH, by this time upgraded to panzer divisional status, was briefed on forthcoming operations. The Division was to form itself into two armoured columns and advance northwards up the Kiev–Zhitomir highway. On the 13th the Heavy Panzer Company came forward in support and took position on the east bank of the Kamenka river. There it was attacked by masses of enemy tanks. At Brusilov Wittmann's platoon and another from the Heavy Panzer Company came under intense fire from anti-tank guns and tanks of a Guards armoured unit, but despite the Russian superiority Wittmann had destroyed ten T 34's and five guns by midday. The Red Army units retreated, and he then carried out a pursuit of the fleeing enemy. His impetuous advance was only halted when a hurricane of fire fired by a fresh group of enemy tanks smashed down upon his platoon. He killed a further eleven machines during the day, and by nightfall he and his crews had put even more Russian tanks out of action.

With the capture of Brusilov on 24 November the LSSAH moved to attack the flank of 60th Red Army. When the assault went in on 6 December the Tigers were in the van of the advance. Pakfronts and SP guns were destroyed, and Soviet units attempting flight were shot to pieces. Just before Christmas the Division was engaged in the defensive battle of Berdichev, and was surrounded at Tortchin by three Soviet armoured and three infantry Corps. In the savage fighting which marked the Soviet offensive and the German counteroffensive, which were carried out in sub-zero temperatures, Wittmann's platoon engaged an armada of T 34s. In the evening of 13 December the Tigers went into action, counterattacking a massive breakthrough by Soviet armour and infantry. Fighting stopped at last light, only to be resumed at dawn the following day.

The number of enemy tanks and guns destroyed by Wittmann grew. On one day he destroyed sixteen enemy vehicles before lunch and a further three, together with three SP guns, during the afternoon. Those victories brought his total of 'kills' to 88, for which he was named in the Wehrmacht communique quoted above. On 20 January he was promoted to the rank of first lieutenant for bravery in the field.

On the morning of 6 February 1944 the LSSAH was sent to bring out a Corps which had been encircled near Cherkassy. In the fighting against 5th Guards Tank Corps Wittmann knocked out a further nine enemy armoured fighting vehicles. By 17 February the German rescue mission was completed, but the Tiger Company had suffered heavy losses and Wittmann took over temporary leadership of the Heavy Panzer Company when its commander was wounded.

At the end of this battle the exhausted Division was taken out of the line and posted to Belgium. In April 1944 Wittmann was posted from his Division and took over No. 2 Company of the 101st Heavy Panzer Battalion. That unit was called Corps troops; a unit whose employment was directed at corps and not at divisional level. The successes Wittmann had gained during his time on the Eastern Front caused him to become known outside the immediate circle of his own Division and the Armed Forces. His face became known to the German civil population, particularly when he was awarded the Oak Leaf to the Knight's Cross.

The Heavy Tank Battalion schwere Panzer Abteilung 101 with which Wittmann fought his battles in Normandy during the summer and early autumn of 1944 was one of the major Corps units of 1st SS Panzer Corps. The order of battle of that formation comprised two élite SS units; 1st SS Panzer Division

'Leibstandarte SS Adolf Hitler', with which Wittmann had once served, and the 12th SS Panzer Division 'Hitler Youth'. At the time of the Normandy landings the 101st Battalion was billeted in Beauvais, and was involved in a long approach march to Normandy which took it via Paris. While there, it was caught in an air raid and Wittmann's No. 2 Company had several vehicles damaged so badly that they had to be sent to the battalion's workshops. The delays to which 101st was subjected, the air raid and the long road march which caused some panzers to fall out with mechanical defects, meant that it did not reach the combat area until six days after the initial landings. Wittmann's Company was allocated positions in a small wood near the hamlet of Montbrocy, south of the main road and about 2km north of Villers Bocage. Here he was to add to the fame he had achieved in the fighting on the Eastern Front.

In order to understand the events which took place on 13 June 1944, we must go back to operations begun by British 2nd Army soon after the Normandy landings. It had been planned that the strategically important city of Caen would be quickly taken, but German panzer counterattacks launched between 6 and 10 June prevented this. Thwarted at one point by determined German opposition, Montgomery moved the point of maximum effort to the sector held by Panzer Lehr Division. This was holding a line running from St Pierre via Tilly sur Seulles to La Sanadiere. Operations had caused touch to be lost between Panzer Lehr and the unit on its left, 352nd Division, and the gap needed to be closed quickly and the line restored before Montgomery could exploit the situation. On 9 June the Army's 2nd Panzer Division was ordered to move forward to bridge the gap, but it would take several days for that unit to reach the area. None of the three Panzer Divisions in the line on 2nd British Army's sector could spare units to guard Panzer Lehr's left flank, and Dietrich, the 1st SS Corps commander, ordered 101st Heavy Panzer Battalion to hold the ground until 2nd Panzer reached the area and took over the task.

Operation Perch was Montgomery's plan to capture Villers Bocage, an important road centre south of Caen, and the offensive was spearheaded by 7th Armoured Division, which he sent on a south-westerly thrust line from Bayeux to capture Villers Bocage. When that village was taken, the German forces defending Caen would be threatened with encirclement. The Germans, just as well as the British, realised the strategic importance of Villers Bocage and were determined to hold it. The stubborn defence put up by Panzer Lehr to protect the Villers Bocage sector forced 7th Armoured to sidestep its units in order to work round the flank of Panzer Lehr to reach the objective.

That was the situation when the 101st Heavy Panzer Battalion was in the Villers Bocage area. Very early in the morning of 13 June a rumour spread that a British armoured Division was driving down Panzer Lehr's left boundary. Wittmann took his group of four Tigers, accompanied by a Panzer IV from the Panzer Lehr, and moved from the right side of the N 175, the main road to Caen, intending to drive down into Villers Bocage. Then, at about 0630, he saw a column of British AFVs climbing uphill out of the village and along the N 175. From wireless messages he knew that the battalion's No. 1 Company on the right side of the road was not ready to go into action, but action needed to be taken. The vehicles which Wittmann saw were from the 4th County of London Yeomanry (CLY), part of a battlegroup formed out of 22nd Armoured Brigade. That Brigade had been given orders from 2nd Army 'to enter the US sector [held by 1st US Infantry Division] and to exploit that operation with successes in the area of Villers Bocage and, if possible, to reach Point 213'.

The British battlegroup had set out as early as 1600 on 12 June, but had met opposition which was not overcome until 2000. It then laagered for the night, and it was not until 0530 on the 13th that the battlegroup resumed its advance. During its move, according to the Brigade War Diary, German armoured cars were seen. Aware that he was now in enemy territory, the Yeomanry's commanding officer asked for time to carry out a thorough reconnaissance, but this was refused him. He was ordered to drive fast and to gain the objective. The advance guard of the 22nd Armoured Brigade, 'A' Squadron of 4th County of London Yeomanry and 'A' Company of 1st Battalion The Rifle Brigade, reached Villers Bocage along the winding, south-westerly road from Avranches. This climbs uphill from the valley of the Seulles river towards the village. On its far side the road straightens out as it rises towards Point 213. In the full light of a fine, warm morning the Brigade had moved out from its overnight laager and by 0800 the point units had passed through Villers Bocage and were halted on the road between the village and Point 213. Each vehicle was halted at correct interval along the road, and the tactical disposition was: 'A' Squadron with the Rifle Brigade's No. 5 Platoon immediately behind it, followed by the headquarters group of 'A' Company and the half-tracks carrying other rifle platoons, and a mortar detachment mounted in carriers bringing up the rear.

Before the column undertook the last bound, which would take it to the crest of Point 213, an O Group was called and 'A' Company's officers walked uphill towards the leading AFVs. O Group was joined at about 0820 by the Yeomanry commanding officer, who brought his regimental headquarters group forward and halted the vehicles at a position some distance behind the Rifle Brigade's mortar detachment. During O Group the tank crews and the riflemen left their tanks and armoured carriers, put out pickets and began to relax. O Group was told that 'A' Squadron had completed its task as point unit, and that 'B' Squadron would take over the lead. At some point during O Group it was considered that the column on the road was creating a partial obstruction. To make room for 'B' Squadron's vehicles as they advanced up the N 175 towards the summit, all the drivers in the point unit were ordered to drive off the road and close their vehicles up head to tail to create less obstruction. While the drivers were moving their vehicles the remainder of the Yeomanry regiment and the 1st Battalion of the Rifles arrived in Villers Bocage and halted in the village.

Wittmann had seen the British column drive uphill and then halt at the junction of the N 175, the main road, and the D 6, a secondary road leading to Tilly sur Seulles. His Tiger was positioned not far from a railway line, and the British advance guard was diagonal to him on his right and about 600m distant. His panzer had gone unnoticed by the British chiefly because it was partly hidden from their sight by the thick bocage hedge and also because of Wittmann's skilful use of ground. Realising that immediate action was called for, he decided that a swift attack would throw the British off balance. He had no time to group his own Company nor to do more than advise No. 1 Company of what he intended to do. He issued orders over the wireless for the other vehicles of his company to follow him, then drove towards the N 175, where he saw, standing on the main road some distance behind, the point units, a small group of Cromwells and Shermans. The four Cromwells were from the CLY regimental headquarters group, and the Shermans were the tanks of the Signals Troop. These vehicles did not carry main armament but were fitted with a dummy gun.

Wittmann decided on a three-stage operation. As a first step his company would take out the Cromwell group. Then it would carry out a reconnaissance in Villers Bocage itself to determine the degree of opposition. Finally, it would drive uphill to destroy the point unit which was still positioned below the crest of Point 213. The Tiger halted on the rue Clemenceau, as the N 175 was named at this point, and faced the Cromwells at close range. Wittmann's first shot knocked out the commanding officer's tank, his second smashed that of the second in command, and the third destroyed the RSM's vehicle. Then he shot up the Shermans. The fourth Cromwell of the headquarters group reversed off the main road into either a small alley or a garden. Probably because of the dense clouds of smoke given off by the burning machines, Wittmann did not see that Cromwell as he made his way into Villers Bocage. Captain Dyas, the commander of the Cromwell, had an excellent opportunity to fire into the flank of Wittmann's Tiger, but could not exploit it. His gunner was outside the tank, and the fleeting chance was lost.

In Villers Bocage, 'B' Squadron, alerted by wireless messages and the sounds of battle, prepared for immediate action as Wittmann's machine rolled downhill, halted and then swung into the main street. The British tank shells ricocheted off the Tiger's thick front armour, but the degree of opposition was enough to give Wittmann the information he needed. There was a strong British force in Villers Bocage and a counterattack in strength would be needed to drive it out. He told his driver to withdraw, and as the panzer turned it confronted Dyas's Cromwell, which had been closing in, intending to shoot the Tiger in the back. The Cromwell fired twice at close range, but neither shot penetrated. Then the 88mm gun on Wittmann's panzer replied, and Dyas's Cromwell brewed up.

A check in the Tiger showed that both ammunition and fuel were low and needed to be replenished, but the vehicles of the point unit were still halted on the road. The chance to destroy them had to be taken. Wittmann moved into the attack, having decided that once he had dealt with the British vehicles he would fill his ammunition racks and fuel tanks. The Tiger was driven across country on an indirect line to the D 6 road and then, bursting through a gap in the bocage hedge, it debouched on to the N 175 close to the men and machines of the point group. Wittmann saw that the British vehicles had been brought so close to each other that they could not use their main armament. They were, in effect, defenceless. His first shot knocked out 'A' Squadron's Firefly, the only machine carrying a gun powerful enough to destroy his Tiger, and then he drove along the line of halted British vehicles, destroying them one after another. It took him less than five minutes to smash them; in 300 seconds he knocked out 27 tanks and other tracked vehicles.

The history of the CLY admits the loss of twenty Cromwells, four Fireflies, three other light tanks, three scout cars and a half-track, but it is unclear from the text whether all of these were destroyed in Wittmann's lone action or whether some were lost during the battle which subsequently raged in and around the village. Although the Rifle Brigade history mentions no vehicle loss, it is believed that at least six half-tracks were destroyed. The British Official History says that 25 tanks, 14 half-tracks and 14 Bren-gun carriers were destroyed in the Villers Bocage battle. The Germans lost at least three Tigers and several other panzers.

It must be assumed that Wittmann's Company did refuel and take on fresh ammunition, because he then led it back downhill into the village. The CLY had not been inactive after he had withdrawn from Villers Bocage; it had sent four tanks from 'B' Squadron across country to intercept and destroy the Tigers. The Cromwells could not negotiate the steep gradient of the railway embankment, and took up ambush positions in the rue Clemenceau, backed by a six-pounder anti-tank gun manned by men of the Queen's Regiment. However, the Cromwells did not use the advantage gained by waiting in a prepared ambush position to open fire upon Wittmann's Tiger as it cruised past. Instead, a shot from the anti-tank gun knocked his machine out. When the British armour finally opened up it was a Firefly which smashed the second Tiger and another Cromwell which then despatched a Mark IV.

Although Wittmann's Tiger had been put out of action, he and his crew escaped without injury. They then marched about 15km until they gained touch with the outposts of Panzer Lehr, and that formation gave him a group of fifteen Panzer IVs. With these he returned to the battle and collaborated with units from 2nd Panzer Division in the capture of Villers Bocage. The main of 2nd Panzer had now begun to reach the battlefield, and went into immediate action. The village was taken. A great number of the documents written about that day's action include citations, notably those from SS General Sepp Dietrich and from Bayerlein, commanding the Panzer Lehr. Those contemporary documents give life to the day's events.

The 101st left the Villers Bocage area on 16 June, and between 9 and 16 July was rested and re-equipped. It then went back into the action until 24 July. During that period Wittmann was promoted to the rank of Hauptsturmfuehrer (captain). He was also offered a post as an instructor so that he could pass on to others his great experience of tank warfare. He refused, stating that he preferred to stay with No. 2 Company. He was then given command of the 101st Battalion.

With the fall of Caen, the capture of the town of Falaise became the next major objective of Montgomery's strategy. The situation had arisen whereby the Allies were throwing a cordon around the German armies in Normandy. Already the Americans were moving fast along the southern side of a pocket which was being created, within which German 7th Army was being encircled. It was now up to the Canadians, on the northern side of the ring, to capture Falaise and thereby trap and reduce the flow of German 7th Army units towards the neck of the pocket. Opposing the Canadians was the 12th SS Panzer Division 'Hitler Youth', with orders to hold the Falaise area to the last. A joint Canadian-British offensive was launched on 7 August, and during the fighting of the following day Wittmann was killed in action.

When Wittmann led his battalion into battle on that day there were certain unusual features. Firstly, he was not mounted in his usual Tiger but in No. 007, one of the battalion headquarters vehicles. Secondly, he did not have his usual crew. Neither Boll, who had served as his gunlayer in so many of the missions on the Eastern Front, nor Wolff, was with him. They had been replaced by Reimers, acting as driver; Wagner as No. 1 on the gun; Weber, the gunlayer and Hirschel, the radio operator. The 101st, and indeed the whole German Army in Normandy, had been fighting without pause since the invasion opened on 6 June. By the first week of August all units had lost heavily and the nerves of those who still manned the line were overstretched by the constant shelling, aerial bombardment and lack of sleep.

The aim of the Canadian-British Operation Totalise was to capture Falaise by driving down the N 158, the main road from Caen. The offensive opened with the saturation bombing of the sector held by 12th SS Panzer Division, carried out during the evening of the 7th by aircraft from both the RAF and the US Eighth Air Force. That air raid was to be followed on the Eighth by another heavy bombardment, and once that had been completed the Canadian-British Divisions would begin their southerly advance towards Falaise.

The battle plan worked out by Crerar, the General Officer Commanding 1st Canadian Army, was for four parallel columns of Canadian units to advance down the right side of the road and for three columns of British troops, serving as part of his Army, to advance down the left side of the road. The offensive opened, and in its initial stages the Northamptonshire Yeomanry of 33rd Independent

Armoured Brigade, supported by 1st Battalion The Black Watch, gained ground by capturing the village of St Aignan. Those two units now held a salient some 5km deep inside German territory.

It was standard German military practice that counterattacks should be launched immediately to regain lost ground. It was also usual practice to launch a pre-emptive strike in an attempt to throw off-balance an enemy attack which had just begun to roll. The 12th SS Division decided to carry out both operations in one stroke. Ten Tigers of Wittmann's No. 2 Company of the 101st Heavy Panzer Battalion, backed by 40 Mark IVs from the 12th SS Division and 10 Jagdpanzer IVs from the same formation, would carry out an attack supported by Kampfgruppe Waldmueller, made up of 1st Battalion of 25th Panzergrenadier Regiment. That grouping would go in to regain the ground lost to the British, the advance being made under a barrage fired by three battalions of 12th SS Artillery Regiment. The point of maximum effort for this massive counterattack would be made on the right side of the main road; the British side. At the same, time pre-emptive blows against the Canadians would throw off-balance the imminent assault by the tanks of 4th Canadian Armoured Division.

Late in the morning of 8 August, Panzermeyer, the commander of 12th SS Panzer, the commander of Battlegroup Waldmueller and Wittmann of the 101st were conducting a final O Group when an RAF 'marker' aircraft flew over. All three men realised its significance. They knew that waves of Allied bombers would be guided in by that single machine, and that the target of the air raid would be the ground held by 12th SS. The SS officers agreed that the time of the attack should be brought forward so that the panzers and the Grenadiers were clear of the target area before the bombers arrived.

The panzer formations of Wittmann's battalion and the 12th SS then set off, moving uphill through the cornfields towards St Aignan, closely followed by Waldmuller's Grenadier Battalion. The British commander, who had been expecting such a reaction, brought down an artillery barrage. This was no deterrent to Wittmann, who merely increased speed, knowing that the gunners could not reduce the range quickly enough to hit him. About 1,800m from St Aignan the Tigers, using the superior range of their 88s, opened fire upon the Shermans of 4th Canadian Armoured Division and caused heavy casualties to a mass of vehicles which had concentrated ready to advance down the road towards the objective; the hamlet of Cintheaux.

Wittmann and a troop of three Tigers were driving along the British side of the N 158 with the village of Gaumesnil on their immediate left. His Tigers were engaging targets on the Canadian side of the road, and it could well be that Wittmann considered these a greater danger than the British units on his right. He knew his Tigers were beyond the range at which Shermans could endanger them, and apparently his assessment of the situation was that the Canadians were the more urgent priority. That must have been his thinking, because although he was partly hidden from the Canadian armour by thick bocage hedges, there was little cover on the British side. He was completely exposed to view across the undulating cornfields, but must have felt no danger from the British armour.

His Tigers, advancing in tactical order, were soon under intense scrutiny by a squadron of the Northamptonshire Yeomanry. The British crews watched as the panzers closed the range to about 800m. At this point confusion sets in as to who killed Wittmann on that August afternoon, for his death was claimed by both the Yeomanry and the Canadians. It is most likely that Northamptons 'killed' his Tiger. The entries for that day in the War Diary of 'A' Squadron record that at '1220hrs three Tiger (VI) [were] reported moving towards 'A' Squadron; and were brewed up at 1240, 1247 and 1252hrs, all without loss'. If it is accepted that Wittmann's vehicle was among those which the Yeomanry claim, then the 'kills' were made by a Firefly tank carrying a 17-pounder gun; the only one on the Allied side which could penetrate the Tiger's armour at a range of 800m. Wittmann could not have known that the British had a Firefly in the area, otherwise his dispositions would have been made to meet that situation.

Relying upon the War Diary, it would seem that shots from the Firefly hit and set alight one of the Tigers. It was then that the other German vehicles returned fire. A second shot from the Firefly struck another of the Tigers, which blew up in a sheet of flame accompanied by a loud explosion. The Firefly then fired two more shots and knocked out the third Tiger. It can be conjectured that the Tiger which blew up in flame and explosion was Wittmann's machine. The force of the detonation was powerful enough to blow off the heavy turret, which landed upside down several metres from the shattered hull.

When it was reported that Wittmann had not returned from the battle, a preliminary search was made by the 12th SS, but without result. His battalion comrades went out again during that day and on the night of 8/9 August, but could not find him. The mystery of whether he had been killed and, if so, how, remained unresolved until March 1983, when a team from the German War Graves Commission, helped and assisted by British and French volunteers, found fragments of bones, uniforms and an identity disc. These proved beyond doubt that the site where they were found was the battlefield burial place of Wittmann and his crew. Because it was impossible for the collection of bones to be individually identified, they were buried in a communal grave in the German War Cemetery at La Cambe. Two things which helped to identify Wittmann positively were an upper set of false teeth and a 6.35mm pistol which he was known to carry in his jacket pocket. The greatest 'ace' in the history of armoured warfare had been killed, but the memory of the man and his deeds remains.

Commander of the Eben Emael Attack

Major Rudolf Witzig

V ery few subaltern officers fighting their first major action carry out an operation which has far-reaching strategic potential. One such man was Rudolf Witzig, who commanded the attack force which captured a modern fortress at the first day of the War in the West in May 1940.

Born in Roehlinghausen on 14 August 1916, Witzig followed the normal educational path for a German boy. While still a teenager he became aware of Germany's economic plight in the terrible years of the depression which followed the ending of the First World War in 1918. In April 1935 he enlisted into the 16th Pioneer Battalion, and through his academic qualifications was soon selected to undergo a course for prospective officers. He was commissioned a second lieutenant in April 1937, then went on to further education in the Army's Pioneer School at Rehagen-Klausdorf, as well as undertaking a course of study at the War Academy. Following those interludes he served for over half a year as a platoon commander in the 31st Pioneer Battalion before applying for a transfer to the Army's Parachute Battalion. The transfer was made effective in August 1938, and Witzig was posted to the battalion's Pioneer platoon, where he carried out standard airborne training and also studied advanced engineering techniques. Thanks to his great knowledge of, and interest in, those disciplines, he passed through the set course and on 1 October 1938 gained the qualifying badge of the Army's Paratroop Battalion.

At that time there were two separate German airborne forces; the Army's battalion and the regiment being raised by the Luftwaffe. This anomaly was resolved in December 1938, when the Army formation was absorbed into the Luftwaffe organisation. Seven months later, in July 1939, Witzig was promoted to the rank of full lieutenant, and in October of that year he took over command of the Paratroop Pioneer Platoon, where his engineering skills gained the attention of Captain Walther Koch, one of the Luftwaffe's most celebrated junior paratroop officers. Koch had been selected to undertake a special mission, and had created a secret élite unit made up of No. 1 Company of 1st Paratroop Regiment, the pioneer platoon of that regiment's 2nd Battalion and the Glider Transport Company. Koch's special assault battalion had a strength of 500 men, and these were trained in assault operations using gliders to carry a complete group of men to a distant target. The men were, of course, all fully qualified parachutists.

Although it might seem improbable, it is true that the hour on which the German Army was to open its attack upon Holland, Belgium and France on 10 May 1940 depended upon the launching and successful outcome of the mission for which Koch's paratroop assault battalion had trained for six months. The Pioneer Platoon of Koch's battalion was commanded by Paratroop Lieutenant Witzig, and the platoon's task was to attack and capture the massive fortress at Eben Emael which lay on the Albert Canal to the west of the river Maas. Once Witzig's pioneers had captured Eben Emael and once the vital bridges across the canal had been seized by Koch's other detachments, the way would be open for 6th German Army to undertake its advance towards Liége and into the heart of Belgium.

Completed in 1935, the modern fortress of Eben Emael stood on a ridge protected to the east and north-east by 40m-high cliffs which dropped sheer into the Albert Canal and thus gave complete protection against conventional ground attacks from those directions. On its southern and south-westerly sides the structure was defended by anti-tank ditches and field fortifications. Beneath the fort lay a mass of interconnecting tunnels linking strongpoints, ammunition stores, a power station and a hospital. The area on the surface of the fort on which the glider pilots were expected to land their aircraft was only 900m long and 800m wide.

Each glider could carry seven or eight men and their equipment, including specially designed hollow-charge grenades. Some of the explosive grenades weighed 50kg and others 22.5kg. The heavier ones were designed to penetrate 25cm of armour plate, the thickness of the cupolas on the roof of the fort, and the lighter were intended to immobilise gun barrels. The fortress guns, many of which were set in retractable rotating cupolas, dominated the area for miles around, so Eben Emael was the one objective which had to be taken without fail. Were it not, the German Army's battle plan, Unternehmen Gelb, would be jeopardised. The success of the Eben Emael operation depended upon the pilots being able to land the eleven gliders of Witzig's group more or less simultaneously on a very small area, as well as on the skill and speed of the Pioneers in placing their charges on the correct cupolas.

There were many pressing problems connected with the glider assault, concerning the guns, the barbed wire covering the area, the restricted size of the landing ground and the few men in Witzig's detachment who were to undertake the operation. But the overriding concern was how little time had been allowed for his platoon to carry out their destructive mission. The Fallschirm High Command allowed Witzig and his men only one hour to land, take out the infantry and anti-aircraft positions, destroy as many of the twenty individual cupolas as possible and block all the exits and entrances to the subterranean areas. Every target was urgent, but the long-range guns dominating the Maas bridges had to be put out of action at all costs, for it would be across those bridges that 6th Army would advance.

It was believed at OKL that the Fallschirmjaeger would have no more than 60 minutes advantage before the Belgian garrison reacted and counterattacked. Thus, the first ten minutes were the most critical, for during that time the guns had to be destroyed. Within those 600 seconds the individual Troops of para-troop pioneers were expected to break out of their gliders, orientate themselves, cover the distance to their principal targets, fix the heavy charges in position and detonate them. Even before the fuses of those principal charges had exploded, the Troops would have gone on to attack the secondary objectives. It was a fear-ful task, and a heavy responsibility on the young Rudolf Witzig. The outcome of the enterprise depended absolutely upon the depth and extent of the training given to him and his pioneers.

The OKW strategy for the attack upon France and the Low Countries called for an advance by two German Army Groups. Army Group 'A', making the principal effort, was to drive through Belgium and Luxembourg with a thrust line towards the lower Somme. Army Group 'B', located to the north of Army Group 'A', was to protect the attacking Army Group's right flank. Army Group 'B' was to take out the frontier defences and go on to capture the important canal bridges and seize Eben Emael. Army Group gave the two latter tasks to 6th Army, for both objectives were in that Army's operational sector. Aware that many of the distant objectives of Army Group 'B' were beyond the range of even the speediest ground troops, thus ruling out the possibility of the targets being captured quickly, OKW proposed to use air-landed and parachute troops to seize the targets in Holland, and glider-borne units to take out the Belgian bridges and the fortress. Rudolf Witzig's report on the operation is given below in an abridged form.

Eben Emael was the most northerly and strongest of the defensive systems around Liege. It dominated the Albert Canal, the east-west road from Maastricht and particularly the vital bridges across the canal at Vroenhoven and Veldwezelt. The fortified area was 800m wide (east to west) and 900m long (north to south), and consisted of a number of infantry and artillery positions, most of which were mutually supporting. A ring of positions outside the central com-plex provided all-round defence, and there was a natural defence formed by high cliffs rising above the Albert Canal and the Gerbach. The canal was a barrier to the east and the Gerbach, together with a parallel anti-tank ditch, formed a double protection to the north and the north-west. The south and south-westerly sides were pro-tected by an anti-tank ditch and barbed wire barricades. The area was covered with small bushes which hid the main gun positions. The fort dominated the approach roads from Maastricht to Veldwezelt, Vroenhoven, Canne, as well as the roads and tracks leading southwards. The fortress formed the major part of the whole Albert Canal defensive system. Wide ditches, whose walls were 7m high, together with positions for close defence, protected the area. An extensive system of underground passages connected the fort internally.

The fort's defences consisted of artillery casemates, each with three 7.5cm guns, another set of three casemates with 7.5cm guns as well as an observation cupola. Then there were two 12cm twin guns in retractable turrets and four 7.5cm twin guns in retractable turrets. Along the canal the defences were anti-tank guns, machine-guns and searchlights. There was a trench system also with anti-tank guns, machine-guns and searchlights. The outer infantry works included machine-guns, anti-tank guns, searchlights and observation towers. In addition there were anti-aircraft machine-gun positions each with four guns, and a number of dummy positions. The garrison numbered 1,200 men. [The Belgian infantry defenders were few in number because Eben Emael was seen as an artillery position. The Belgian main infantry forces were located east of the Maas.]

In order that 6th Army might pass quickly between Roermond and Liége, it was essential to take out the frontier defences, to capture the Albert Canal bridges intact and to neutralise Eben Emael. For the last two operations paratroop drops would not have guaranteed success, and accordingly the German High Command chose gliders as the means to reach the objectives. Those machines had a number of advantages. They made no sound, they would be invisible against the night sky and they could carry a complete Troop of men. The same number of Jaeger dropped by parachute would have had the disadvantage of being dispersed; a "stick" jumping from a Ju 52 in seven seconds at a height of 90m would be spread across a 300m area. There was also the danger that an alert sentry might see the white parachutes descending through the night and raise the alarm.

A DFS glider, carrying men or a ton of equipment, could be cast off 25km from its objective by its towing aircraft and, in skilled hands, be piloted to within 20m of its objective. There would no time lost in having to collect the men together. Each Troop would be carried in a single glider, and upon landing would break out of the flimsy fuselage to attack its given targets. In addition to the usual infantry weapons, special pieces of Pioneer equipment were carried collapsible assault ladders, flamethrowers and hollow-charge grenades which were being used for the first time to test their capabilities in smashing the armour-plate cupolas of the gun emplacements.

There were twenty individual targets to be taken out, but with a total attack force of only 85 men, including the glider pilots who had been trained as intensely as the Pioneers, the platoon would have to concentrate quickly and destroy simultaneously the main artillery and anti-aircraft cupolas, particularly those whose guns dominated the area to the north, where the canal bridges were located across which 6th Army was to pass. It was calculated that the Pioneer Troops would have only an hour to carry out all their tasks, for it was anticipated that after that period the Belgians would have overcome the initial shock and would begin to fight back. By blowing up the principal entrance and the smaller ones the enemy could be stopped from coming out to fight. In the event of the Paratroop Pioneer Platoon not gaining its objectives its Troops had orders to hold the ground they had captured until a back-up unit, the Army's 51st Pioneer Battalion, could be rushed forward. If it was thought necessary, Stuka attacks would be made to block the principal entrance.

The issue of the operation order on 9 May was a relief after the six months of intensive training. Koch's assault battalion, the groups which would take out the Albert Canal bridges and the Pioneer Platoon grouped on the airfields around Cologne and emplaned shortly before 0430. It had been planned that all four glider groups would touch down on their objectives simultaneously at 0525, five minutes before the German Army opened the War in the West. The 'tug' aircraft towing the gliders took off, made a curve to the south to gain height and then flew along a flight path illuminated by fires towards the cast-off point. There were incidents involving the gliders of the Pioneer Platoon, when the ropes on two of the machines broke. What made the loss of one glider particularly worrying was that it carried the Platoon Commander (Lieutenant Witzig) and in an enterprise having so tight a deadline the loss of one fifth of the platoon's effectives meant extra work for the remaining Troops. The nine remaining gliders swooped down out of the night and into a light fog which covered the area. The machines were met with scattered machine-gun fire, but upon touchdown the Troops moved into action and began their planned tasks of destruction. Within ten minutes the soldiers, working almost precisely to the battle plan schedule, had successfully attacked nine objectives. Seven armour-plate cupolas had been attacked and destroyed by the hollow-charge grenades, and nine 7.5cm guns in three casemates had been put out of action. All of those successes had been accomplished in the southern area of the fortress by seven Troops numbering 55 men. During that time other Troops had been employed in attacking targets in the northern sector of the fort.

The two gliders whose tow ropes had broken both came down inside Germany, and by the time the original Ju 52 tug aircraft had returned, landed, and taken off again with its glider in tow, three hours had elapsed. When the platoon commander's machine landed, he found that the main tasks had been completed and the principal objectives taken. The Belgian defenders had opened artillery fire against Troops caught in the open, and what was thought to be a Belgian infantry attack had been mounted. This proved subsequently to have been no more than an aggressive reconnaissance patrol. The Pioneer Platoon held the ground in the northern edge of the fortress and sent out fighting patrols equipped with hollow-charge grenades to block the entrances to a number of emplacements and complete the work of demolition.

On 11 May at about 0700 the leading group of 51st Pioneer Battalion crossed the Albert Canal and made contact with the Paratroop Platoon. At about midday, when other groups from the 51st came across the water, the last flickers of Belgian resistance ended and the garrison surrendered. That garrison numbered 750 men in total and had been housed in strongly fortified positions. The garrison surrendered to a paratroop group of less than a hundred men. The Pioneer Platoon lost six men killed and fifteen men wounded, four of whom had been injured as a result of the shock of the glider landings.

The OKW communique issued on 11 May gave details of the paratroop operations of the previous day. In part, it stated: '... the fort [Eben Emael] was put out of action by an élite group of Luftwaffe personnel under the command of Oberleutnant Witzig'. The success of Assault Battalion Koch in gaining its objectives resulted in all the senior officers of the battalion being recommended and awarded for the Knight's Cross of the Iron Cross. In Witzig's case there was an administrative difficulty. Most awards in the German forces were graded by class. For a man to receive the Knight's Cross he had to possess both Second and First Classes of the Iron Cross, and Witzig had neither. The problem was overcome by granting him the Knight's Cross on 10 May and the other two classes retrospectively. In addition to the crosses, Witzig, in common with the other men who had fought in the action, was promoted, and rose from lieutenant to captain.

The signals sent by Koch's battalion to its headquarters for onward transmission to OKW are interesting. The signals from the Troops which took out the bridges are not included below; only those received from the Pioneer Platoon at Eben Emael.

10 May 1940. Eben Emael

0542. Target reached. Everything in order.
0835. We are beating back the enemy. The high ground is being attacked.
1050. The western high ground has been taken. All the enemy casemates are out of action.
1240. We are under heavy artillery fire.
1320. An enemy reconnaissance patrol has been flung back. Everything in order.
1810. Enemy counterattack on the southern corner has been beaten back. We need artillery support.

11 May 1940. 6th Army HQ

0820. There is no contact with the Troops at Eben Emael. There are unconfirmed reports that they are on their way back after completing the mission.

Witzig's star was in the ascendant, and there followed a posting to the Luftwaffe High Command in Berlin, where he served as adjutant to Reichsmarschall Goering. Witzig then returned to active duty and took over command of No. 9 Company in the 3rd Battalion of the Air Landing Assault regiment, and was with that formation when it took part, as a contingent of Battlegroup West, in the invasion of Crete. The objectives of Battlegroup West were the town and airfield of Maleme, which had to be taken and held for it was upon Maleme airfield that the air-landing component, the 5te Gebirgs Division, was to disembark. Witzig led his men into action supporting the regiment's 1st Battalion and elements of 2nd Battalion which were attacking the commanding height, Point 107. During the successful assault upon that objective he was wounded and evacuated by air, first to Athens and then, when the wound failed to heal quickly enough, to a hospital in Germany.

The successes gained by the Airborne Division in Crete led to Hitler issuing an order to expand the airborne arm of Service. As a result of that growth, the pioneer unit became the Corps Pioneer Battalion, and on 10 May 1942

Colonel Barenthin, commanding Paratroop Corps troops, handed over command of that unit to Rudolf Witzig. In the spring of 1942 Witzig received orders for his battalion to proceed via Italy to Africa, where it was to form part of Ramcke's Brigade, which was serving in the desert. Following the battle of El Alamein, the Axis forces began a retreat out of Egypt and then out of Libya into Tunisia. Because of the confused situation in North Africa, as well as shortages of supplies and equipment among the forces serving there, there were delays in transporting Witzig's Pioneer Battalion from Europe. During this waiting period he was called to a conference with Field Marshal Kesselring and told that he and his men now had a new destination. Instead of going to Italian North Africa, they were to be flown to the French colony of Tunisia and, specifically, to Bizerta.

Such was the confusion arising from the Allied invasion of Algeria and Tunisia that Kesselring's order could not be carried out. By the time Witzig had returned to his headquarters some of his unit had been moved to Greece, while Nos. 3 and 4 Companies had returned to Italy. It seemed likely that the battalion's move overseas would be subject to even further delays, but eventually space was found on a six-engined flying boat which took off from Piraeus on 15 November, carrying the advance party of battalion headquarters, the signals group and No. 1 Company. On the following day that advance guard was joined by other detachments from the battalion. Then Nos. 3 and 4 Companies arrived from Italy and, while the battalion was concentrating, orders were received that, although it was not completely raised, the battalion was to send two of its Companies into action. The need for haste arose because the flimsy German perimeter in western Tunisia was close to collapse, and every available man had to be rushed forward to hold the line. The Companies of Witzig's Battalion were sent out with orders to advance as far westwards as possible, to try to reach Tabarka and halt the Allied advance upon the Tunisian capital.

The Pioneer Battalion had no vehicles; these had had to be left behind in Italy, and all that was available to the remaining Companies were six motorcycle combinations and two field kitchens without prime movers. But new units which Hitler had ordered to be rushed to the Tunisian bridgehead had arrived, and these included a Company of Panzer IVs. These were added to the battalion's strength, together with a Company of Italians equipped with SP anti-tank guns, a platoon of 2cm flak and a battery of 10.5cm guns, the whole being formed into Battlegroup 'Witzig'. There were no personnel carriers for the Jaeger Pioneers, who had to find places where they could on the outsides of the battlegroup's vehicles.

Late in the afternoon of 16 November Witzig led his group westwards, following the route taken by the two advance guard Companies, and on the morning of 17 November, outside the small town of Tabarka, his group first brushed with the enemy. The Allied outpost line withdrew to previously prepared positions, and from these and from the high ground along the road from Sedjenane they had excellent observation of the Axis battlegroup as it rolled towards Djebel Abiod, a small village some 100km west of Bizerta. The village and the surrounding ground was held by three Companies of 6th Battalion The Queen's Own Royal West Kent Regiment, supported by a few 25-pounders. The battle began at 1430, when the British artillery opened fire, and within minutes eight of Witzig's AFVs were alight. But the German paratroops reacted swiftly, leapt from the vehicles on which they had been riding and returned fire. The line reached during that first engagement at Djebel Abiod was, at that time, the farthest point westwards that Witzig's battlegroup advanced.

After that first engagement, the battalion went over to the defensive and in time was absorbed into the von Broich Division then being created. The German front, until then made up of splinter groups, was slowly coalescing as more and more units reached the perimeter and were organised into formal establishments. The onset of winter weather then slowed the pace of military operations on both sides, and in that period of relative calm the Pioneers improved their front-line positions, using explosives to blast out slit trenches in the rocky ground. Those defensive posts created the so-called 'Jefna' position. The term 'relative calm' is deceptive, as the days, and more particularly the nights, were filled with patrol activity, but there were no major military operations. Later in the year there was an increase in the strength of Witzig's battalion when its No. 2 Company, which had been on detached duty with Ramcke's battlegroup in Libya, came back on strength.

The battalion took a prominent part in the offensive around Medjez el Bab on 26 February. Witzig led it along the small Sedjenane River to the north of the main westward-leading road, and in the hills around Sedjenane the Paratroop Pioneers were soon engaged in hand-to-hand combat against British infantry forces. During the battle a number of British AFVs were destroyed using satchel charges and other close-quarter weapons. Fighting died away slowly as the German advance was halted, but during 8 March the delayed operation was reactivated. The pause in the fighting had been used by units of the British First Army to regroup, and when the Pioneer Battalion opened its fresh attack this collapsed in the face of Allied artillery. Witzig ordered all of his Companies to withdraw except for No. 1 Company, which was told to hold the positions it had gained. He intended it to be the springboard when he resumed the stalled attack, but this was not to be. Before he could open a fresh assault a British counterattack swept in and overran No. 1 Company.

In Witzig's opinion there could now be no question of the German assault being resumed, but von Manteuffel, who had succeeded von Broich as divisional commander, insisted upon it. Deeply concerned at the heavy losses suffered by his battalion, Witzig spoke out and advised against a new offensive, but Manteuffel insisted upon it. The new assault was made, but despite initial gains of territory it collapsed and Allied pressure forced the battalion back as far as Jefna.

By April the strength of Witzig's battalion had sunk to just himself and one other officer, four NCOs and 27 men.

The end of the campaign in Africa was fast approaching, and on 6 May Witzig was given authority to take his battalion out of Tunisia and try and reach Italy by ship. There then followed days racing from one port to another to find a vessel, but that activity ended when the capture of Tunis on 7 May separated Witzig and one small group in the north of Tunisia from the main body of the battalion south of the capital city. The groups then subdivided into Sections. They sought, and some found, passage on craft heading for Europe. Major Witzig and his group received special orders and priority treatment, a high-speed motorboat being sent to carry them to Sicily. The war in Africa was ended.

Upon his return to Germany, Witzig was given a short spell of leave and was then posted to Wittenberg an der Elbe, where a new Fallschirm Pioneer Battalion was being created to replace the original one which had been destroyed in Tunisia. The battalion was raised and posted first to the Erveux area, 80km west of Paris, and then to an area near Vichy. It remained in that area, and the only change during the time it spent there was that the German Airborne organisation expanded from a two-corps establishment to become an Army. As a consequence the Pioneer establishment was increased to become a regiment; the 21st Paratroop Pioneer Regiment. Witzig's battalion thereupon became the 1st Battalion of the new regiment. Not only did he retain command of his battalion, but he also led the newly formed Regiment.

The fact that an Allied invasion would be made in north-west Europe was clear to all the Pioneers, and although the invasion came in June it was not until the first days of July that the Pioneer regiment was ordered into action. It moved towards the battlefront, but not as a single unit. Witzig's 1st Battalion had already been posted to Salzwedel, where it was held to counter a possible Allied air landing in Scandinavia, as well as to protect the flow of iron ore to Germany.

In June 1944, the month during which the invasion of Europe was launched, 1st Battalion of the Pioneer Regiment, commanded by Major Witzig, was posted from Salzwedel to the Eastern Front, where it came under the command of Paratroop Battlegroup Schirmer. This posting had been made necessary because Soviet military advances which had struck German Army Group Centre had not only brought about its almost total destruction but also separated it for a short time from Army Group North. The Red Army formations which had broken through had raced on so quickly across Germany's eastern provinces that they also cut the communication land lines between Army Group North's fighting echelons and its rear supply depots. As a consequence, the combat formations of that Army Group had had to be supplied by sea until the land route was restored.

The Russian offensive posed a frightening threat to the eastern borders of the Reich, and demanded the employment of every available unit to seal the battle line. Among those brought in by the trawl or taken from quieter sectors of the Eastern Front was Witzig's 1st Battalion of the Paratroop Pioneer Regiment. It was rushed by train to East Prussia and thence to Lithuania, where it went into the line on 29 June, to the east of Kovno. The first contact with the enemy came in the form of a long and heavy bombardment, but surprisingly this was not followed up by an infantry attack, which was the usual pattern of Soviet tactics. Reconnaissance patrols soon established that there was no immediate crisis on the battalion's sector, and it was then ordered to take up new positions along the Kovno-Duena road and, specifically, at a village named Jonava.

It was here that German High Command expected a major Russian armoured assault would be launched. The battalion foot-marched, reaching its objective during the evening of 25 July. High Command was, of course, aware that a single battalion, even one of such an élite arm of Service as the Fallschirmjaeger, could not be expected to hold a major Russian assault without support, and Witzig's formation was reinforced with an Army battlegroup. To the Paratroop Pioneer Major it seemed obvious that the Red Army's main effort on his sector would be made along the Kovno-Duena road, and it was on the left side of that highway that he placed Lieutenant Kubillus's No. 1 Company. Kubillus sent forward one of his platoons to form a slender outpost line, supporting this with a heavy machine-gun group. On the right side of the road Witzig placed No. 2 Company under Lieutenant Walther. The right flank platoon of that Company was in touch with the left wing Company of a neighbouring infantry unit. Thus, the battalion's right wing could be considered firm and safe. Lieutenant Schuermann's No. 4 Company formed the battalion reserve. The unit's remaining Company, No. 3, under the command of Lieutenant von Albert, was not at that time serving with the battalion but had been detached and was acting as Corps reserve.

Into Witzig's sector there then rolled a few SPs and other mobile anti-tank guns. These AFVs took up position in a wood behind the battalion, from where it was expected they would give long-range support. For close-quarter tank-busting Witzig's men had one Panzerschreck for every four men, as well as a large number of Panzerfausts.

Shortly before last light on 25 July, Nos. 1 and 2 Companies in the line took up all-round defence and kept a vigilant watch; the Russians were less than a kilometre distant. The Companies had little chance to rest. Throughout the night the sound of tank engines and tracks was loud and continuous. As he made the rounds of the trench line, Witzig warned his men: 'When the Ivans come they will be in overwhelming numbers'. Patrols from both Companies went out at first light and discovered that several of the German listening posts dug-in forward of the outpost line had been attacked during the night, the men in the trenches either being killed or taken prisoner. The day passed with the pioneers expecting hourly to be attacked, but the Russians made no move. That night, for a second time, there came the sound of tank engines in the darkness. 'Stand to' next morning produced the sight of a long line of Soviet AFVs facing Witzig and his men, just over a kilometre distant. Behind the line of steel the Pioneers could see row upon row of 'Stalin organs', field artillery pieces and anti-tank guns. It was a psychological demonstration of naked power by the Soviets; evidence of the strength they could afford to fling against a unit as small as a single paratroop battalion.

A heavy midsummer silence hung over the battlefield; then, when it seemed that it would never be broken, with a terrible roar the Russian guns and rocket projectors opened up and deluged the Pioneer trench line with a storm of steel. For more than an hour the bombardment lasted. Wounded Pioneers going back to the RAP then saw to their surprise that the SPs which should have been supporting the battalion had begun to pull back, although no one could say why they were withdrawing or where they were being taken. The Russian barrage eventually began to lessen, although it did not cease entirely. The guns had spoken. Now it was the turn of the armour, and behind the first line of tanks there were arrayed rows of others on which Red Army infantry were mounted.

The first line of tanks moved forward, gathered speed and prepared to charge at and over the thin, short line of trenches of No. 1 Company. The Company commander's fire orders were brief. The enemy was to be allowed to approach to within 200m, and only then would fire be opened. Soon the Russian vehicles were within range, and the Paratroop Pioneers left their trenches and attacked the armour at close range with panzerfausts, bazookas and satchel charges. One after another, groups of T 34s burst into flame as they were struck and knocked out. Kubillus, No. 1 Company commander, destroyed first one vehicle and then a second, but was then hit and seriously wounded by machine-gun fire. A Corporal who had already knocked out three tanks took over command of the Company, and under his leadership fifteen more enemy machines were destroyed. The fierceness of the German resistance halted the Soviet attack against No. 1 Company, but then across ground littered with burning armoured vehicles a mass of Red Army infantry stormed forward into an attack, only to die in the fire of the Company's heavy machine-guns. A quick check of the Company positions showed that only 30 men were still standing. The others had been killed or wounded.

Reports came in from the outpost line of No. 2 Company on the right-hand side of the road that no fewer than 50 Russian tanks were about to make an attack, and that behind the armour there were columns of Russian infantry marching forward to take part in the assault. Eight of the 50 enemy vehicles raced down with infantry hanging on their outsides. German machine-gun fire forced the Red soldiers to leap from the turrets, and then the armoured machines came under panzerfaust fire and were destroyed one after the other.

But those eight machines had only been bait to attract No. 2 Company's attention. While the Pioneers had been fighting them, the remaining Russian machines began to outflank the paratroop positions. The attacking tank group was reinforced by other enemy machines which raced into No. 2 Company's area from the direction of the main road. That group was attacked and destroyed in its turn, but then fresh enemy vehicles advanced from all sides to beef up the main attack. Soon it was clear that the Company's resistance was coming to an end. When it did, the Paratroop Pioneers of No. 2 Company pulled back and regrouped around a farmhouse behind their positions.

A battle of equal intensity was still being fought in No. 1 Company area, and groups of Red Army tanks covered with infantry roared across the line of German slit trenches. Russian machine-gun teams bypassed Pioneers still holding out, and set up their weapons to fire into the backs of the defenders. No. 1 Company was forced to pull back through standing corn and then across a piece of open ground to reach a large wood, where the remnant of the battalion had been ordered to rally. Russian machine-guns set up in the cornfield opened fire and had soon turned the area into a killing ground, and No. 1 Company lost no fewer than eighteen men killed in trying to cross it. Only twelve men on that Company reported in, and Witzig set up a sentry line to guide any remaining individual soldiers towards the battalion area.

Ordered to withdraw and moving in single file, No. 2 Company made its way along a series of ditches, and for the greater part of its retirement was under fire from Soviet infantry, machine-gunners and tanks. When the shelter of the ditches came to an end, the men faced a perilous passage across the flat and open 'killing ground' to reach the shelter of the trees.

In the wood, Major Witzig began to group the survivors; those who had fought their way through to him. He led the column past Russian tank units and Red Army infantry groups marching on a parallel course to his battalion. On the morning of the second day's march Witzig and his remnant reached the German lines. Although the Paratroop Pioneer Battalion was all but destroyed, it had achieved a notable victory. The losses which the Red Army had suffered on this particular sector had been so severe that for more than two days there was no further forward movement by the Soviets.

The Paratroop Pioneer survivors took part in the retreat of the German Army towards the East Prussian frontier, and even though there were only 54 survivors of Nos. 1 and 2 Companies, this was not the end of the battalion or its battles. Those few survivors carried on fighting until October, when they were shipped back to Mecklenburg. There Major Witzig took leave of his men to command the newly raised 18th Paratroop Regiment, and the battalion he had commanded so well was broken up.

The regiment which Rudolf Witzig now led formed part of 6th Paratroop Division, whose raising had been ordered in April 1944. The heavy losses which the incompletely raised Division suffered during the fighting in Normandy meant that it had to be broken up and created anew. When the units of the reconstituted 6th Division had been assembled and grouped, the formation went into the line in southern Holland, and was moved from the area of Arnhem to positions between the Maas and the Rhein. On 25 November Witzig was advised that he had been awarded the Oak Leaf to the Knight's Cross for his leadership in the operations in Lithuania.

The 18th Regiment remained in action until February 1945, when it moved to the heavily forested Reichswald area of Western Germany and relieved a badly shattered Army unit. During the third week of February the 6th Para Division was ordered to extend the length of its front, and Witzig's 18th Regiment took over part of the sector of 21st Regiment near Kleve. There the 18th was engaged in bitter fighting against British and Canadian flamethrowing tanks, and had to give ground against units from both armies, which attacked it in overwhelming strength. The ensuing withdrawal was only the first of many which had to be carried out during March 1945.

From the 12th of that month the 6th Para Division fought a defensive battle along the Rhine between Emmerich and Rees with Witzig's 18th Regiment on the left, supported by the remnant of 17th Regiment. Under a barrage which lasted twelve hours the Allies crossed the Rhine and the armada of US tanks which came over the river struck into the flank of Witzig's regiment, forcing it to retreat north-eastwards. That retreat opened a gap in the German line which it was impossible to close, and it was against that open flank that a British tank attack came in on 17 April. Under its impact the 6th was fragmented. Small groups of paratroops carried on the fight, but by 8 May the war was over and Witzig, together with the other officers and men of 6th Paratroop Division, passed into captivity. There was some good news to soften the bitterness of defeat. Major Witzig was informed that in the last days of the war his name had been added to the Luftwaffe's Roll of Honour.

Witzig was fortunate in that he spent only a few months as a prisoner of war, being released in September 1945. He lived for several years in retirement, but in January 1956 he was invited to rejoin the forces. He served as a Lieutenant Colonel in the Bundeswehr, and commanded the headquarters of a Pioneer regiment. From that post he went on to lead 2nd Pioneer Battalion, and also served on the Inspectorate of Weapons and Equipment. Promotion to colonel in 1965 brought him a new post on the staff of the Pioneer School in Munich. He retired from the forces in 1974, and since then has devoted his life to leading the pan-German Paratroop Organisation and playing a leading part in the Confédération Européene des Anciens Combattants, bringing together old soldiers of former enemy nations.

Bibliography

Published Works

Alman, K., *Die Ritterkreuztraeger des Afrika Korps*

Austermann, H., *Von Eben Emael bis Edewechter Damm*

Bielefeld and Essame, *The Battle for Normandy*, Batsford

Blumenson, *Break-out and Pursuit*, US Army, 1961

Boehmler-Haupt, *Fallschirmjaeger*

Bundesarchiv Zentralnachweisstelle, *Ranglists der Generaele der Luftwaffe 1939–45*

Ellis, *Victory in the West*, HMSO, 1968

Esebeck, H. von, *Helden der Wueste*, Heimbuecherei, Berlin, 1942

— *Sand, Sonne, Sieg*, Heimbuecherei, Berlin, 1942

Gericke, *Hurra! Wir springen*

Goerlitz, W., *Model*

Goetzel, *Generaloberst Kurt Student und seine Fallschirmjaeger*

Greiner, H., *Kampf um Rom; Inferno am Po*

Heydte, F. von, *Muss ich Sterben, Will ich Fallen*

Hillgruber, *KTB der OKW*, Bernard & Graefe

Huebner, *Das Sturmbatallion der Fallschirmjaeger Armee*

Jung, *Die Ardennen Offensive 1944–1945*

Kesselring, A., *Soldat bis zum letzten Tag*

— *Die deutsche Luftwaffe im Bilanz des Zweiten Weltkrieges*

Lehmann, R., *Die Leibstandarte*, Munin, various dates

Liddell-Hart, B., *The Rommel Papers*

Manstein, *Lost Victories*

Mellenthin, F. W., *Panzer Battles*, Vowinckel, 1953

Middelldorf, E., *Taktik im russischen Feldzug*, E.S. Mittler, 1956

Munzel, O., *Panzertaktik*, Vowinckel, 1959

Nehring, W. K., *Die Geschichte der deutsch Panzerwaffe, 1916–1945*, Motorbuch Verlag, 1974

OKW, *Kriegstagebuecher 1940–1945*

Playfair, I., and Molony, C., *The Mediterranean and the Middle East*, Vols 1–4, HMSO, 1956/66

Ramcke, B., *Fallschirmjaeger damals und danach*

Rendulic, L., *Gekaempft, gesiegt, geschlagen*

— *The Fighting Qualities of the Russian Soldier*

Selbstverlag, *Geschichte des Panzer Korps 'Grossdeutschland'*, Berlin, 1958

Tessin, G., *Verbaende und Truppen der deutsch. Wehrmacht und Waffen SS, 1939–1945*, Biblio Verlag

Traditionsverband der Division, *Geschichte der 3ten Panzer Division*, Richter, Berlin, 1967

Tschimpke, A., *Die Gespenster Division der NSDAP*, Zentralverlag, 1941.

Weber, Th., *Die Memoiren Generalfeldmarschall Kesselring; Ein neuer Beitrag*

Weidinger, O., *Das Reich*
— *Kameraden bis zum Ende*

Yerger, M., *August Krag*
— *'Das Reich'*, Vol. 1
— *Knights of Steel* ('Das Reich' Division)
— *Otto Kumm*
— *Otto Weidinger*

Histories of several divisions and corps, notably 1st Panzer, 3rd Panzer, 7th Panzer, 1st SS Panzer, 2md SS Panzer, 'Grossdeutschland' Panzer Corps, as well as official histories of the American and British forces in Africa, Italy and north-west Europe.

Unpublished Sources

AFRIKA KORPS
KTB. Afrika Korps & Panzer Armee Afrika

ARMY GROUP 'B'
KTB. 1944

BAOR
Intelligence Reviews. Various dates.

7TH ARMY
KTB. 1944

SIMON
Experiences gained in combat against Russian infantry.

SIMON
Soviet Infantry and armoured forces.

Also interviews and correspondence with former German soldiers.

Index

Aa canal, 19
Aachen, 100, 101
Aalen, 191
Aalten, 35
Agedabia, 158
Aisne, 110
Alam, Halfa, 31, 113
Alaric, Operation, 32
Alarm Brigade Grossdeutschland, 63
Alarm Group Schmelter, 63, 64
Albert Canal, 35, 179, 180, 184, 216–20
Alexayovka, 201
Algeria, 48, 160, 222
Alpine Fortress, 144
Alps, 146
Annaberg, 16, 166
Antwerp, 36, 100, 102
Archangelskoye, 136
Ardennes, 35, 73, 102, 109
Argentan, 194
Armentières, 155
Armoured Battlegroup Langkeit, 56, 59
Arnhem, 35, 100, 185, 228
Arnim, General Jurgen von, 114
Arras, 154, 155
Assault Battalion Koch, 180
Astrakhan, 78, 80, 168
Athens, 182
Austrian Consular Academy, 27
Avdeyevka, 189
Avesnes, 153
Avranches, 126
Azov, Sea of, 75, 81

Bad Toelz, 201
Badoglio, Marshal, 51, 50
Baku, 79
Balaton, 24
Balck, General Hermann, 24
Baranov, 116

Barbarossa, Operation, 46, 90, 110, 130, 201
Bardia, 158
Bardiyev, 116
Barenthin, Colonel, 222
Barkmann, 9
Bastogne, 24
Battlegroup Peiper, 24
Bavaria, 25, 26
Bavarian State Police, 15
Bayerlein, General Fritz, 99, 103, 211
Bayeux, 161
Bayreuth, 40
Beauvais, 208
Beck, General Ludwig, 73, 108, 152
Berchtesgaden, 138
Beresina, 90
Berghof, 83
Berlin, 71
Berlin University, 27
Birch Tree, Operation 141
Bir Fuka, 124
Bir Hachim, 112, 159
Birch Tree, 140
Bittrich, 66
Bizerta, 222, 223
Blaskowitz, General Johannes von, 185
Blau, Unternehmen, 59, 93, 94
Blitzkrieg, 12, 108, 111
Bobruisk, 90, 130, 132
Bock, Field Marshal Fedor von, 46, 109
Bologna, 52
bomb plot, 84, 162
Bosnia, 138
Brac, 137
Brandenburg, 138
Brauchitsch, Field Marshal Walter von, 85
Braunschweig, 123, 186
Breslau, 72, 84, 166, 170
Brest, 126, 127
Brest-Litovsk, 109, 90

Brittany, 125, 126
Brusilov, 204, 206, 207
Bryansk, 111
Budapest, 24
Budweis, 197
Bug, river, 90
Buipavas, 127
Bulgaria, 19
Bulge, Battle of the, 8, 23, 35, 101, 102, 196
Burkhardt, 123
Burluk, 59
Busch, Field Marshal Ernst, 84
Busse, General, 69
Byelgorod, 81
Byeloi, 93
Bzura, river, 18

Caen, 192, 193, 208, 212
Cairo, 113
Calabria, 184
Canal du Nord, 154
Canea, 28, 29, 120, 122, 182
Cannam, Brigadier General, 127
Canne, 218
Carentan, 33
Carpathian mountains, 77, 97, 129
carrier pigeons, 23
Cassino, 184
Catholic church, 27
Caucasus mountains, 78, 80, 106, 183
Chambois, 194, 195
Champosoult, 195
Charanovka, 61
Charzysk, 183
Chemin des Dames, 15
Cherbourg, 156
Cherkassy, 84
Cherevichenko, Lieutenant General, 75
Chernowitz, 83
Cholm, 9
Choltitz, von, 99
Churchill, Winston S., 44, 157
Cintheaux, 213
Citadel, Operation, see Zitadelle
Citavecchia, 125
Clark, Mark, 51
Cologne, 126
Gaedke, Colonel, 136
Corinth, 20, 181
Cotentin Peninsula, 33, 194
Cottbus, 65
Courland, 72, 141
Crete, 8, 28, 119–23, 181–5, 221
Crimea, 20, 74, 77, 106

cuff titles, 25
Curgies, 15
Cyrenaica, 158
Czechoslovakia, 42, 89

Dachau, 186
Damm, 69
Danube, 25, 141–3
Danzig, 104
Deir el Shein, 31
Denmark, 180
Desna, river, 96, 188
Deutsch Brod, 118
Dietl, General Edouard, 138–40
Dietrich, Josef 'Sepp': early years, 13; First
    World War service, 13–15; in Bavarian
    State Police, 15; Annaberg action, 16;
    joins Nazi Party, 16; enlists in SS, 16; 'SS
    Headquarters Guard Dietrich', 17; in Leib-
    standarte Adolf Hitler, 17; with Guder-
    ian's XVI Corps, 17; in Polish campaign,
    18; in Holland, 18; in France, 19; in Balkan
    campaign, 19; in Greece, 20; in Operation
    Barbarossa, 20; in France and formation
    of SS Corps, 21; at Kharkov, 21; raises
    new SS Corps, 22; and Normandy cam-
    paign, 22; in Battle of the Bulge, 23;
    attends Berlin conference, January 1945,
    24; with 'Spring Awakening' in Hungary,
    24; disgrace and disgust, 25; at Vienna,
    25; surrenders to Americans, 25; trials,
    imprisonment and death, 25; other refer-
    ences, 211
Dinant, 102, 152
Dives, river, 99
Djebel Abiod, 223
Dnieper, river, 75, 82, 90, 114, 115, 130, 191
Dniester, 83
Dodecanese, 125
Doenitz, 52
Doetinchen, 100
Don, 78
Donets, 59, 60, 82
Dordrecht, 180, 181
Dorler, 151
Dresden, 42, 84, 149, 187
Drut, river, 130, 131
Drvar, 138
Dunkirk, 19, 43, 110, 155, 156
Dusseldorf, 103
Dynamo, Operation, 43

'Eagle Day', 45
Eastchurch, 45

Eben Emael, 8, 179, 180, 216–21
Eberbach, General, 99
Eifel, 36
Eindhoven, 100
El Alamein, 31, 124, 159, 222
Elba, 32, 125
Elsenborn, 38
Emmerich, 228
Enns, river, 144, 145
Erdmann, Major, 35, 36, 37
Espeler, 151
Evreux, 224

Falaise, 22, 35, 98, 99, 194, 196, 212
Fallschirm Armee Waffen Schule, 35
Falster, 180
Fatesh, 111
Finland, 139, 140
First World War, 9, 11, 13, 14, 26, 40, 71, 73,
    104, 106, 119, 129, 146, 163, 175
Flanders, 13, 19, 89, 119, 150, 156
Fliegerzentrale, 175
Florisdorfer, 196
Flying Equipment Test and Research Centre,
    176
Foni, 148
Forli, 52
Frankfurt, 63, 66, 69
Freikorps, 11, 15, 17, 107, 165
French North Africa, Anglo-American inva-
    sion of, 48
Freya, 44
Frontier Defence Force, 72, 106
Fuchsbauer, Lieutenant, 15
Fuka Pass, 124

Gaedke, General, 144
Galatas, 28, 29, 122
Gallwitz, von, 72
Gariboldi, General Italo, 157
Gaumesnil, 213
Gavrilovka, 20
Gazala, 31, 124, 159, 112
Gelb, Unternehmen, 150, 151, 179, 216
General, Staff, 11, 12, 27, 41, 72, 87, 88,
    107, 108, 130
Genoa, 125
Genthin, 86
Georges, General Alphonse, 153
Gerbach, 217
Gericke, 121, 125
Geyr von Schweppenburg, General Leo,
    Baron, 108
Gibraltar, 48, 183

Gloggau, 117
Goebbels, Paul Josef, 143, 144
Goering, Reichsmarschall Hermann, 8, 20,
    27, 41, 43, 44–6, 48, 42, 123, 176, 177,
    181, 184, 221
Gollnick, General, 136
Golovin, 206
Gouarec, 126
Gran Sasso, 50
Greece, 20, 157, 181, 182, 222, 200
Gresnoya, 203
Greve, 100
Gross-Born, 119
Grosstein, 163
Gshatsk, 92
Guderian, General Heinz, 9, 17, 19, 24, 90,
    107–12, 153, 172
Gumrak, 168
Guzzoni, General Alfredo, 50

Hague, 19, 27, 181
Hainburg, 142
Halfaya, 159
Hansen, General, 74, 75
Harpe, Colonel General, 116
Hartenstein, 100
Haumburg an der Salle, 86
Hauptmann, Behr, 79
Hausser, SS General, 17, 21, 22, 99, 170
Hawangen, 13
Heidrich, Colonel, 123
Heilbronn, 23
Heraklion, 182
Herkules, Unternehmen, 47
**Heydte, Friedrich August Freiherr von
    der:** early years, 26; joins cavalry, 26;
    studies law, 27; at Vienna Consular Acad-
    emy, 27; General Staff course, 27; in
    France, 28; joins Fallschirmjaeger, 28;
    campaign in Crete, 28; on Leningrad front,
    30; deployment to Libya, 31; at Alam
    Halfa, 31; dysentery and return to Ger-
    many, 32; Brittany and 2nd Paratroop
    Division, 32; and Operation Alaric, 32;
    injured in car crash, 33; training in Nor-
    mandy, 33; and Carentan defence, 33–5;
    in Battle of the Bulge, 35–9; capture, 39;
    service in Bundeswehr and death, 139;
    other references, 8, 23, 123
Hill 107, 120
Himmler, Reichsfuehrer SS Heinrich, 17, 25,
    187
Hindenburg, Field Marshal Paul von, 105
Hitler, Adolf: and Dietrich, 24, 25; and

Manstein, 80, 83; and Model, 92–3; and Rommel, 150;
Hoepner, General Erich, 74
Hoth, General Hermann, 78, 150, 151
Hotton, 151
Houx, 152
Hube, 168, 169
Hudel, 65, 69
Huertgen forest, 103
Hungary, 24, 25

Imperial Balloon Arm, 40
India, 80
Infantry Attack, 150
Innsbruck University, 27
Ishun, 75
Isono, 147
Italy, 49, 53, 161, 184

Jakantov, 190
'Jefna', position, 223
Jonava, 225

Kalinin, 91, 92
Kalista, 91
Kamenka, river, 203
Kampfgruppe Gersdorf, 63
Kampfgruppe Langkeit, 63, 65, 69
Kandalakscha, 140
Karachev, 95, 111
Karaguendo, 140
Kasatin, 115
Katarra Pass, 20
Kazan, 175
Kemenez-Podolsk, 83
Kempf, General Werner, 20
Kempten, 13
Kerch Peninsula, 76
Kesselring, Albert: early years, 40; joins artillery, 40; First World War service, 40; Reichswehr Staff appointments, 41; posted to Luftwaffe, 41; work on infrastructure of the new Luftwaffe, 41; Chief of Luftwaffe General Staff, 42; with Luftflotte 1 in Poland, 42; GOC Luftflotte 2 and war in the West, 1940, 43; and Battle of Britain, 44–6; and Operation Barbarossa, 47; appointed Supreme Commander South, 47; in Tunisia, 48–9; in Sicily, 50; and rescue of Mussolini, 50; defence of Italy, 51–2; injured in car accident, 52; Supreme Commander West, 52; surrenders, 53; trial, imprisonment and death, 53; other references, 8, 102, 113, 114, 160, 161, 222

Kharkov, 21, 22, 59, 80, 81, 170, 190, 191, 201, 202
Kiev, 21, 82, 90, 111, 125, 203, 205, 206
Kirkenes, 140
Kleist, Field Marshal Paul Ewald von, 55, 75, 78, 79, 110
Kleve, 228
Klidi Pass, 20
Klissura Pass, 20
Kluge, Field Marshal Gunther Hans von, 77, 96, 98, 161, 109
Koch, Major Walter, 215, 216, 219
Kodern, 90
Koenigsberg, 54
'Koenigsberg' defensive line, 92
Kolomak, 190
Kolosyoki, 138, 140
Kolovrat, 147, 148
Korosten, 205
Kortuky, 205
Kos, 125
Kovno, 225
Krivoi Rog, 61
Krn, 147
Kroh, 123
Kubillus, Lieutenant, 225, 226
Kuebler, 74
Kufstein, 25
Kunersdorf, 67
Kursk, 81, 82, 95, 96, 114, 190, 202, 203

La Crozon, 127
La Haye des Puits, 194
La Sanadiere, 208
Lakselv, 140
Lambach, 144
Landshut, 26
Langres, 110
Langkeit, Willi: early years, 54; joins Army, 54; in Polish campaign, 54; in Operation Barbarossa, 54; in battle for Rostov, 55–9; and Mius river defences, 59; at the Donets river, 59–60; advance to Stalingrad, 60; wounded, 61; Pavlovka–Vodyana battles, 61–2; commands Panzer regiment of 'Grossdeutschland' Division, 62; Pruth–Moldau battles, 62–3; with battlegroups in East Prussia, 63–9; and 'Kurmark' Panzergrenadier Division on the Oder, 69; surrender and captivity, 70; in Frontier Defence Force, 70
Lapland, 138, 140
Lauban, 117
Le Cateau, 154

Le Moulins, 194
Lederer, Colonel, 114
Leeb, Field Marshal Wilhelm Ritter von, 73, 74
Leitmeritz, 198
Lemgo, 185
Leningrad, 30, 77, 183
Leros, 125, 184
Lewinski family, 71
Libau, 172
Libya, 31, 47–9, 113, 157, 183, 222, 223
Lichterfelde, 163, 175
Liddell Hart, Sir Basil, 71
Liége, 179, 216, 218
Liegnitz, 73, 84
Lille, 155
Linz, 144
Lippspringe, 37
Lippstadt, 102
Lissa, 137
Lithuania, 225, 228
Llubljana Gap, 146
Lodz, 116, 130
Loehr, Field Marshal, 142
Lombardy, 147
London, 46, 130
Lossberg, General von, 72
Ludendorff, General Erich, 105
Ludin, river, 56
Luico, 147
Luneburg, 85
Lutschky, 202
Lutz, General, 107
Lutzow, 173
Lyons, 19
Lyubotin, 190

Maas, 99, 100, 101, 102, 109, 152, 153, 180, 181, 216, 217, 228
Maastricht, 217, 218
Maginot Line, 153, 154, 178
Main, 67
Major, Petereit, 64
Maleme, 120, 121, 182, 183, 221
Malin, 205
Malmedy, 36
Malmuck, 78
Malo-Archangelsk, 96
Malta, 47, 183
Mannerheim, Marshal Carol Gustaf Emil, Baron, 139
Manstein, Erich von: adoption and early years, 71; joins Guards, 71; First World War service, 71–2; post-war Staff and regi-
mental positions, 72; joins Truppenamt, 72; with General Staff, 72; Chief of Staff to Army Group South in Polish campaign, 73; plans Western campaign, 73–4; with LVI Panzer Corps in Operation Barbarossa, 74; commands 11th Army, 74; operations around Perekop, 74–5; in Crimea theatre, 75–6; conducts siege of Sevastopol, 75–6; death of son, Gero, 77; defends Crimea, 77; in command of Army Group Don, 77; attempts to relieve Stalingrad, 78–80; disagreements with Hitler, 80; and Battle of Kursk, 81–2; in further disagreements with Hitler and dismissal, 83; eye operation, 84; surrender, trial and imprisonment, 85; as advisor to West German Army, 85; death, 85; other references, 8, 18, 22, 95, 114, 170, 180, 202
Manstein, Gero, von, 77
Manteuffel, Hasso Eccard von, 24, 102, 223, 62
Mardilly, 194
Maria Theresa Military Academy, 129
Mariupol, 20
Market Garden, Operation, 100
Marksteft, 40
Marne, 99, 164
Maspelt, 151
Matajur, 147
Mechili, 158
Mecklenburg, 185, 227
Medjez el Bab, 223
Meindl, General, 121
Melitopol, 74
Melun, 164
Memel, 98
Memmingen, 13
Mercury, Operation, 182
Messvatay, 56
Metz, 40
Middleton, General Troy, 127, 128
Milch, General Erhard, 42
Mius, river, 55, 59, 114, 183
Model, Otto Moritz Walter: early years, 86; joins Army, 86; First World War service (wounded), 87; General Staff course, 87; helps put down putsch attempt, 88–9; writes paper and lectures on military history and tactics, 88; on missions to Russia, 88; involved in proposals for new army and Reischskuratorium, 88; General Staff, 88; administrative roles, 1938–40; injured in car accident, 89; commands 3rd Panzer Division, 89; in Operation Barbarossa, 90;

with XXXXI Panzer Corps on Moscow front,
91; GOC 9th Army, 92; operations around
Rzhev, 92; altercations with Hitler, 92–3;
wounded, 93; in Unternehmen Blau and
third battle for Rzhev, 93; withdrawal from
Rzhev salient, 94–5; commands Army
Group South, 95; and Battle of Kursk,
95–7; and Army Group North, 97; pro-
moted generalfeldmarschall, 97; and Army
Group Centre, 97; Supreme Commander
West, 98; orders Maas–Mosel defensive
line, 99; and Battle of Arnhem, 100; and
Battle of the Bulge, 101–2; suicide, 103;
other references, 8, 36, 52, 81, 83, 115,
133, 135
Modlin, 18
Moerdijk, 180, 181
Moldau, river, 63
Monschau, 39
Mont d'Areem, 126
Mont Le Ban, 151
Montbrocy, 208
Monte Cragonza, 149
Monte Hevnik, 148
Monte Kuk, 147, 148
Monte Matajeur, 149
Monte Mrzli, 147
Monte Stol, 147
Montgomery, Field Marshal Sir Bernard, 51,
85, 124, 208, 212
Moritz, 15
Mors, Major, 125
Mortain, 22, 194
Moscow, 91, 188
Mosel, 99, 101
Mosel, Colonel von der, 127
Mount Kemmel, 106
Mount Ormel, 195
Mount St Leger, 195
Muehlen, 105
Muehlensee, 105
Munich, 16, 26, 150, 73
Münster, 35
Mussolini, Benito, 20, 32, 47, 50, 125, 156,
160, 184

Nackitchevan, 58
Nazi Party, 16, 64, 166, 176
Negrebovka, 191
Nehring, Walter Kurt Josef: early life, 104;
joins Army, 104; brief aviation career and
accident, 105–6; wounded, 106; in Volunteer Frontier Defence Force, 106; General
Staff qualification, 107; friendship with
Guderian, 107; and evolution of armoured
warfare, 107; raises XIX (Mot) Corps, 109;
Polish campaign, 109; collaborates with
Guderian in Western campaign, 110; commands 18th Panzer Division, 110; in Oper-
ation Barbarossa, 111; to Afrika Korps,
112; at Tobruk, 113–14; at Battle of Alam
Halfa, 113; wounded, 113; in Tunisia,
113–14; commands XXIV Panzer Corps,
114; at Battle of Kursk, 114–15; in
defence, 115; commands 4th Panzer
Army, 116; illness, 116; with XXIV Corps
again and as 'wandering pocket', 116; at
Gloggau, 117; in Upper Silesia, 117; sur-
renders to Americans, 118; imprisonment
and release, 118; other references, 48, 49,
167
Neisse, 86
Neu Bischofsee, 67
Neuendorf, 65
Neumark, 175
Neusalz, 117
Neva, river, 30
Niemoeller, Pastor, 88
Nijmegen, 100
Normandy, 22, 33, 100, 161, 162, 191–4,
196, 208, 212, 227
'Northern Lights', 140
Norway, 180
Novocherkasak, 60
Noyers, 192
Nuremberg, 85, 145

Oberland Frei Korps, 16
Oder, river, 16, 24, 63, 66, 67, 69, 117
Oesel, 119
Oise, 110
Olkovatka, 96
Oosterbeek, 100
Orel, 95, 96, 97, 134, 137
Oserany, 130, 131
Oskar of Prussia, Prince, 87
Ostia, 125
Ourthe, river, 151

Paderborn, 35, 36, 37
Paget, Reginald, 85
Paris, 98, 110, 164, 208
Patton, General George S., 144, 145
Paulus, Field Marshal Friedrich, 77, 79, 78,
79, 80, 168
Pavlovka, 61
Peel position, 179
Pelz, General, 36

Perch, Operation, 208
Perekop, Isthmus, 74
Periers, 33
Philippeville, 153
Piastov, 18
Pilsen, 198
Pinnow, 66
Piraeus, 222
Platania ridge, 122
Ploen, 71
Ploernel, 201
Ploesti, 62
Pointe de Capucins, 127
Poland, 9, 15, 17, 18, 19, 42, 54, 73, 89, 109,
   130, 150, 178, 187
Ponyri, 96
Posen, 63
Potsdam, 150, 175
Potshniki, 204
Prague, 89, 110, 150, 197, 198
Prokharovka, 190
Pruth, river, 63
Psyol, river, 202, 203
Pueckler, Obergruppenfuehrer, 197

Quattara Depression, 124

Radomyshl, 205
Ramcke, Hermann Bernhard: early years,
   119; joins Imperial Marines, 119; First
   World War service, 119; joins Fallschirmjaeger, 119; in Greek campaign, 119–20;
   and Crete campaign, 120–2; on training
   duties, 123; to Afrika Korps, 123; escapes
   from El Alamein, 124; raises new Fallschir-
   mjaeger formation, 124–5; in Italian cam-
   paign, 125; on Eastern Front, 125; and
   Normandy/Brittany campaign, 126;
   defence of Brest, 127; surrenders, 128; in
   and out of prison camp, 128; other refer-
   ences, 31, 182, 183
Rapallo Treaty, 12, 175
Rastenburg, 81, 137
Ratingen, 103
Rechlin, 176, 177
Rehagen-Klausdorf, 215
Reichsarbeitsdienst, 88
Reichskuratorium, 88
Reichsstrasse 50, 140
Reichstag, 16
Reichswald, 101, 228
Reinhardt, General Georg Hans, 18
Rendulic, Lothar: early years, 129; joins
   Austrian Army, 129; First World War ser-

vice, 129; General Staff Academy, 130; as
Austrian Military Attaché in London, 130;
as Chief of Staff to XVII Corps, 130; with
14th Division in Operation Barbarossa,
130; with 52nd Division, 130–3; with XXXV
Corps, 133; and Battle of Kursk, 133–7; in
Yugoslavia, 137; to Lapland, 138–41; as
Supreme Commander Courland, 141; with
Army Group South, 141–2; at Vienna,
142–3; and Goebbels' 'split' story, 144;
surrenders to Americans, trial, imprison-
ment and death, 145; other references, 25
Rennenkampf, General, 104, 105
Reppen, 65, 66, 67, 68
Rethymnon, 182
Rhine, 100, 101
Ribemount, 110
Richthofen, Field Marshal Wolfram von, 43
Ridgeway, General Matthew Bunker, 103
Riga, 172, 173, 174
Ringl, General, 29, 120, 122, 119
Roehlinghausen, 215
Roehm, Ernst, 17
Roermond, 218
Rogachev, 130, 131
Rogosana, 203
Rokiczany, 199
Rolshevski, 126
Rome, 32, 53, 114, 125, 161
Rommel, Erwin: early life, 146; First World
   War service, 146; at Battle of Caporetto,
   147–9; awarded Pour le Mérite, 149; inter-
   war regimental and instructional posts,
   149–50; commands Fuehrer Begleit Battal-
   ion, 150; with 7th Panzer Division in
   France and Flanders, 150–6; crosses Our-
   the, 151; crosses Maas, 152–3; at
   Avesnes, 153–4; and Arras counter-attack,
   155; penetrates Weygand Line, 156; takes
   Cherbourg, 156; commands Afrika Korps,
   156; to Agedabia, 158; his 'dash to the
   wire', 159; and Gazala Line, 159; captures
   Tobruk, 159; at Battle of El Alamein,
   159–60; retreats to Tunisia, 160; in Italy,
   160–1; commands in North-West Europe,
   161; injury and suicide, 162; other refer-
   ences, 8, 9, 48, 51, 49, 80, 110, 112, 114,
   123, 181
Rossochovatka, 62
Rostov, 55, 59, 74, 79
Rotterdam, 19, 180, 181
Rovaniemi, 140
Rudel, Colonel, 68
Ruhr, 52, 102, 103

Rundstedt, Field Marshal Karl von, 52, 73, 85, 184, 161
Ruweisat Ridge, 124, 31
Rynok, 168
Rzhev, 92, 93, 94

St Aignan, 213
St Lô, 35
St Malo, 126
St Michel du Mont, 33
St Omer, 19
St Pierre, 208
St Valéry, 156
St Vith, 102
SA, 16
Saar, 101
Saarland, 17
Salerno, 51, 184
Salmuth, General Hans von, 74, 99
Salonika, 120
Salzburg, 144
Salzwedel, 224
Sambre, 154
Samsonov, General, 104, 105
Saporozhne, 80
Sardinia, 49
Scarpe, river, 155
Scheldt, 100
Scherer, 9
Schirmer, 224
Schlieffen Plan, 73
Schnee Eifel, 36, 196
Schoerner, Field Marshal Ferdinand, 172, 197
Schuchten bei Treuberg, 54
Schuermann, Lieutenant, 225
Sdvish, river, 204
Sedjenane, 222
Seeckt, General Hans von, 41
Seeland, 180
Seeloewe, 44, 45
Seine, 22, 44, 99
Semmering, 142, 143
Sennelager, 35
Serbia, 72
Seulles, river, 209
Sevastopol, 74, 75, 76
Seves, river, 33, 34
Seythen, 105
Sicily, 48, 49, 50, 51, 82, 125, 133, 160, 184
Sidi Abd el Rahman, 31
Sidi Rezegh, 159
Siegfried Line, 98, 100, 101, 102, 196
Silesia, 73, 109
Sivry, 153

Skopin, 112
Skorzeny, 23
Slovakia, 73
Smolensk, 77, 188
Soissons, 15
Sollum, 158
Somme, 44, 72, 99, 109, 110, 217
Sonnenblume, Unternehmen, 157
Soviet Russia, pact with, 12
Spanish Civil War, 89
Spartakova, 168
Speer, Albert, 84, 103
Sperrle, General Hugo, 44
'Spring Awakening', 24
'Springer Geist', 35, 177, 182
Ssuchinitshy, 112
Ssush, river, 134
Ssusnitche, 133
Stadler, Standartenfuehrer, 192
Stalingrad, 59, 60, 61, 77, 78, 79, 93, 94, 95, 168, 169, 170
Stary Zamsc, 129
Steiermark, 142, 143
Steinau, 117
Steiner, 17
Stendal, 177
Sternberg, 66
Stettin, 72
Strachwitz, Hyazinth von: early years, 163; in Gards du Korps cavalry, 163; First World War service, 163; capture and imprisonment, 164–5; injured in escape attempt, 165; feigns madness, 165; post-war convalescence, 165; with Freikorps against the Poles, 165–6; at Annaberg, 166; enters Panzer regiment, 166; and Polish campaign, 166; and campaign in France, 166–7; and Operation Barbarossa, 167; in thrust to the Volga, 167–8; operations about Stalingrad, 169–70; wounded, 170; with 'Grossdeutschland' at Kharkov, 170–1; as GOC 1st Panzer Division, 172; in operations about Riga, 172–4; injured in car crash, 174; in Syria, 174; death, 174; other references, 8
Strasbourg, 24, 71
Strauss, 85
Stretzin, 104
Student, Karl: early years, 175; joins Army, 175; First World War service in air force, 175; post-war Fliegerzentrale post, 175; as Director of Luftwaffe Technical Training School, 176; at Flying Equipment Test and Research Centre, 176; raises Airborne

Division, 177; and evolution of Fallschirmjaeger, 177–8; commands 7th Airborne Division, 178; and Western campaign, 179; wounded, 181; in Crete operations, 181–3; on Leningrad front, 183; and expansion of the airborne forces in ground roles, 183–4; commands new airborne army, 184; capture, trial, retirement and death, 185; other references, 8, 19, 35, 48, 120, 122, 123, 120, 125
Stumme, General Georg, 160
Stuttgart-Cannstatt, 26
Styrty, 205
Suchiy, Torez, 59
Suda Bay, 182
Sudetenland, 17
Suez canal, 48, 112, 159, 124
Sussmann, General, 120
Switzerland, 165
Syria, 174
Systshevka, 92

Tabarka, 222
Tabor, 118
Taganrog, 20
Tebourba, 114
Teutonic Knights, 104
Tichvin, 30
Tilly sur Seulles, 208
Timoshenko, Marshal Semën, 188
'Tirschtiegel', positions, 63, 64
Tito, Josip Broz, 137, 138
Tobruk, 112, 113, 123, 158, 159
Tolbhukin, Marshal Fedor, 142
Tolmein, 147
Tortchin, 206, 207
Toucques, river, 99
Toulouse, 191
Traunstein, 26
Tripoli, 123, 156, 157, 158
Tripolitania, 89, 157
Troya, bridge, 197
Trubchevsk, 111
Truman, President Harry S., 145
Trun, 194
Truppenamt, 72
Truppendienst Taschenbuc, 147
Tsolakoglou, General, 20
Tuapse, 183
Tuccum, 173
Tula, 91, 112
Tunis, 49, 113, 224
Tunisia, 32, 48, 49, 113, 114, 160, 184, 222, 224

Typhoon, Operation, 91

Ukraine, 55, 106, 111
Uman, 20, 167

Valenciennes, 15
Valkemburg, 181
Vannes, 125
Vedeces, river, 153
Vehicle Training Command, 107
Veldwezelt, 217, 218
Velence, 24
Venice, 53
Verchnopenye, 203
Verfuegungs, Truppen, 17, 187
Versailles, 11, 12, 26, 87, 88, 107, 108, 175, 176
Vewrba, 167
Via Balbia, 124
Victor Emmanuel, King of Italy, 50
Vienna, 25, 27, 129, 130, 141, 142, 143, 196
Villers Bocage, 192, 208, 210, 211, 212
Vinnitsa, 82
Vistula, 18, 109
Viterbo, 32
Vladimirovka, 61
Vodyana, 62
Vogelthal, 200
Volga, 59, 60, 61, 78, 79, 80, 91, 93, 94, 168
Volunteer Frontier Defence Force, 106
Vroenhoven, 217, 218

Waalhaven, 181
Wagner, Anton, 147
Walker, General, 145
Waplitz, 105
Warsaw, 18, 98, 111
Wattenberg, 19
Wavell, Field Marshal Sir Archibald, 156, 157, 158
Weichs, General Maximilian, Baron, 133, 134
Weidenheim ner Ulm, 146
Weidinger, Otto: early years, 186; joins SS, 186; with 'Deutschland' Standarte, 186–7; with VT Divisions, 187; in Operation Barbarossa, 188; on Eastern Front, 188–9; at Battle of Kursk, 189–90; at Kharkov, 191; formation of Kampfgruppe Weidinger, 191; to Normandy, 192; commands 'Der Fuehrer' Regiment, 192; and bocage fighting, 192–6; in Hungary, 196; at Prague, 197; surrenders to Americans, 199; imprisonment and death, 199; other references, 9, 11

Weimar Republic, 12, 41, 87, 106, 119
Westphal, General Siegfried, 51
Westphalia, 87
Wever, 45
Weygand Line, 54
Wiener Neustadt, 129, 150
Wisliceny, SS Obersturmbandfuehrer Günther, 191
Wittenberg an der Elbe, 224
Wittmann, Michael: early life, 200; joins Leibstandarte SS 'Adolf Hitler', 200; and campaigns in Greece and Balkans, 200–1; and Operation Barbarossa, 200–1; at Kharkov, 201–2; at Battle of Kursk, 202–3; and operations in Kiev area, 203; about Brusilov, 204–7; to Belgium, 207; fighting in Normandy, 207–14; at Villers Bocage, 208–12; at Falaise, 212–14; death in action, 214; other references, 8, 9, 11
Witzig, Rudolf: early years, 215; joins Army's Paratroop Battalion, 215; and capture of Eben Emael, 216–21; and campaign in Crete, 221; with Ramcke at El Alamein, 222; in Tunisia, 222; at Medjez el Bab, 223; raises new Fallschirm Pioneer Battalion, 224; to Lithuania, 225; in Holland, 228; capture, 228; service in Bundeswehr and retirement, 228; activities in Confédération Européene des Anciens Combattants, 228; other references, 8, 180
Wolfsberg, 100
Wolfsschanze, 81
Wormhoudt, 19
Württemberg, 146
Würzburg, 186

Yelnya, 188, 189
Yerger, Mark, 190
Youth Training Programme, 88
Yperburg, 181
Ypres, 13
Yugoslav Army of National Liberation, 137
Yugoslavia, 52, 137, 188

Zaga, 147
Zell am See, 25
Zhitomir, 203, 205, 206
Zhukov, Marshal Georgi, 63, 64
Zitadelle, Unternehmen, 22, 81, 82, 93–6, 114, 115, 133, 134, 189, 190, 191, 202,
Zisterdorf, 143
Zoppot, 104

Acknowledgements

I acknowledge with grateful thanks the help of the following persons and institutions: Vizeleutnant Helmuth Eberl, Vienna; John Harding, Army Historical Branch; Marian Harding, National Army Museum; Lieutenant Colonel Hannes Hauser, Kameradschaft, Regiment 'DF'; Sir Tom Normanton, London and Hampshire; Colonel Hubert Meyer, Kameradschaft 1sten SS Panzer Division; Gill Pratt, Vienna; Dr. Manfred Rauchensteiner, Director of the Heeresgeschichtliches Museum, Vienna; The family of the late General Dr. Rendulic; Hilary Roberts, Department of Photographs, Imperial War Museum; Julie Robertshaw, Department of Printed Books, Imperial War Museum; Adi Strauch, Fallschirmjaegerkameradschaft Kiel; Colonel Rudolf Witzig, Fallschirmjaeger Pionier Kameradschaft; Captain Georg Seegerer, Kameradschaft Regiment 'DF'; The family of the late Lieutenant Colonel Otto Weidinger; Mark Yerger, Lancaster, PA, USA; and members of the Old Comrades' Associations of 1st, 3rd and 7th Panzer Divisions; of the 1st and 2nd SS Panzer Divisions; and of the Panzer Corps Grossdeutschland.